Student Solutions Manual

OPTIONS FUTURES, AND OTHER DERIVATIVES

Sixth Edition

John C. Hull

PEARSON

Prentice
Hall

Upper Saddle River, New Jersey 07458

D0543345

VP/Editorial Director: Jeff Shelstad
Executive Editor: David Alexander
Project Manager: Francesca Calogero
Associate Director, Manufacturing: Vincent Scelta
Production Editor & Buyer: Carol O'Rourke
Printer/Binder: Hamilton Printing

10 9 8 7 6 5 4 3 2 1
ISBN 0-13-149906-8

Contents

Preface

This book contains solutions to the questions and problems that appear at the ends of chapters in my book *Options, Futures, and Other Derivatives*, 6th edition. The questions and problems have been designed to help readers study on their own and test their understanding of the material. They range from quick checks on whether a key point is understood to much more challenging applications of analytical techniques. Some problems prove or extend results presented in the book. To maximize the benefits from this book readers are urged to sketch out their own solutions to the problems before consulting mine.

I would like to thank my Research Assistant, Andrew King, for all his work on this book. He greatly improved the finished product.

I welcome comments on either *Options, Futures, and Other Derivatives*, 6th edition or this book. My e-mail address is

hull@rotman.utoronto.ca

John C. Hull
Joseph L. Rotman School of Management
University of Toronto

Chapter 1

Introduction

SOLUTIONS TO QUESTIONS AND PROBLEMS

Problem 1.1.

When a trader enters into a long forward contract, she is agreeing to *buy* the underlying asset for a certain price at a certain time in the future. When a trader enters into a short forward contract, she is agreeing to *sell* the underlying asset for a certain price at a certain time in the future.

Problem 1.2.

A trader is *hedging* when she has an exposure to the price of an asset and takes a position in a derivative to offset the exposure. In a *speculation* the trader has no exposure to offset. She is betting on the future movements in the price of the asset. *Arbitrage* involves taking a position in two or more different markets to lock in a profit.

Problem 1.3.

In the first case the trader is obligated to buy the asset for $50. (The trader does not have a choice.) In the second case the trader has an option to buy the asset for $50. (The trader does not have to exercise the option.)

Problem 1.4.

Selling a call option involves giving someone else the right to buy an asset from you. It gives you a payoff of

$$-\max(S_T - K, 0) = \min(K - S_T, 0)$$

Buying a put option involves buying an option from someone else. It gives a payoff of

$$\max(K - S_T, 0)$$

In both cases the potential payoff is $K - S_T$. When you write a call option, the payoff is negative or zero. (This is because the counterparty chooses whether to exercise.) When you buy a put option, the payoff is zero or positive. (This is because you choose whether to exercise.)

Problem 1.5.

(a) The investor is obligated to sell pounds for 1.5000 when they are worth 1.4900. The gain is $(1.5000 - 1.4900) \times 100,000 = \$1,000$.

(b) The investor is obligated to sell pounds for 1.5000 when they are worth 1.5200. The loss is $(1.5200 - 1.5000) \times 100,000 = \$2,000$.

Problem 1.6.

(a) The trader sells for 50 cents per pound something that is worth 48.20 cents per pound. Gain $= (\$0.5000 - \$0.4820) \times 50,000 = \$900$.

(b) The trader sells for 50 cents per pound something that is worth 51.30 cents per pound. Loss $= (\$0.5130 - \$0.5000) \times 50,000 = \$650$.

Problem 1.7.

You have sold a put option. You have agreed to buy 100 shares for $40 per share if the party on the other side of the contract chooses to exercise the right to sell for this price. The option will be exercised only when the price of stock is below $40. Suppose, for example, that the option is exercised when the price is $30. You have to buy at $40 shares that are worth $30; you lose $10 per share, or $1,000 in total. If the option is exercised when the price is $20, you lose $20 per share, or $2,000 in total. The worst that can happen is that the price of the stock declines to almost zero during the three-month period. This highly unlikely event would cost you $4,000. In return for the possible future losses, you receive the price of the option from the purchaser.

Problem 1.8.

The over-the-counter market is a telephone- and computer-linked network of financial institutions, fund managers, and corporate treasurers where two participants can enter into any mutually acceptable contract. An exchange-traded market is a market organized by an exchange where traders either meet physically or communicate electronically and the contracts that can be traded have been defined by the exchange. When a market maker quotes a bid and an offer, the bid is the price at which the market maker is prepared to buy and the offer is the price at which the market maker is prepared to sell.

Problem 1.9.

One strategy would be to buy 200 shares. Another would be to buy 2,000 options. If the share price does well the second strategy will give rise to greater gains. For example, if the share price goes up to $40 you gain $[2,000 \times (\$40 - \$30)] - \$5,800 = \$14,200$ from the second strategy and only $200 \times (\$40 - \$29) = \$2,200$ from the first strategy. However, if the share price does badly, the second strategy gives greater losses. For example, if the share price goes down to $25, the first strategy leads to a loss of $200 \times (\$29 - \$25) = \$800$, whereas the second strategy leads to a loss of the whole $5,800 investment. This example shows that options contain built in leverage.

Problem 1.10.

You could buy 5,000 put options (or 50 contracts) with a strike price of $25 and an expiration date in 4 months. This provides a type of insurance. If at the end of 4 months the stock price proves to be less than $25 you can exercise the options and sell the shares for $25 each. The cost of this strategy is the price you pay for the put options.

Problem 1.11.

A stock option provides no funds for the company. It is a security sold by one trader to another. The company is not involved. By contrast, a stock when it is first issued is a claim sold by the company to investors and does provide funds for the company.

Problem 1.12.

If a trader has an exposure to the price of an asset, she can hedge with a forward contract. If the exposure is such that the trader will gain when the price decreases and lose when the price increases, a long forward position will hedge the risk. If the exposure is such that the trader will lose when the price decreases and gain when the price increases, a short forward position will hedge the risk. Thus either a long or a short forward position can be entered into for hedging purposes. If the trader has no other exposure to the price of the underlying asset, entering into a forward contract is speculation.

Problem 1.13.

Ignoring the time value of money, the holder of the option will make a profit if the stock price in March is greater than $52.50. This is because the payoff to the holder of the option is, in these circumstances, greater than the $2.50 paid for the option. The option will be exercised if the stock price at maturity is greater than $50.00. Note that if the stock price is between $50.00 and $52.50 the option is exercised, but the holder of the option takes a loss overall. The profit from a long position is as shown in Figure S1.1.

Problem 1.14.

Ignoring the time value of money, the seller of the option will make a profit if the stock price in June is greater than $56.00. This is because the cost to the seller of the option is in these circumstances less than the price received for the option. The option will be exercised if the stock price at maturity is less than $60.00. Note that if the stock price is between $56.00 and $60.00 the seller of the option makes a profit even though the option is exercised. The profit from the short position is as shown in Figure S1.2.

Figure S1.1: Profit from long position in Problem 1.13

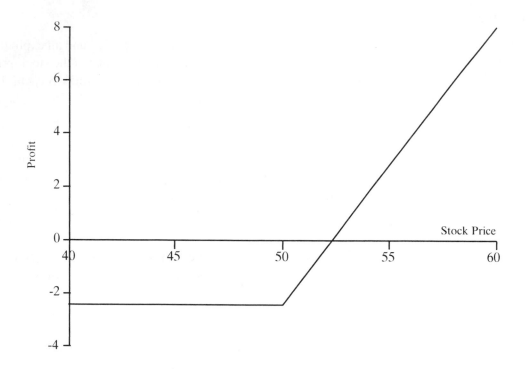

Problem 1.15.

The trader receives an inflow of $2 in May. Since the option is exercised, the trader also has an outflow of $5 in September. The $2 is the cash received from the sale of the option. The $5 is the result of buying the stock for $25 in September and selling it to the purchaser of the option for $20.

Problem 1.16.

The trader makes a gain if the price of the stock is above $26 in December. (This ignores the time value of money.)

Problem 1.17.

A long position in a four-month put option can provide insurance against the exchange rate falling below the strike price. It ensures that the foreign currency can be sold for at least the strike price.

Figure S1.2: Profit from short position in Problem 1.14

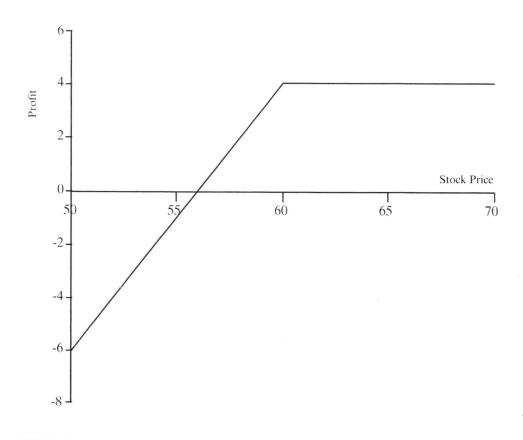

Problem 1.18.

The company could enter into a long forward contract to buy 1 million Canadian dollars in six months. This would have the effect of locking in an exchange rate equal to the current forward exchange rate. Alternatively the company could buy a call option giving it the right (but not the obligation) to purchase 1 million Canadian dollar at a certain exchange rate in six months. This would provide insurance against a strong Canadian dollar in six months while still allowing the company to benefit from a weak Canadian dollar at that time.

Problem 1.19.

(a) The trader sells 100 million yen for $0.0080 per yen when the exchange rate is $0.0074 per yen. The gain is 100×0.0006 millions of dollars or $60,000.

(b) The trader sells 100 million yen for $0.0080 per yen when the exchange rate is $0.0091 per yen. The loss is 100×0.0011 millions of dollars or $110,000.

Problem 1.20.

Most traders who use the contract will wish to do one of the following:

(a) Hedge their exposure to long-term interest rates

(b) Speculate on the future direction of long-term interest rates

(c) Arbitrage between cash and futures markets

This contract is discussed in Chapter 6.

Problem 1.21.

The statement means that the gain (loss) to the party with a short position in an option is always equal to the loss (gain) to the party with the long position. The sum of the gains is zero.

Problem 1.22.

The terminal value of the long forward contract is:

$$S_T - F_0$$

where S_T is the price of the asset at maturity and F_0 is the forward price of the asset at the time the portfolio is set up. (The delivery price in the forward contract is F_0.)

The terminal value of the put option is:

$$\max\left(F_0 - S_T, 0\right)$$

The terminal value of the portfolio is therefore

$$S_T - F_0 + \max\left(F_0 - S_T, 0\right)$$

$$= \max\left(0, S_T - F_0\right]$$

This is the same as the terminal value of a European call option with the same maturity as the forward contract and an exercise price equal to F_0. This result is illustrated in the Figure S1.3. The profit equals the terminal value less the amount paid for the option.

Problem 1.23.

Suppose that the yen exchange rate (yen per dollar) at maturity of the ICON is S_T. The payoff from the ICON is[1]

$$1,000 \qquad\qquad \text{if} \qquad S_T > 169$$

$$1,000 - 1,000\left(\frac{169}{S_T} - 1\right) \quad \text{if} \quad 84.5 \leq S_T \leq 169$$

$$0 \qquad\qquad \text{if} \qquad S_T < 84.5$$

---

[1]There was a typo in the first printing of the book. The expression given for the payoff should be $1,000 - \max[0, 1,000(\frac{169}{S_T} - 1)]$.

Figure S1.3: Payoff from portfolio in Problem 1.22

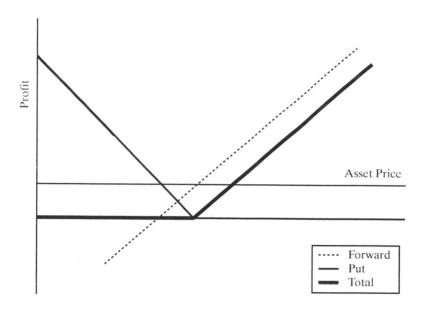

When $84.5 \leq S_T \leq 169$ the payoff can be written

$$2,000 - \frac{169,000}{S_T}$$

The payoff from an ICON is the payoff from:

(a) A regular bond

(b) A short position in call options to buy 169,000 yen with an exercise price of 1/169

(c) A long position in call options to buy 169,000 yen with an exercise price of 1/84.5

This is demonstrated by the following table:

	Terminal Value of Regular Bond	Terminal Value of Short Calls	Terminal Value of Long Calls	Terminal Value of Whole Position
$S_T > 169$	1,000	0	0	1000
$84.5 \leq S_T \leq 169$	1000	$-169,000\left(\frac{1}{S_T} - \frac{1}{169}\right)$	0	$2000 - \frac{169,000}{S_T}$
$S_T < 84.5$	1000	$-169,000\left(\frac{1}{S_T} - \frac{1}{169}\right)$	$169,000\left(\frac{1}{S_T} - \frac{1}{84.5}\right)$	0

Problem 1.24.

Suppose that the forward price for the contract entered into on July 1, 2005 is F_1 and that the forward price for the contract entered into on September 1, 2005 is F_2 with both F_1 and F_2 being measured as dollars per yen. If the value of one Japanese yen (measured in U.S. dollars) is S_T on January 1, 2006, then the value of the first contract (in millions of dollars) at that time is

$$10(S_T - F_1)$$

while the value of the second contract (per yen sold) at that time is:

$$10(F_2 - S_T)$$

The total payoff from the two contracts is therefore

$$10(S_T - F_1) + 10(F_2 - S_T) = 10(F_2 - F_1)$$

Thus if the forward price for delivery on January 1, 2006 increases between July 1, 2005 and September 1, 2005 the company will make a profit.

Problem 1.25.

(a) The trader buys a 180-day call option and takes a short position in a 180-day forward contract. If S_T is the terminal spot rate, the profit from the call option is

$$\max(S_T - 1.57, 0) - 0.02$$

The profit from the short forward contract is

$$1.6018 - S_T$$

The profit from the strategy is therefore

$$\max(S_T - 1.57, 0) - 0.02 + 1.6018 - S_T$$

or

$$\max(S_T - 1.57, 0) + 1.5818 - S_T$$

This is

$$1.5818 - S_T \quad \text{when} \quad S_T < 1.57$$
$$0.0118 \quad \text{when} \quad S_T > 1.57$$

This shows that the profit is always positive. The time value of money has been ignored in these calculations. However, when it is taken into account the strategy is still likely to be profitable in all circumstances. (We would require an extremely high interest rate for $0.0118 interest to be required on an outlay of $0.02 over a 180-day period.)

(b) The trader buys 90-day put options and takes a long position in a 90 day forward contract. If S_T is the terminal spot rate, the profit from the put option is

$$\max{(1.64 - S_T, 0)} - 0.020$$

The profit from the long forward contract is

$$S_T - 1.6056$$

The profit from this strategy is therefore

$$\max{(1.64 - S_T, 0)} - 0.020 + S_T - 1.6056$$

or

$$\max{(1.64 - S_T, 0)} + S_T - 1.6256$$

This is

$$S_T - 1.6256 \quad \text{when} \quad S_T > 1.64$$
$$0.0144 \quad\quad \text{when} \quad S_T < 1.64$$

The profit is therefore always positive. Again, the time value of money has been ignored but is unlikely to affect the overall profitability of the strategy. (We would require interest rates to be extremely high for $0.0144 interest to be required on an outlay of $0.02 over a 90-day period.)

Chapter 2

Mechanics of Futures Markets

SOLUTIONS TO QUESTIONS AND PROBLEMS

Problem 2.1.

The *open interest* of a futures contract at a particular time is the total number of long positions outstanding. (Equivalently, it is the total number of short positions outstanding.) The *trading volume* during a certain period of time is the number of contracts traded during this period.

Problem 2.2.

A *commission broker* trades on behalf of a client and charges a commission. A *local* trades on his or her own behalf.

Problem 2.3.

There will be a margin call when $1,000 has been lost from the margin account. This will occur when the price of silver increases by $1,000/5,000 = \$0.20$. The price of silver must therefore rise to $5.40 per ounce for there to be a margin call. If the margin call is not met, your broker closes out your position.

Problem 2.4.

The total profit is $(\$20.50 - \$18.30) \times 1,000 = \$2,200$. Of this $(\$19.10 - \$18.30) \times 1,000 = \$800$ is realized on a day-by-day basis between September 2006 and December 31, 2006. A further $(\$20.50 - \$19.10) \times 1,000 = \$1,400$ is realized on a day-by-day basis between January 1, 2007, and March 2007. A hedger would be taxed on the whole profit of $2,200 in 2007. A speculator would be taxed on $800 in 2006 and $1,400 in 2007.

Problem 2.5.

A *stop order* to sell at $2 is an order to sell at the best available price once a price of $2 or less is reached. It could be used to limit the losses from an existing long position. A *limit order* to sell at $2 is an order to sell at a price of $2 or more. It could be used to instruct a broker that a short position should be taken, providing it can be done at a price more favorable than $2.

Problem 2.6.

The margin account administered by the clearinghouse is marked to market daily, and the clearinghouse member is required to bring the account back up to the prescribed level daily. The margin account administered by the broker is also marked to market daily. However, the account does not have to be brought up to the initial margin level on a daily basis. It has to be brought up to the initial margin level when the balance in the account falls below the maintenance margin level. The maintenance margin is usually about 75% of the initial margin.

Problem 2.7.

In futures markets prices are quoted as the number of U.S. dollars per unit of foreign currency. Spot and forward rates are quoted in this way for the British pound, euro, Australian dollar, and New Zealand dollar. For other major currencies, spot and forward rates are quoted as the number of units of foreign currency per U.S. dollar.

Problem 2.8.

These options make the contract less attractive to the party with the long position and more attractive to the party with the short position. They therefore tend to reduce the futures price.

Problem 2.9.

The most important aspects of the design of a new futures contract are the specification of the underlying asset, the size of the contract, the delivery arrangements, and the delivery months.

Problem 2.10.

A margin is a sum of money deposited by an investor with his or her broker. It acts as a guarantee that the investor can cover any losses on the futures contract. The balance in the margin account is adjusted daily to reflect gains and losses on the futures contract. If losses are above a certain level, the investor is required to deposit a further margin. This system makes it unlikely that the investor will default. A similar system of margins makes it unlikely that the investor's broker will default on the contract it has with the clearinghouse member and unlikely that the clearinghouse member will default with the clearinghouse.

Problem 2.11.

There is a margin call if $1,500 is lost on one contract. This happens if the futures price of orange juice falls by 10 cents to 150 cents per lb. $2,000 can be withdrawn from the margin account if there is a gain on one contract of $1,000. This will happen if the futures price rises by 6.67 cents to 166.67 cents per lb.

Problem 2.12.

If the futures price is greater than the spot price during the delivery period, an arbitrageur buys the asset, shorts a futures contract, and makes delivery for an immediate profit. If the futures price is less than the spot price during the delivery period, there is no similar perfect arbitrage strategy. An arbitrageur can take a long futures position but cannot force immediate delivery of the asset. The decision on when delivery will be made is made by the party with the short position. Nevertheless companies interested in acquiring the asset will find it attractive to enter into a long futures contract and wait for delivery to be made.

Problem 2.13.

A market-if-touched order is executed at the best available price after a trade occurs at a specified price or at a price more favorable than the specified price. A stop order is executed at the best available price after there is a bid or offer at the specified price or at a price less favorable than the specified price.

Problem 2.14.

A stop-limit order to sell at 20.30 with a limit of 20.10 means that as soon as there is a bid at 20.30 the contract should be sold providing this can be done at 20.10 or a higher price.

Problem 2.15.

The clearinghouse member is required to provide $20 \times \$2,000 = \$40,000$ as initial margin for the new contracts. There is a gain of $(50,200 - 50,000) \times 100 = \$20,000$ on the existing contracts. There is also a loss of $(51,000 - 50,200) \times 20 = \$16,000$ on the new contracts. The member must therefore add

$$40,000 - 20,000 + 16,000 = \$36,000$$

to the margin account.

Problem 2.16.

Suppose F_1 and F_2 are the forward exchange rates for the contracts entered into July 1, 2006 and September 1, 2006, and S is the spot rate on January 1, 2007. (All exchange rates are measured as dollars per pound). The payoff from the first contract is $10(S - F_1)$ million dollars and the payoff from the second contract is $10(F_2 - S)$ million dollars. The total payoff is therefore $10(S - F_1) + 10(F_2 - S) = 10(F_2 - F_1)$ million dollars.

Problem 2.17.

The 1.8204 forward quote is the number of Swiss francs per dollar. The 0.5479 futures quote is the number of dollars per Swiss franc. When quoted in the same way as the futures price the forward price is $1/1.8204 = 0.5493$. The Swiss franc is therefore more valuable in the forward market than in the futures market. The forward market is therefore more attractive for an investor wanting to sell Swiss francs.

Problem 2.18.

Hog futures are traded on the Chicago Mercantile Exchange. (See Table 2.2). The broker will request some initial margin. The order will be relayed by telephone to your broker's trading desk on the floor of the exchange (or to the trading desk of another broker).

It will be sent by messenger to a commission broker who will execute the trade according to your instructions. Confirmation of the trade eventually reaches you. If there are adverse movements in the futures price your broker may contact you to request additional margin.

Problem 2.19.

Speculators are important market participants because they add liquidity to the market. However, contracts must be useful for hedging as well as speculation. This is because regulators generally only approve contracts when they are likely to be of interest to hedgers as well as speculators.

Problem 2.20.

The most actively traded contracts as measured by open interest are

Grains and Oilseeds:	Corn (CBT)
Livestock:	Cattle-Live (CME)
Food and Fiber:	Sugar–World (CSCE)
Metals:	Gold (CMX)
Petroleum:	Crude Oil (NYM)

Problem 2.21.

The contract would not be a success. Parties with short positions would hold their contracts until delivery and then deliver the cheapest form of the asset. This might well be viewed by the party with the long position as garbage! Once news of the quality problem became widely known no one would be prepared to buy the contract. This shows that futures contracts are feasible only when there are rigorous standards within an industry for defining the quality of the asset. Many futures contracts have in practice failed because of the problem of defining quality.

Problem 2.22.

If both sides of the transaction are entering into a new contract, the open interest increases by one. If both sides of the transaction are closing out existing positions, the open interest decreases by one. If one party is entering into a new contract while the other party is closing out an existing position, the open interest stays the same.

Problem 2.23.

The total profit is

$$40,000 \times (0.6120 - 0.5830) = \$1,160$$

If you are a hedger this is all taxed in 2007. If you are a speculator

$$40,000 \times (0.6120 - 0.5880) = \$960$$

is taxed in 2006 and

$$40,000 \times (0.5880 - 0.5830) = \$200$$

is taxed in 2007.

Problem 2.24.

The farmer can short 3 contracts that have 3 months to maturity. If the price of cattle falls, the gain on the futures contract will offset the loss on the sale of the cattle. If the price of cattle rises, the gain on the sale of the cattle will be offset by the loss on the futures contract. Using futures contracts to hedge has the advantage that it can at no cost reduce risk to almost zero. Its disadvantage is that the farmer no longer gains from favorable movements in cattle prices.

Problem 2.25.

The mining company can estimate its production on a month by month basis. It can then short futures contracts to lock in the price received for the gold. For example, if a total of 3,000 ounces are expected to be produced in January 2006 and February 2006, the price received for this production can be hedged by shorting a total of 30 February 2006 contracts.

Chapter 3
Hedging Strategies Using Futures

SOLUTIONS TO QUESTIONS AND PROBLEMS

Problem 3.1.

A *short hedge* is appropriate when a company owns an asset and expects to sell that asset in the future. It can also be used when the company does not currently own the asset but expects to do so at some time in the future. A *long hedge* is appropriate when a company knows it will have to purchase an asset in the future. It can also be used to offset the risk from an existing short position.

Problem 3.2.

Basis risk arises from the hedger's uncertainty as to the difference between the spot price and futures price at the expiration of the hedge.

Problem 3.3.

A *perfect hedge* is one that completely eliminates the hedger's risk. A perfect hedge does not always lead to a better outcome than an imperfect hedge. It just leads to a more certain outcome. Consider a company that hedges its exposure to the price of an asset. Suppose the asset's price movements prove to be favorable to the company. A perfect hedge totally neutralizes the company's gain from these favorable price movements. An imperfect hedge, which only partially neutralizes the gains, might well give a better outcome.

Problem 3.4.

A minimum variance hedge leads to no hedging when the coefficient of correlation between the futures price changes and changes in the price of the asset being hedged is zero.

Problem 3.5.

(a) If the company's competitors are not hedging, the treasurer might feel that the company will experience less risk if it does not hedge. (See Table 3.1.)

(b) The shareholders might not want the company to hedge.

(c) If there is a loss on the hedge and a gain from the company's exposure to the underlying asset, the treasurer might feel that he or she will have difficulty justifying the hedging to other executives within the organization.

Problem 3.6.

The optimal hedge ratio is

$$0.8 \times \frac{0.65}{0.81} = 0.642$$

This means that the size of the futures position should be 64.2% of the size of the company's exposure in a three-month hedge.

Problem 3.7.

The formula for the number of contracts that should be shorted gives

$$1.2 \times \frac{20,000,000}{1080 \times 250} = 88.9$$

Rounding to the nearest whole number, 89 contracts should be shorted. To reduce the beta to 0.6, half of this position, or a short position in 44 contracts, is required.

Problem 3.8.

A good rule of thumb is to choose a futures contract that has a delivery month as close as possible to, but later than, the month containing the expiration of the hedge. The contracts that should be used are therefore (a) July, (b) September, and (c) March.

Problem 3.9.

No. Consider, for example, the use of a forward contract to hedge a known cash inflow in a foreign currency. The forward contract locks in the forward exchange rate — which is in general different from the spot exchange rate.

Problem 3.10.

The basis is the amount by which the spot price exceeds the futures price. A short hedger is long the asset and short futures contracts. The value of his or her position therefore improves as the basis increases. Similarly it worsens as the basis decreases.

Problem 3.11.

The simple answer to this question is that the treasurer should (a) estimate the company's future cash flows in Japanese yen and U.S. dollars and (b) enter into forward and futures contracts to lock in the exchange rate for the U.S. dollar cash flows.

However, this is not the whole story. As the gold jewelry example in Table 3.1 shows, the company should examine whether the magnitudes of the foreign cash flows depend on the exchange rate. For example, will the company be able to raise the price of its product in U.S. dollars if the yen appreciates? If the company can do so, its foreign exchange exposure may be quite low. The key estimates required are those showing the overall effect on the company's profitability of changes in the exchange rate at various times in the future. Once these estimates have been produced the company can choose between using futures and options to hedge its risk. The results of the analysis should be presented carefully to other executives. It should be explained that a hedge does not ensure that profits will be higher. It means that profit will be more certain. When futures/forwards are used both the downside and upside are eliminated. With options a premium is paid to eliminate only the downside.

Problem 3.12.

If the hedge ratio is 0.8, the company takes a long position in 16 NYM December oil futures contracts on June 8 when the futures price is \$18.00. It closes out its position on November 10. The spot price and futures price at this time are \$20.00 and \$19.10. The gain on the futures position is

$$(19.10 - 18.00) \times 16,000 = 17,600$$

The effective cost of the oil is therefore

$$20,000 \times 20 - 17,600 = 382,400$$

or \$19.12 per barrel. (This compares with \$18.90 per barrel when the company is fully hedged.)

Problem 3.13.

The statement is not true. The minimum variance hedge ratio is

$$\rho \frac{\sigma_S}{\sigma_F}$$

It is 1.0 when $\rho = 0.5$ and $\sigma_S = 2\sigma_F$. Since $\rho < 1.0$ the hedge is clearly not perfect.

Problem 3.14.

The statement is true. Using the notation in the text, if the hedge ratio is 1.0, the hedger locks in a price of $F_1 + b_2$. Since both F_1 and b_2 are known this has a variance of zero and must be the best hedge.

Problem 3.15.

A company that knows it will purchase a commodity in the future is able to lock in a price close to the futures price. This is likely to be particularly attractive when the futures price is less than the spot price.

Problem 3.16.

The optimal hedge ratio is

$$0.7 \times \frac{1.2}{1.4} = 0.6$$

The beef producer requires a long position in $200000 \times 0.6 = 120,000$ lbs of cattle. The beef producer should therefore take a long position in 3 December contracts closing out the position on November 15.

Problem 3.17.

Suppose that the weather is bad and the farmer's production is lower than expected. Other farmers are likely to have been affected similarly. Corn production overall will be low and as a consequence the price of corn will be relatively high. The farmer is likely to be overhedged relative to actual production. The farmer's problems arising from the bad harvest will be made worse by losses on the short futures position. This problem emphasizes the importance of looking at the big picture when hedging. The farmer is correct to question whether hedging price risk while ignoring other risks is a good strategy.

Problem 3.18.

A short position in

$$1.3 \times \frac{50,000 \times 30}{50 \times 1,500} = 26$$

contracts is required.

Problem 3.19.

If the company uses a hedge ratio of 1.5 in Table 3.5 it would at each stage short 150 contracts. The gain from the futures contracts would be

$$1.50 \times 1.70 = \$2.55 \text{ per barrel}$$

and the company would be $0.85 per barrel better off.

Problem 3.20.

Suppose that you enter into a short futures contract to hedge the sale of a asset in six months. If the price of the asset rises sharply during the six months, the futures price will also rise and you may get margin calls. The margin calls will lead to cash outflows. Eventually the cash outflows will be offset by the extra amount you get when you sell the asset, but there is a mismatch in the timing of the cash outflows and inflows. Your cash outflows occur earlier than your cash inflows. A similar situation could arise if you used a long position in a futures contract to hedge the purchase of an asset and the asset's price fell sharply. An extreme example of what we are talking about here is provided by Metallgesellschaft (see Business Snapshot 3.2).

Problem 3.21.

It may well be true that there is just as much chance that the price of oil in the future will be above the futures price as that it will be below the futures price. This means that the use of a futures contract for speculation would be like betting on whether a coin comes up heads or tails. But it might make sense for the airline to use futures for hedging rather than speculation. The futures contract then has the effect of reducing risks. It can be argued that an airline should not expose its shareholders to risks associated with the future price of oil when there are contracts available to hedge the risks.

Problem 3.22.

Goldman Sachs can borrow 1 ounce of gold and sell it for $400. It invests the $400 at 5% so that it becomes $420 at the end of the year. It must pay the lease rate of 1.5% on $400. This is $6 and leaves it with $414. It follows that if it agrees to buy the gold for less than $414 in one year it will make a profit.

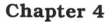

Chapter 4

Interest Rates

SOLUTIONS TO QUESTIONS AND PROBLEMS

Problem 4.1.

(a) The rate with continuous compounding is

$$4\ln\left(1 + \frac{0.14}{4}\right) = 0.1376$$

or 13.76% per annum.

(b) The rate with annual compounding is

$$\left(1 + \frac{0.14}{4}\right)^4 - 1 = 0.1475$$

or 14.75% per annum.

Problem 4.2.

LIBOR is the London InterBank Offer Rate. It is the rate a bank quotes for deposits it is prepared to place with other banks. LIBID is the London InterBank Bid rate. It is the rate a bank quotes for deposits from other banks. LIBOR is greater than LIBID.

Problem 4.3.

Suppose the bond has a face value of $100. Its price is obtained by discounting the cash flows at 10.4%. The price is

$$\frac{4}{1.052} + \frac{4}{1.052^2} + \frac{104}{1.052^3} = 96.74$$

If the 18-month zero rate is R, we must have

$$\frac{4}{1.05} + \frac{4}{1.05^2} + \frac{104}{(1 + R/2)^3} = 96.74$$

which gives $R = 10.42\%$.

Problem 4.4.

(a) With annual compounding the return is

$$\frac{1100}{1000} - 1 = 0.1$$

or 10% per annum.

(b) With semi-annual compounding the return is R where

$$1000 \left(1 + \frac{R}{2}\right)^2 = 1100$$

i.e.,

$$1 + \frac{R}{2} = \sqrt{1.1} = 1.0488$$

so that $R = 0.0976$. The percentage return is therefore 9.76% per annum.

(c) With monthly compounding the return is R where

$$1000 \left(1 + \frac{R}{12}\right)^{12} = 1100$$

i.e.,

$$\left(1 + \frac{R}{12}\right) = \sqrt[12]{1.1} = 1.00797$$

so that $R = 0.0957$ The percentage return is therefore 9.57% per annum.

(d) With continuous compounding the return is R where:

$$1000e^R = 1100$$

i.e.,

$$e^R = 1.1$$

so that $R = \ln 1.1 = 0.0953$. The percentage return is therefore 9.53% per annum.

Problem 4.5.

The forward rates with continuous compounding are as follows:

Qtr 2:	8.4%
Qtr 3:	8.8%
Qtr 4:	8.8%
Qtr 5:	9.0%
Qtr 6:	9.2%

Problem 4.6.

The forward rate is 9.0% with continuous compounding or 9.102% with quarterly compounding. From equation (4.9), the value of the FRA is therefore

$$[1,000,000 \times 0.25 \times (0.095 - 0.09102)]e^{-0.086 \times 1.25} = 893.56$$

or $893.56.

Problem 4.7.

When the term structure is upward sloping, $c > a > b$. When it is downward sloping, $b > a > c$.

Problem 4.8.

Duration provides information about the effect of a small parallel shift in the yield curve on the value of a bond portfolio. The percentage decrease in the value of the portfolio equals the duration of the portfolio multiplied by the amount by which interest rates are increased in the small parallel shift. The duration measure has the following limitation. It applies only to parallel shifts in the yield curve that are small.

Problem 4.9.

The rate of interest is R where:

$$e^R = \left(1 + \frac{0.15}{12}\right)^{12}$$

i.e.,

$$R = 12 \ln\left(1 + \frac{0.15}{12}\right)$$

$$= 0.1491$$

The rate of interest is therefore 14.91% per annum.

Problem 4.10.

The equivalent rate of interest with quarterly compounding is R where

$$e^{0.12} = \left(1 + \frac{R}{4}\right)^4$$

or

$$R = 4(e^{0.03} - 1) = 0.1218$$

The amount of interest paid each quarter is therefore:

$$10,000 \times \frac{0.1218}{4} = 304.55$$

or \$304.55.

Problem 4.11.

The bond pays \$2 in 6, 12, 18, and 24 months, and \$102 in 30 months. The cash price is

$$2e^{0.04 \times 0.5} + 2e^{0.042 \times 1.0} + 2e^{0.044 \times 1.5} + 2e^{0.046 \times 2} + 102e^{0.048 \times 2.5} = 98.04$$

Problem 4.12.

The bond pays \$4 in 6, 12, 18, 24, and 30 months, and \$104 in 36 months. The bond yield is the value of y that solves

$$4e^{-0.5y} + 4e^{-1.0y} + 4e^{-1.5y} + 4e^{-2.0y} + 4e^{-2.5y} + 104e^{-3.0y} = 104$$

Using the *Goal Seek* tool in Excel $y = 0.06407$ or 6.407%.

Problem 4.13.

Using the notation in the text, $m = 2$, $d = e^{-0.07 \times 2} = 0.8694$. Also

$$A = e^{-0.05 \times 0.5} + e^{-0.06 \times 1.0} + e^{-0.065 \times 1.5} + e^{-0.07 \times 2.0} = 3.6935$$

The formula in the text gives the par yield as

$$\frac{(100 - 100 \times 0.8694) \times 2}{3.6935} = 7.072$$

To verify that this is correct we calculate the value of a bond that pays a coupon of 7.072% per year (that is 3.05365 every six months). The value is

$$3.536e^{-0.05 \times 0.5} + 3.5365e^{-0.06 \times 1.0} + 3.536e^{-0.065 \times 1.5} + 103.536e^{-0.07 \times 2.0} = 100$$

verifying that 7.072% is the par yield.

Problem 4.14.

The forward rates with continuous compounding are as follows:

Year 2:   4.0%
Year 3:   5.1%
Year 4:   5.7%
Year 5:   5.7%

Problem 4.15.

The forward rate is 5.1% with continuous compounding or $e^{0.051 \times 1} - 1 = 5.232\%$ with annual compounding. The 3-year interest rate is 3.7% with continuous compounding. From equation (4.10), the value of the FRA is therefore

$$[1,000,000 \times (0.05232 - 0.05) \times 1]e^{-0.037 \times 3} = 2,078.85$$

or $2,078.85.

Problem 4.16.

Taking a long position in two of the 4% coupon bonds and a short position in one of the 8% coupon bonds leads to the following cash flows

$$\text{Year } 0: \ 90 - 2 \times 80 = -70$$
$$\text{Year } 10: \ 200 - 100 = 100$$

because the coupons cancel out. $100 in 10 years time is equivalent to $70 today. The 10-year rate, R, (continuously compounded) is therefore given by

$$100 = 70e^{10R}$$

The rate is

$$\frac{1}{10}\ln\frac{100}{70} = 0.0357$$

or 3.57% per annum.

Problem 4.17.

If long-term rates were simply a reflection of expected future short-term rates, we would expect the term structure to be downward sloping as often as it is upward sloping. (This is based on the assumption that half of the time investors expect rates to increase and half of the time investors expect rates to decrease). Liquidity preference theory argues that long term rates are high relative to expected future short-term rates. This means that the term structure should be upward sloping more often than it is downward sloping.

Problem 4.18.

The par yield is the yield on a coupon-bearing bond. The zero rate is the yield on a zero-coupon bond. When the yield curve is upward sloping, the yield on an N-year coupon-bearing bond is less than the yield on an N-year zero-coupon bond. This is because the coupons are discounted at a lower rate than the N-year rate and drag the yield down below this rate. Similarly, when the yield curve is downward sloping, the yield on an N-year coupon bearing bond is higher than the yield on an N-year zero-coupon bond.

Problem 4.19.

There are three reasons (see Business Snapshot 4.1).

(i) Treasury bills and Treasury bonds must be purchased by financial institutions to fulfill a variety of regulatory requirements. This increases demand for these Treasury instruments driving the price up and the yield down.

(ii) The amount of capital a bank is required to hold to support an investment in Treasury bills and bonds is substantially smaller than the capital required to support a similar investment in other very-low-risk instruments.

(iii) In the United States, Treasury instruments are given a favorable tax treatment compared with most other fixed-income investments because they are not taxed at the state level.

Problem 4.20.

A repo is a contract where an investment dealer who owns securities agrees to sell them to another company now and buy them back later at a slightly higher price. The other company is providing a loan to the investment dealer. This loan involves very little credit risk. If the borrower does not honor the agreement, the lending company simply keeps the securities. If the lending company does not keep to its side of the agreement, the original owner of the securities keeps the cash.

Problem 4.21.

A FRA is an agreement that a certain specified interest rate, R_K, will apply to a certain principal, L, for a certain specified future time period. Suppose that the rate observed in the market for the future time period at the beginning of the time period proves to be R_M. If the FRA is an agreement that R_K will apply when the principal is invested, the holder of the FRA can borrow the principal at R_M and then invest it at R_K. The net cash flow at the end of the period is then an inflow of $R_K L$ and an outflow of $R_M L$. If the FRA is an agreement that R_K will apply when the principal is borrowed, the holder of the FRA can invest the borrowed principal at R_M. The net cash flow at the end of the period is then an inflow of $R_M L$ and an outflow of $R_K L$. In either case we see that the FRA involves the exchange of a fixed rate of interest, R_K, on the principal of L for the floating rate of interest observed in the market, R_M.

Problem 4.22.

(a) The bond's price is

$$8e^{-0.11} + 8e^{-0.11 \times 2} + 8e^{-0.11 \times 3} + 8e^{-0.11 \times 4} + 108e^{-0.11 \times 5} = 86.80$$

(b) The bond's duration is

$$\frac{1}{86.80} \left[8e^{-0.11} + 2 \times 8e^{-0.11 \times 2} + 3 \times 8e^{-0.11 \times 3} + 4 \times 8e^{-0.11 \times 4} + 5 \times 108e^{-0.11 \times 5} \right]$$

$$= 4.256 \text{ years}$$

(c) Since, with the notation in the chapter

$$\Delta B = -BD\Delta y$$

the effect on the bond's price of a 0.2% decrease in its yield is

$$86.80 \times 4.256 \times 0.002 = 0.74$$

The bond's price should increase from 86.80 to 87.54.

(d) With a 10.8% yield the bond's price is

$$8e^{-0.108} + 8e^{-0.108 \times 2} + 8e^{-0.108 \times 3} + 8e^{-0.108 \times 4} + 108e^{-0.108 \times 5} = 87.54$$

This is consistent with the answer in (c).

Problem 4.23.

The 6-month rate (with continuous compounding) is $2\ln(1 + 6/94) = 12.38\%$. The 12-month rate is $\ln(1 + 11/89) = 11.65\%$.

For the 1.5-year bond we must have

$$4e^{-0.1238 \times 0.5} + 4e^{-0.1165 \times 1.0} + 104e^{-1.5R} = 94.84$$

where R is the 1.5-year spot rate. It follows that

$$3.76 + 3.56 + 104e^{-1.5R} = 94.84$$

$$e^{-1.5R} = 0.8415$$

$$R = 0.115$$

or 11.5%. For the 2-year bond we must have

$$5e^{-0.1238 \times 0.5} + 5e^{-0.1165 \times 1.0} + 5e^{-0.115 \times 1.5} + 105e^{-2R} = 97.12$$

where R is the 2-year spot rate. It follows that

$$e^{-2R} = 0.7977$$
$$R = 0.113$$

or 11.3%.

Chapter 5

Determination of Forward and Futures Prices

SOLUTIONS TO QUESTIONS AND PROBLEMS

Problem 5.1.

The investor's broker borrows the shares from another client's account and sells them in the usual way. To close out the position, the investor must purchase the shares. The broker then replaces them in the account of the client from whom they were borrowed. The party with the short position must remit to the broker dividends and other income paid on the shares. The broker transfers these funds to the account of the client from whom the shares were borrowed. Occasionally the broker runs out of places from which to borrow the shares. The investor is then short squeezed and has to close out the position immediately.

Problem 5.2.

The forward price of an asset today is the price at which you would agree to buy or sell the asset at a future time. The value of a forward contract is zero when you first enter into it. As time passes the underlying asset price changes and the value of the contract may become positive or negative.

Problem 5.3.

The forward price is

$$30e^{0.12 \times 0.5} = \$31.86$$

Problem 5.4.

The futures price is

$$350e^{(0.08-0.04) \times 0.3333} = \$354.7$$

Problem 5.5.

Gold is an investment asset. If the futures price is too high, investors will find it profitable to increase their holdings of gold and short futures contracts. If the futures price is too low, they will find it profitable to decrease their holdings of gold and go long in the futures market. Copper is a consumption asset. If the futures price is too high, a strategy of buy copper and short futures works. However, because investors do not in general hold the asset, the strategy of sell copper and buy futures is not available to them. There is therefore an upper bound, but no lower bound, to the futures price.

Problem 5.6.

Convenience yield measures the extent to which there are benefits obtained from ownership of the physical asset that are not obtained by owners of long futures contracts. The *cost of carry* is the interest cost plus storage cost less the income earned. The futures price, F_0, and spot price, S_0, are related by

$$F_0 = S_0 e^{(c-y)T}$$

where c is the cost of carry, y is the convenience yield, and T is the time to maturity of the futures contract.

Problem 5.7.

A foreign currency provides a known interest rate, but the interest is received in the foreign currency. The value in the domestic currency of the income provided by the foreign currency is therefore known as a percentage of the value of the foreign currency. This means that the income has the properties of a known yield.

Problem 5.8.

The futures price of a stock index is always less than the expected future value of the index. This follows from Section 5.14 and the fact that the index has positive systematic risk. For an alternative argument, let μ be the expected return required by investors on the index so that $E(S_T) = S_0 e^{(\mu-q)T}$. Because $\mu > r$ and $F_0 = S_0 e^{(r-q)T}$, it follows that $E(S_T) > F_0$.

Problem 5.9.

(a) The forward price, F_0, is given by equation (5.1) as:

$$F_0 = 40e^{0.1\times1} = 44.21$$

or \$44.21. The initial value of the forward contract is zero.

(b) The delivery price K in the contract is \$44.21. The value of the contract, f, after six months is given by equation (5.5) as:

$$f = 45 - 44.21e^{-0.1\times0.5}$$

$$= 2.95$$

i.e., it is \$2.95. The forward price is:

$$45e^{0.1\times0.5} = 47.31$$

or \$47.31.

Problem 5.10.

Using equation (5.3) the six month futures price is

$$150e^{(0.07-0.032)\times0.5} = 152.88$$

or \$152.88.

Problem 5.11.

The futures contract lasts for five months. The dividend yield is 2% for three of the months and 5% for two of the months. The average dividend yield is therefore

$$\frac{1}{5}(3\times2+2\times5) = 3.2\%$$

The futures price is therefore

$$300e^{(0.09-0.032)\times0.4167} = 307.34$$

or \$307.34.

Problem 5.12.

The theoretical futures price is

$$400e^{(0.10-0.04)\times4/12} = 408.08$$

The actual futures price is only 405. This shows that the index futures price is too low relative to the index. The correct arbitrage strategy is

1. Buy futures contracts
2. Short the shares underlying the index.

Problem 5.13.

The settlement prices for the futures contracts are

| Mar | 0.08920 |
| June | 0.08812 |

The June 2004 price is about 1.2% below the March 2004 price. This suggests that the short-term interest rate in the Mexico exceeded short-term interest rates in the United States by about 1.2% per three months or about 4.8% per year.

Problem 5.14.

The theoretical futures price is

$$0.6500e^{(0.08-0.03)\times2/12} = 0.6554$$

The actual futures price is too high. This suggests that an arbitrageur should buy Swiss francs and short Swiss francs futures.

Problem 5.15.

The present value of the storage costs for nine months are

$$0.06 + 0.06e^{-0.10 \times 0.25} + 0.06e^{-0.10 \times 0.5} = 0.176$$

or $0.176. The futures price is from equation (5.11) given by F_0 where

$$F_0 = (9.000 + 0.176)e^{0.1 \times 0.75} = 9.89$$

i.e., it is $9.89 per ounce.

Problem 5.16.

If

$$F_2 > F_1 e^{r(t_2 - t_1)}$$

an investor could make a riskless profit by

1. Taking a long position in a futures contract which matures at time t_1

2. Taking a short position in a futures contract which matures at time t_2

When the first futures contract matures, the asset is purchased for F_1 using funds borrowed at rate r. It is then held until time t_2 at which point it is exchanged for F_2 under the second contract. The costs of the funds borrowed and accumulated interest at time t_2 is $F_1 e^{r(t_2 - t_1)}$ A positive profit of

$$F_2 - F_1 e^{r(t_2 - t_1)}$$

is then realized at time t_2. This type of arbitrage opportunity cannot exist for long. Hence:

$$F_2 \leq F_1 e^{r(t_2 - t_1)}$$

Problem 5.17.

In total the gain or loss under a futures contract is equal to the gain or loss under the corresponding forward contract. However the timing of the cash flows is different. When the time value of money is taken into account a futures contract may prove to be more valuable or less valuable than a forward contract. Of course the company does not know in advance which will work out better. The long forward contract provides a perfect hedge. The long futures contract provides a slightly imperfect hedge.

  (a) In this case the forward contract would lead to a slightly better outcome. The company will make a loss on its hedge. If the hedge is with a forward contract the whole of the loss will be realized at the end. If it is with a futures contract the loss will be realized day by day throughout the contract. On a present value basis the former is preferable.

(b) In this case the futures contract would lead to a slightly better outcome. The company will make a gain on the hedge. If the hedge is with a forward contract the gain will be realized at the end. If it is with a futures contract the gain will be realized day by day throughout the life of the contract. On a present value basis the latter is preferable.

(c) In this case the futures contract would lead to a slightly better outcome. This is because it would involve positive cash flows early and negative cash flows later.

(d) In this case the forward contract would lead to a slightly better outcome. This is because, in the case of the futures contract, the early cash flows would be negative and the later cash flow would be positive.

Problem 5.18.

From the discussion in Section 5.14 of the text, the forward exchange rate is an unbiased predictor of the future exchange rate when the exchange rate has no systematic risk. To have no systematic risk the exchange rate must be uncorrelated with the return on the market.

Problem 5.19.

Suppose that F_0 is the futures price at time zero for a contract maturing at time T and F_1 is the futures price for the same contract at time t_1. It follows that

$$F_0 = S_0 e^{(r-q)T}$$

$$F_1 = S_1 e^{(r-q)(T-t_1)}$$

where S_0 and S_1 are the spot price at times zero and t_1, r is the risk-free rate, and q is the dividend yield. These equations imply that

$$\frac{F_1}{F_0} = \frac{S_1}{S_0} e^{-(r-q)t_1}$$

Define the excess return of the index over the risk-free rate as x. The total return is $r+x$ and the return realized in the form of capital gains is $r+x-q$. It follows that $S_1 = S_0 e^{(r+x-q)t_1}$ and the equation for F_1/F_0 reduces to

$$\frac{F_1}{F_0} = e^{xt_1}$$

which is the required result.

Problem 5.20.

Suppose we buy N units of the asset and invest the income from the asset in the asset. The income from the asset causes our holding in the asset to grow at a continuously compounded rate q. By time T our holding has grown to Ne^{qT} units of the asset. Analogously to footnotes 2 and 4 of Chapter 5, we therefore buy N units of the asset at time zero at a cost of S_0 per unit and enter into a forward contract to sell Ne^{qT} unit for F_0 per unit at time T. This generates the following cash flows:

$$\text{Time } 0: \quad -NS_0$$
$$\text{Time } T: \quad NF_0e^{qT}$$

Because there is no uncertainty about these cash flows, the present value of the time T inflow must equal the time zero outflow when we discount at the risk-free rate. This means that

$$NS_0 = (NF_0e^{qT})e^{-rT}$$

or

$$F_0 = S_0e^{(r-q)T}$$

This is equation (5.3).

If $F_0 > S_0e^{(r-q)T}$, an arbitrageur should borrow money at rate r and buy N units of the asset. At the same time the arbitrageur should enter into a forward contract to sell Ne^{qT} units of the asset at time T. As income is received, it is reinvested in the asset. At time T the loan is repaid and the arbitrageur makes a profit of $N(F_0e^{qT} - S_0e^{rT})$ at time T.

If $F_0 < S_0e^{(r-q)T}$, an arbitrageur should short N units of the asset investing the proceeds at rate r. At the same time the arbitrageur should enter into a forward contract to buy Ne^{qT} units of the asset at time T. When income is paid on the asset, the arbitrageur owes money on the short position. The investor meets this obligation from the cash proceeds of shorting further units. The result is that the number of units shorted grows at rate q to Ne^{qT}. The cumulative short position is closed out at time T and the arbitrageur makes a profit of $N(S_0e^{rT} - F_0e^{qT})$.

Problem 5.21.

To understand the meaning of the expected future price of a commodity, suppose that there are N different possible prices at a particular future time: P_1, P_2, ..., P_N. Define q_i as the (subjective) probability the price being P_i (with $q_1 + q_2 + \ldots + q_N = 1$). The expected future price is

$$\sum_{i=1}^{N} q_i P_i$$

Different people may have different expected future prices for the commodity. The expected future price in the market can be thought of as an average of the opinions of different market participants. Of course, in practice the actual price of the commodity at the future time may prove to be higher or lower than the expected price.

Keynes and Hicks argue that speculators on average make money from commodity futures trading and hedgers on average lose money from commodity futures trading. If speculators tend to have short positions in crude oil futures, the Keynes and Hicks argument implies that futures prices overstate expected future spot prices. Table 2.2 shows crude oil futures prices decline fast. The Keynes and Hicks argument therefore implies a very fast decline for the expected price of crude oil over the period following February 4, 2004 if speculators are short.

Problem 5.22.

When the geometric average of the price relatives is used, the changes in the value of the index do not correspond to changes in the value of a portfolio that is traded. Equation (5.8) is therefore no longer correct. The changes in the value of the portfolio is monitored by an index calculated from the arithmetic average of the prices of the stocks in the portfolio. Since the geometric average of a set of numbers is always less than the arithmetic average, equation (5.8) overstates the futures price. It is rumored that at one time (prior to 1988), equation (5.8) did hold for the Value Line Index. A major Wall Street firm was the first to recognize that this represented a trading opportunity. It made a financial killing by buying the stocks underlying the index and shorting the futures.

Problem 5.23.

(a) The relationship between the futures price F_t and the spot price S_t at time t is

$$F_t = S_t e^{(r-r_f)(T-t)}$$

Suppose that the hedge ratio is h. The price obtained with hedging is

$$h(F_0 - F_t) + S_t$$

where F_0 is the initial futures price. This is

$$hF_0 + S_t - hS_t e^{(r-r_f)(T-t)}$$

If $h = e^{(r_f - r)(T-t)}$, this reduces to hF_0 and a zero variance hedge is obtained.

(b) When t is one day, h is approximately $e^{(r_f - r)T} = S_0/F_0$. The appropriate hedge ratio is therefore S_0/F_0.

(c) When a futures contract is used for hedging, the price movements in each day should in theory be hedged separately. This is because the daily settlement means that a futures contract is closed out and rewritten at the end of each day. From (b) the correct hedge ratio at any given time is, therefore, S/F where S is the spot price and F is the futures price. Suppose there is an exposure to N units of the foreign currency and M units of the foreign currency underlie one futures contract. With a hedge ratio of 1 we should trade N/M contracts. With a hedge ratio of S/F we should trade

$$\frac{SN}{FM}$$

contracts. In other words we should calculate the number of contracts that should be traded as the dollar value of our exposure divided by the dollar value of one futures contract (This is not the same as the dollar value of our exposure divided by the dollar value of the assets underlying one futures contract.) Since a futures contract is settled daily, we should in theory rebalance our hedge daily so that the outstanding number of futures contracts is always $(SN)/(FM)$. This is known as tailing the hedge. (See footnote 5 of Chapter 3 of the text.)

Chapter 6

Interest Rate Futures

SOLUTIONS TO QUESTIONS AND PROBLEMS

Problem 6.1.

There are 33 calendar days between July 7, 2004 and August 9, 2004. There are 184 calendar days between July 7, 2004 and January 7, 2005. The interest earned per $100 of principal is therefore $3.5 \times 33/184 = \$0.6277$. For a corporate bond we assume 32 days between July 7 and August 9, 2004 and 180 days between July 7, 2004 and January 7, 2005. The interest earned is $3.5 \times 32/180 = \$0.6222$.

Problem 6.2.

There are 89 days between October 12, 2004, and January 9, 2005. There are 182 days between October 12, 2004, and April 12, 2005. The cash price of the bond is obtained by adding the accrued interest to the quoted price. The quoted price is $102\frac{7}{32}$ or 102.21875. The cash price is therefore

$$102.21875 + \frac{89}{182} \times 6 = \$105.15$$

Problem 6.3.

The conversion factor for a bond is equal to the quoted price the bond would have per dollar of principal on the first day of the delivery month on the assumption that the interest rate for all maturities equals 6% per annum (with semiannual compounding). The bond maturity and the times to the coupon payment dates are rounded down to the nearest three months for the purposes of the calculation. The conversion factor defines how much an investor with a short bond futures contract receives when bonds are delivered. If the conversion factor is 1.2345 the amount investor receives is calculated by multiplying 1.2345 by the most recent futures price and adding accrued interest.

Problem 6.4.

The Eurodollar futures price has increased by 6 basis points. The investor makes a gain per contract of $25 \times 6 = \$150$ or $300 in total.

Problem 6.5.

Suppose that a Eurodollar futures quote is 95.00. This gives a futures rate of 5% for the three-month period covered by the contract. The convexity adjustment is the amount by which futures rate has to be reduced to give an estimate of the forward rate for the period The convexity adjustment is necessary because a) the futures contract is settled daily and b) the futures contract expires at the beginning of the three months. Both of these lead to the futures rate being greater than the forward rate.

Problem 6.6.

From equation (6.4) the rate is

$$\frac{3.2 \times 90 + 3 \times 350}{440} = 3.0409$$

or 3.0409%.

Problem 6.7.

The value of a contract is $108\frac{15}{32} \times 1,000 = \$108,468.75$. The number of contracts that should be shorted is

$$\frac{6,000,000}{108,468.75} \times \frac{8.2}{7.6} = 59.7$$

Rounding to the nearest whole number, 60 contracts should be shorted. The position should be closed out at the end of July.

Problem 6.8.

The cash price of the Treasury bill is

$$100 - \frac{90}{360} \times 10 = \$97.50$$

The annualized continuously compounded return is

$$\frac{365}{90} \ln\left(1 + \frac{2.5}{97.5}\right) = 10.27\%$$

Problem 6.9.

The number of days between January 27, 2003 and May 5, 2003 is 98. The number of days between January 27, 2003 and July 27, 2003 is 181. The accrued interest is therefore

$$6 \times \frac{98}{181} = 3.2486$$

The quoted price is 110.5312. The cash price is therefore

$$110.5312 + 3.2486 = 113.7798$$

or $113.78.

Problem 6.10.

The cheapest-to-deliver bond is the one for which

Quoted Price $-$ Futures Price $\times$ Conversion Factor

is least. Calculating this factor for each of the 4 bonds we get

Bond 1: $125.15625 - 101.375 \times 1.2131 = 2.178$
Bond 2: $142.46875 - 101.375 \times 1.3792 = 2.652$
Bond 3: $115.96875 - 101.375 \times 1.1149 = 2.946$
Bond 4: $144.06250 - 101.375 \times 1.4026 = 1.874$

Bond 4 is therefore the cheapest to deliver.

Problem 6.11.

There are 177 days between February 4 and July 30 and 182 days between February 4 and August 4. The cash price of the bond is, therefore:

$$110 + \frac{177}{182} \times 6.5 = 116.32$$

The rate of interest with continuous compounding is $2 \ln 1.06 = 0.1165$ or 11.65% per annum. A coupon of 6.5 will be received in 5 days ($= 0.01366$ years) time. The present value of the coupon is

$$6.5 e^{-0.01366 \times 0.1165} = 6.490$$

The futures contract lasts for 62 days ($= 0.1694$ years). The cash futures price if the contract were written on the 13% bond would be

$$(116.32 - 6.490) e^{0.1694 \times 0.1165} = 112.02$$

At delivery there are 57 days of accrued interest. The quoted futures price if the contract were written on the 13% bond would therefore be

$$112.02 - 6.5 \times \frac{57}{184} = 110.01$$

Taking the conversion factor into account the quoted futures price should be:

$$\frac{110.01}{1.5} = 73.34$$

Problem 6.12.

If the bond to be delivered and the time of delivery were known, arbitrage would be straightforward. When the futures price is too high, the arbitrageur buys bonds and shorts an equivalent number of bond futures contracts. When the futures price is too low, the arbitrageur sells bonds and goes long an equivalent number of bond futures contracts.

Uncertainty as to which bond will be delivered introduces complications. The bond that appears cheapest-to-deliver now may not in fact be cheapest-to-deliver at maturity. In the case where the futures price is too high, this is not a major problem since the party with the short position (i.e., the arbitrageur) determines which bond is to be delivered. In the case where the futures price is too low, the arbitrageur's position is far more difficult since he or she does not know which bond to buy; it is unlikely that a profit can be locked in for all possible outcomes.

Problem 6.13.

The forward interest rate for the time period between months 6 and 9 is 9% per annum with continuous compounding. This is because 9% per annum for three months when combined with $7\frac{1}{2}$% per annum for six months gives an average interest rate of 8% per annum for the nine-month period.

With quarterly compounding the forward interest rate is

$$4(e^{0.09/4} - 1) = 0.09102$$

or 9.102%. This assumes that the day count is actual/actual. With a day count of actual/360 the rate is $9.102 \times 360/365 = 8.977$. The three-month Eurodollar quote for a contract maturing in six months is therefore

$$100 - 8.977 = 91.02$$

This assumes no difference between futures and forward prices.

Problem 6.14.

The forward rates calculated form the first two Eurodollar futures are 4.17% and 4.38%. These are expressed with an actual/360 day count and quarterly compounding. With continuous compounding and an actual/365 day count they are $(365/90)\ln(1 + 0.0417/4) = 4.2060\%$ and $(365/90)\ln(1 + 0.0438/4) = 4.4167\%$. It follows from equation (6.4) that the 398 day rate is

$$\frac{4 \times 300 + 4.2060 \times 98}{398} = 4.0507$$

or 3.0254%. The 489 day rate is

$$\frac{4.0507 \times 398 + 4.4167 \times 91}{489} = 4.1188$$

or 4.1188%. We are assuming that the first futures rate applies to 98 days rather than the usual 91 days. The third futures quote is not needed.

Problem 6.15.

Duration-based hedging schemes assume parallel shifts in the yield curve. Since the 12-year rate tends to move by less than the 4-year rate, the portfolio manager may find that he or she is over-hedged.

Problem 6.16.

The company treasurer can hedge the company's exposure by shorting Eurodollar futures contracts. The Eurodollar futures position leads to a profit if rates rise and a loss if they fall.

The duration of the commercial paper is twice that of the Eurodollar deposit underlying the Eurodollar futures contract. The contract price of a Eurodollar futures contract is 980,000. The number of contracts that should be shorted is, therefore,

$$\frac{4,820,000}{980,000} \times 2 = 9.84$$

Rounding to the nearest whole number 10 contracts should be shorted.

Problem 6.17.

The treasurer should short Treasury bond futures contract. If bond prices go down, this futures position will provide offsetting gains. The number of contracts that should be shorted is

$$\frac{10,000,000 \times 7.1}{91,375 \times 8.8} = 88.30$$

Rounding to the nearest whole number 88 contracts should be shorted.

Problem 6.18.

The answer in Problem 6.17 is designed to reduce the duration to zero. To reduce the duration from 7.1 to 3.0 instead of from 7.1 to 0, the treasurer should short

$$\frac{4.1}{7.1} \times 88.30 = 50.99$$

or 51 contracts.

Problem 6.19.

You would prefer to own the Treasury bond. Under the 30/360 day count convention there is one day between October 30, 2006 and November 1, 2006. Under the actual/actual (in period) day count convention, there are two days. Therefore you would earn approximately twice as much interest by holding the Treasury bond. This assumes that the quoted prices of the two bonds are the same.

Problem 6.20.

The Eurodollar futures contract price of 88 means that the Eurodollar futures rate is 12% per annum. This is the forward rate for the 60- to 150-day period with quarterly compounding and an actual/360 day count convention.

Problem 6.21.

Using the notation of Section 6.4, $\sigma = 0.011$, $T_1 = 6$, and $T_2 = 6.25$. The convexity adjustment is

$$\frac{1}{2} \times 0.011^2 \times 6 \times 6.25 = 0.002269$$

or about 23 basis points. The futures rate is 4.8% with quarterly compounding and an actual/360 day count. This becomes $4.8 \times 365/360 = 4.867\%$ with an actual/actual day count. It is $4\ln(1 + .04867/4) = 4.84\%$ with continuous compounding. The forward rate is therefore $4.84 - 0.23 = 4.61\%$ with continuous compounding.

Problem 6.22.

Suppose that the contracts apply to the interest rate between times T_1 and T_2. There are two reasons for a difference between the forward rate and the futures rate. The first is that the futures contract is settled daily whereas the forward contract is settled once at time T_2. The second is that without daily settlement a futures contract would be settled at time T_1 not T_2. Both reasons tend to make the futures rate greater than the forward rate.

Chapter 7

Swaps

SOLUTIONS TO QUESTIONS AND PROBLEMS

Problem 7.1.

A has an apparent comparative advantage in fixed-rate markets but wants to borrow floating. B has an apparent comparative advantage in floating-rate markets but wants to borrow fixed. This provides the basis for the swap. There is a 1.4% per annum differential between the fixed rates offered to the two companies and a 0.5% per annum differential between the floating rates offered to the two companies. The total gain to all parties from the swap is therefore $1.4 - 0.5 = 0.9\%$ per annum. Because the bank gets 0.1% per annum of this gain, the swap should make each of A and B 0.4% per annum better off. This means that it should lead to A borrowing at LIBOR $- 0.3\%$ and to B borrowing at 13%. The appropriate arrangement is therefore as shown in Figure S7.1.

Figure S7.1: Swap for Problem 7.1

Problem 7.2.

X has a comparative advantage in yen markets but wants to borrow dollars. Y has a comparative advantage in dollar markets but wants to borrow yen. This provides the basis for the swap. There is a 1.5% per annum differential between the yen rates and a 0.4% per annum differential between the dollar rates. The total gain to all parties from the swap is therefore $1.5 - 0.4 = 1.1\%$ per annum. The bank requires 0.5% per annum, leaving 0.3% per annum for each of X and Y. The swap should lead to X borrowing dollars at $9.6 - 0.3 = 9.3\%$ per annum and to Y borrowing yen at $6.5 - 0.3 = 6.2\%$ per annum. The appropriate arrangement is therefore as shown in Figure S7.2. All foreign exchange risk is borne by the bank.

Figure S7.2: Swap for Problem 7.2

Problem 7.3.

In four months \$6 million ($= 0.5 \times 0.12 \times \$100$ million) will be received and \$4.8 million ($= 0.5 \times 0.096 \times \$100$ million) will be paid. (We ignore day count issues.) In 10 months \$6 million will be received, and the LIBOR rate prevailing in four months' time will be paid. The value of the fixed-rate bond underlying the swap is

$$6e^{-0.1 \times 4/12} + 106e^{-0.1 \times 10/12} = \$103.328 \text{ million}$$

The value of the floating-rate bond underlying the swap is

$$(100 + 4.8)e^{-0.1 \times 4/12} = \$101.364 \text{ million}$$

The value of the swap to the party paying floating is $\$103.328 - \$101.364 = \$1.964$ million. The value of the swap to the party paying fixed is $-\$1.964$ million.

These results can also be derived by decomposing the swap into forward contracts. Consider the party paying floating. The first forward contract involves paying \$4.8 million and receiving \$6 million in four months. It has a value of $1.2e^{-0.1 \times 4/12} = \$1.161$ million. To value the second forward contract, we note that the forward interest rate is 10% per annum with continuous compounding, or 10.254% per annum with semiannual compounding. The value of the forward contract is

$$100 \times (0.12 \times 0.5 - 0.10254 \times 0.5)e^{-0.1 \times 10/12} = \$0.803 \text{ million}$$

The total value of the forward contracts is therefore $\$1.161 + \$0.803 = \$1.964$ million.

Problem 7.4.

A swap rate for a particular maturity is the average of the bid and offer fixed rates that a market maker is prepared to exchange for LIBOR in a standard plain vanilla swap with that maturity. The swap rate for a particular maturity is the LIBOR/swap par yield for that maturity.

Problem 7.5.

The swap involves exchanging the sterling interest of $20 \times 0.14 = 2.8$ million for the dollar interest of $30 \times 0.1 = \$3$ million. The principal amounts are also exchanged at the end of the life of the swap. The value of the sterling bond underlying the swap is

$$\frac{2.8}{(1.11)^{1/4}} + \frac{22.8}{(1.11)^{5/4}} = 22.739 \text{ million pounds}$$

The value of the dollar bond underlying the swap is

$$\frac{3}{(1.08)^{1/4}} + \frac{33}{(1.08)^{5/4}} = \$32.916 \text{ million}$$

The value of the swap to the party paying sterling is therefore

$$32.916 - (22.739 \times 1.65) = -\$4.604 \text{ million}$$

The value of the swap to the party paying dollars is $+\$4.604$ million. The results can also be obtained by viewing the swap as a portfolio of forward contracts. The continuously compounded interest rates in sterling and dollars are 10.436% per annum and 7.696% per annum. The 3-month and 15-month forward exchange rates are $1.65e^{-(0.10436-0.07696) \times 0.25} = 1.6387$ and $1.65e^{-(0.10436-0.07696) \times 1.25} = 1.5944$. The values of the two forward contracts corresponding to the exchange of interest for the party paying sterling are therefore

$$(3 - 2.8 \times 1.6387)e^{-0.07696 \times 0.25} = -\$1.558 \text{ million}$$

$$(3 - 2.8 \times 1.5944)e^{-0.07696 \times 1.25} = -\$1.330 \text{ million}$$

The value of the forward contract corresponding to the exchange of principals is

$$(30 - 20 \times 1.5944)e^{-0.07696 \times 1.25} = -\$1.716 \text{ million}$$

The total value of the swap is $-\$1.558 - \$1.330 - \$1.716 = -\$4.604$ million.

Problem 7.6.

Credit risk arises from the possibility of a default by the counterparty. Market risk arises from movements in market variables such as interest rates and exchange rates. A complication is that the credit risk in a swap is contingent on the values of market variables. A company's position in a swap has credit risk only when the value of the swap to the company is positive.

Problem 7.7.

The rate is not truly fixed because, if the company's credit rating declines, it will not be able to roll over its floating rate borrowings at LIBOR plus 150 basis points. The effective fixed borrowing rate then increases. Suppose for example that the treasurer's spread over LIBOR increases from 150 basis points to 200 basis points. The borrowing rate increases from 5.2% to 5.7%.

Figure S7.3: Swap for Problem 7.9

Problem 7.8.

At the start of the swap, both contracts have a value of approximately zero. As time passes, it is likely that the swap values will change, so that one swap has a positive value to the bank and the other has a negative value to the bank. If the counterparty on the other side of the positive-value swap defaults, the bank still has to honor its contract with the other counterparty. It is liable to lose an amount equal to the positive value of the swap.

Problem 7.9.

The spread between the interest rates offered to X and Y is 0.8% per annum on fixed rate investments and 0.0% per annum on floating rate investments. This means that the total benefit to all parties from the swap is 0.8% per annum. Of this 0.2% per annum will go to the bank. This leaves 0.3% per annum for each of X and Y. In other words, company X should be able to get a fixed-rate return of 8.3% per annum while company Y should be able to get a floating-rate return LIBOR + 0.3% per annum. The required swap is shown in Figure S7.3. The bank earns 0.2%, company X earns 8.3%, and company Y earns LIBOR + 0.3%. This assumes that company X can continue to roll over the funds at LIBOR.

Problem 7.10.

At the end of year 3 the financial institution was due to receive $500,000 ($= 0.5 \times 10\%$ of $10 million) and pay $450,000 ($= 0.5 \times 9\%$ of $10 million). The immediate loss is therefore $50,000. To value the remaining swap we assume than forward rates are realized. All forward rates are 8% per annum. The remaining cash flows are therefore valued on the assumption that the floating payment is $0.5 \times 0.08 \times 10,000,000 = \$400,000$ and the net payment that would be received is $500,000 - 400,000 = \$100,000$. The total cost of default is therefore the cost of foregoing the following cash flows:

year 3:	$50,000
year $3\frac{1}{2}$:	$100,000
year 4:	$100,000
year $4\frac{1}{2}$:	$100,000
year 5:	$100,000

Discounting these cash flows to year 3 at 4% per six months we obtain the cost of the default as $413,000.

Problem 7.11.

When interest rates are compounded annually

$$F_0 = S_0 \left(\frac{1+r}{1+r_f} \right)^T$$

where F_0 is the T-year forward rate, S_0 is the spot rate, r is the domestic risk-free rate, and r_f is the foreign risk-free rate. As $r = 0.08$ and $r_f = 0.03$, the spot and forward exchange rates at the end of year 6 are

1 year forward:	0.8388
2 year forward:	0.8796
3 year forward:	0.9223
4 year forward:	0.9670

The value of the swap at the time of the default can be calculated on the assumption that forward rates are realized. The cash flows lost as a result of the default are therefore as follows:

Year	Dollar Paid	Swiss Franc Received	Forward Rate	Dollar Equivalent of Swiss Franc Received	Cash Flow Lost
6	560,000	300,000	0.8000	240,000	(320,000)
7	560,000	300,000	0.8388	251,600	(308,400)
8	560,000	300,000	0.8796	263,900	(296,100)
9	560,000	300,000	0.9223	276,700	(283,300)
10	7,560,000	10,300,000	0.9670	9,960,100	2,400,100

Discounting the numbers in the final column to the end of year 6 at 8% per annum, the cost of the default is $679,800.

Note that, if this were the only contract entered into by company Y, it would make no sense for the company to default at the end of year six as the exchange of payments at that time has a positive value to company Y. In practice company Y is likely to be defaulting and declaring bankruptcy for reasons unrelated to this particular contract and payments on the contract are likely to stop when bankruptcy is declared.

Problem 7.12.

Company A has a comparative advantage in the Canadian dollar fixed-rate market. Company B has a comparative advantage in the U.S. dollar floating-rate market. (This may be because of their tax positions.) However, company A wants to borrow in the U.S. dollar floating-rate market and company B wants to borrow in the Canadian dollar fixed-rate market. This gives rise to the swap opportunity.

The differential between the U.S. dollar floating rates is 0.5% per annum, and the differential between the Canadian dollar fixed rates is 1.5% per annum. The difference between the differentials is 1% per annum. The total potential gain to all parties from the swap is therefore 1% per annum, or 100 basis points. If the financial intermediary requires 50 basis points, each of A and B can be made 25 basis points better off. Thus a swap can be designed so that it

Figure S7.4: Swap for Problem 7.12

provides A with U.S. dollars at LIBOR + 0.25% per annum, and B with Canadian dollars at 6.25% per annum. The swap is shown in Figure S7.4.

Principal payments flow in the opposite direction to the arrows at the start of the life of the swap and in the same direction as the arrows at the end of the life of the swap. The financial institution would be exposed to some foreign exchange risk which could be hedged using forward contracts.

Problem 7.13.

The financial institution will have to buy 1.1% of the AUD principal in the forward market for each year of the life of the swap. Since AUD interest rates are higher than dollar interest rates, AUD is at a discount in forward markets. This means that the AUD purchased for year 2 is less expensive than that purchased for year 1; the AUD purchased for year 3 is less expensive than that purchased for year 2; and so on. This works in favor of the financial institution and means that its spread increases with time. The spread is always above 20 basis points.

Problem 7.14.

Consider a plain-vanilla interest rate swap involving two companies X and Y. We suppose that X is paying fixed and receiving floating while Y is paying floating and receiving fixed.

The quote suggests that company X will usually be less creditworthy than company Y. (Company X might be a BBB-rated company that has difficulty in accessing fixed-rate markets directly; company Y might be a AAA-rated company that has no difficulty accessing fixed or floating rate markets.) Presumably company X wants fixed-rate funds and company Y wants floating-rate funds.

The financial institution will realize a loss if company Y defaults when rates are high or if company X defaults when rates are low. These events are relatively unlikely since (a) Y is unlikely to default in any circumstances and (b) defaults are less likely to happen when rates are low. For the purposes of illustration, suppose that the probabilities of various events are as follows:

Default by Y:	0.001
Default by X:	0.010
Rates high when default occurs:	0.7
Rates low when default occurs:	0.3

The probability of a loss is

$$0.001 \times 0.7 + 0.010 \times 0.3 = 0.0037$$

If the roles of X and Y in the swap had been reversed the probability of a loss would be

$$0.001 \times 0.3 + 0.010 \times 0.7 = 0.0073$$

Assuming companies are more likely to default when interest rates are high, the above argument shows that the observation in quotes has the effect of decreasing the risk of a financial institution's swap portfolio. It is worth noting that the assumption that defaults are more likely when interest rates are high is open to question. The assumption is motivated by the thought that high interest rates often lead to financial difficulties for corporations. However, there is often a time lag between interest rates being high and the resultant default. When the default actually happens interest rates may be relatively low.

Problem 7.15.

In an interest-rate swap a financial institution's exposure depends on the difference between a fixed-rate of interest and a floating-rate of interest. It has no exposure to the notional principal. In a loan the whole principal can be lost.

Problem 7.16.

The bank is paying a floating-rate on the deposits and receiving a fixed-rate on the loans. It can offset its risk by entering into interest rate swaps (with other financial institutions or corporations) in which it contracts to pay fixed and receive floating.

Problem 7.17.

The floating payments can be valued in currency A by (i) assuming that the forward rates are realized, and (ii) discounting the resulting cash flows at appropriate currency A discount rates. Suppose that the value is V_A. The fixed payments can be valued in currency B by discounting them at the appropriate currency B discount rates. Suppose that the value is V_B. If Q is the current exchange rate (number of units of currency A per unit of currency B), the value of the swap in currency A is $V_A - QV_B$. Alternatively, it is $V_A/Q - V_B$ in currency B.

Problem 7.18.

The two-year swap rate is 5.4%. This means that a two-year LIBOR bond paying a semiannual coupon at the rate of 5.4% per annum sells for par. If R_2 is the two-year LIBOR zero rate

$$2.7e^{-0.05 \times 0.5} + 2.7e^{-0.05 \times 1.0} + 2.7e^{-0.05 \times 1.5} + 102.7e^{-R_2 \times 2.0} = 100$$

Solving this gives $R_2 = 0.05342$. The 2.5-year swap rate is assumed to be 5.5%. This means that a 2.5-year LIBOR bond paying a semiannual coupon at the rate of 5.5% per annum sells for par. If $R_{2.5}$ is the 2.5-year LIBOR zero rate

$$2.75e^{-0.05 \times 0.5} + 2.75e^{-0.05 \times 1.0} + 2.75e^{-0.05 \times 1.5} + 2.75e^{-0.05342 \times 2.0} + 102.75e^{-R_{2.5} \times 2.5} = 100$$

Solving this gives $R_{2.5} = 0.05442$. The 3-year swap rate is 5.6%. This means that a 3-year LIBOR bond paying a semiannual coupon at the rate of 5.6% per annum sells for par. If R_3 is the three-year LIBOR zero rate

$$2.8e^{-0.05 \times 0.5} + 2.8e^{-0.05 \times 1.0} + 2.8e^{-0.05 \times 1.5} +$$
$$+ 2.8e^{-0.05342 \times 2.0} + 2.8e^{-0.05442 \times 2.5} + 102.8e^{-R_3 \times 3.0} = 100$$

Solving this gives $R_3 = 0.05544$. The zero rates for maturities 2.0, 2.5, and 3.0 years are therefore 5.342%, 5.442%, and 5.544%, respectively.

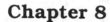

Chapter 8
Mechanics of Options Markets

SOLUTIONS TO QUESTIONS AND PROBLEMS

Problem 8.1.

The investor makes a profit if the price of the stock on the expiration date is less than $37. In these circumstances the gain from exercising the option is greater than $3. The option will be exercised if the stock price is less than $40 at the maturity of the option. The variation of the investor's profit with the stock price in Figure S8.1.

Problem 8.2.

The investor makes a profit if the price of the stock is below $54 on the expiration date. If the stock price is below $50, the option will not be exercised, and the investor makes a profit of $4. If the stock price is between $50 and $54, the option is exercised and the investor makes a profit between $0 and $4. The variation of the investor's profit with the stock price is as shown in Figure S8.2.

Figure S8.1: Investor's profit in Problem 8.1

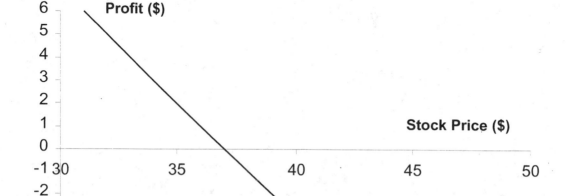

Figure S8.2: Investor's profit in Problem 8.2

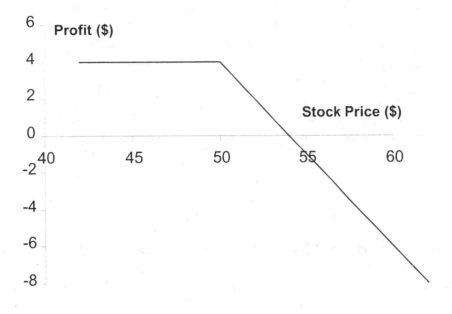

Problem 8.3.

The payoff to the investor is

$$- \max\left(S_T - K, 0\right) + \max\left(K - S_T, 0\right)$$

This is $K - S_T$ in all circumstances. The investor's position is the same as a short position in a forward contract with delivery price K.

Problem 8.4.

When an investor buys an option, cash must be paid up front. There is no possibility of future liabilities and therefore no need for a margin account. When an investor sells an option, there are potential future liabilities. To protect against the risk of a default, margins are required.

Problem 8.5.

On April 1 options trade with expiration months of April, May, August, and November. On May 30 options trade with expiration months of June, July, August, and November.

Problem 8.6.

The strike price is reduced to $30, and the option gives the holder the right to purchase twice as many shares.

Problem 8.7.

Executive stock options last a long time (often 10 years or more). There is a vesting period during which the options cannot be exercised. If the executive leaves the company during the vesting period the options are forfeited. If the executive leaves the company after the end of the vesting period, in-the-money options are exercised immediately while out-of-the-money options are forfeited. The options cannot be sold to another party by the executive.

Problem 8.8.

The Philadelphia Exchange offers European and American options with standard strike prices and times to maturity. Options in the over-the-counter market have the advantage that they can be tailored to meet the precise needs of the treasurer. Their disadvantage is that they expose the treasurer to some credit risk. Exchanges organize their trading so that there is virtually no credit risk.

Problem 8.9.

Ignoring the time value of money, the holder of the option will make a profit if the stock price at maturity of the option is greater than $105. This is because the payoff to the holder of the option is, in these circumstances, greater than the $5 paid for the option. The option will be exercised if the stock price at maturity is greater than $100. Note that if the stock price is between $100 and $105 the option is exercised, but the holder of the option takes a loss overall. The profit from a long position is as shown in Figure S8.3.

Problem 8.10.

Ignoring the time value of money, the seller of the option will make a profit if the stock price at maturity is greater than $52.00. This is because the cost to the seller of the option is in these circumstances less than the price received for the option. The option will be exercised if the stock price at maturity is less than $60.00. Note that if the stock price is between $52.00 and $60.00 the seller of the option makes a profit even though the option is exercised. The profit from the short position is as shown in Figure S8.4.

Problem 8.11.

The terminal value of the long forward contract is:

$$S_T - F_0$$

where S_T is the price of the asset at maturity and F_0 is the forward price of the asset at the time the portfolio is set up. (The delivery price in the forward contract is also F_0.)

The terminal value of the put option is:

$$\max(F_0 - S_T, 0)$$

The terminal value of the portfolio is therefore

$$S_T - F_0 + \max(F_0 - S_T, 0)$$

Figure S8.3: Profit from long position in Problem 8.9

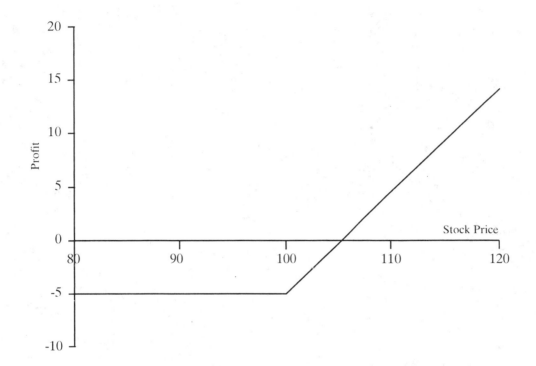

$$= \max\left(0, S_T - F_0\right)$$

This is the same as the terminal value of a European call option with the same maturity as the forward contract and an exercise price equal to F_0. This result is illustrated in the Figure S8.5.

We have shown that the forward contract plus the put is worth the same as a call with the same strike price and time to maturity as the put. The forward contract is worth zero at the time the portfolio is set up. It follows that the put is worth the same as the call at the time the portfolio is set up.

Problem 8.12.

Figure S8.6 shows the variation of the trader's position with the asset price. We can divide the alternative asset prices into three ranges:

(a) When the asset price less than $40, the put option provides a payoff of $40 - S_T$ and the call option provides no payoff. The options cost $7 and so the total profit is $33 - S_T$.

(b) When the asset price is between $40 and $45, neither option provides a payoff. There is a net loss of $7.

Figure S8.4: Profit from short position in Problem 8.10

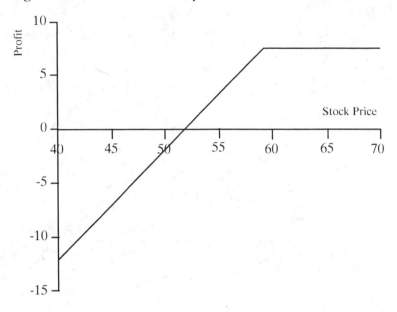

Figure S8.5: Profit from portfolio in Problem 8.11

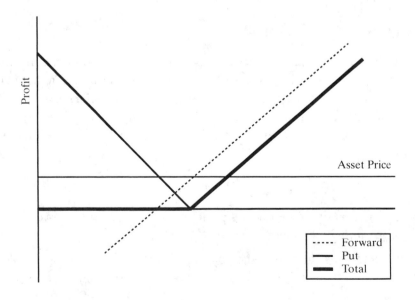

Figure S8.6: Profit from trading strategy in Problem 8.12

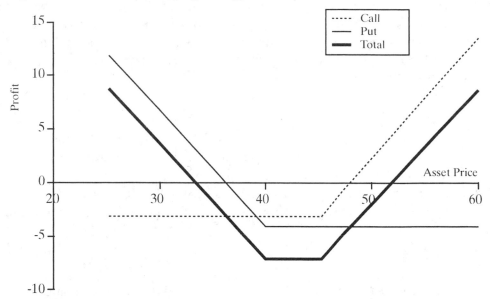

(c) When the asset price greater than \$45, the call option provides a payoff of $S_T - 45$ and the put option provides no payoff. Taking into account the \$7 cost of the options, the total profit is $S_T - 52$.

(d) The trader makes a profit (ignoring the time value of money) if the stock price is less than \$33 or greater than \$52. This type of trading strategy is known as a strangle and is discussed in Chapter 10.

Problem 8.13.

The holder of an American option has all the same rights as the holder of a European option and more. It must therefore be worth at least as much. If it were not, an arbitrageur could short the European option and take a long position in the American option.

Problem 8.14.

The holder of an American option has the right to exercise it immediately. The American option must therefore be worth at least as much as its intrinsic value. If it were not an arbitrageur could lock in a sure profit by buying the option and exercising it immediately.

Problem 8.15.

Writing a put gives a payoff of $\min(S_T - K, 0)$. Buying a call gives a payoff of $\max(S_T - K, 0)$. In both cases the potential payoff is $S_T - K$. The difference is that for a written put the counterparty chooses whether you get the payoff (and will allow you to get it only when it is negative to you). For a long call you decide whether you get the payoff (and you choose to get it when it is positive to you).

Problem 8.16.

Forward contracts lock in the exchange rate that will apply to a particular transaction in the future. Options provide insurance that the exchange rate will not be worse than some level. The advantage of a forward contract is that uncertainty is eliminated as far as possible. The disadvantage is that the outcome with hedging can be significantly worse than the outcome with no hedging. This disadvantage is not as marked with options. However, unlike forward contracts, options involve an up-front cost.

Problem 8.17.

   (a) The option contract becomes one to buy $500 \times 1.1 = 550$ shares with an exercise price $40/1.1 = 36.36$.

   (b) There is no effect. The terms of an options contract are not normally adjusted for cash dividends.

   (c) The option contract becomes one to buy $500 \times 4 = 2,000$ shares with an exercise price of $40/4 = \$10$.

Problem 8.18.

The exchange has certain rules governing when trading in a new option is initiated. These mean that the option is close-to-the-money when it is first traded. If all call options are in the money it is therefore likely that the stock price has risen since trading in the option began.

Problem 8.19.

An unexpected cash dividend would reduce the stock price on the ex-dividend date. This stock price reduction would not be anticipated by option holders. As a result there would be a reduction in the value of a call option and an increase the value of a put option. (Note that the terms of an option are adjusted for cash dividends only in exceptional circumstances.)

Problem 8.20.

   (a) March, April, June and September

   (b) July, August, September, December

   (c) August, September, December, March.

Longer dated options may also trade.

Problem 8.21.

A "fair" price for the option can reasonably be assumed to be half way between the bid and the offer price quoted by a market maker. An investor typically buys at the market maker's offer and sells at the market maker's bid. Each time he or she does this there is a hidden cost equal to half the bid-offer spread.

Problem 8.22.

The two calculations are necessary to determine the initial margin. The first gives

$$500 \times (3.5 + 0.2 \times 57 - 3) = 5,950$$

The second gives

$$500 \times (3.5 + 0.1 \times 57) = 4,600$$

The initial margin is the greater of these, or $5,950. Part of this can be provided by the initial amount of $500 \times 3.5 = \$1,750$ received for the options.

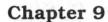

Chapter 9

Properties of Stock Options

SOLUTIONS TO QUESTIONS AND PROBLEMS

Problem 9.1.

The six factors affecting stock option prices are the stock price, strike price, risk-free interest rate, volatility, time to maturity, and dividends.

Problem 9.2.

The lower bound is

$$28 - 25e^{-0.08 \times 0.3333} = \$3.66$$

Problem 9.3.

The lower bound is

$$15e^{-0.06 \times 0.08333} - 12 = \$2.93$$

Problem 9.4.

Delaying exercise delays the payment of the strike price. This means that the option holder is able to earn interest on the strike price for a longer period of time. Delaying exercise also provides insurance against the stock price falling below the strike price by the expiration date. Assume that the option holder has an amount of cash K and that interest rates are zero. Exercising early means that the option holder's position will be worth S_T at expiration. Delaying exercise means that it will be worth $\max(K, S_T)$ at expiration.

Problem 9.5.

An American put when held in conjunction with the underlying stock provides insurance. It guarantees that the stock can be sold for the strike price, K. If the put is exercised early, the insurance ceases. However, the option holder receives the strike price immediately and is able to earn interest on it between the time of the early exercise and the expiration date.

Problem 9.6.

An American call option can be exercised at any time. If it is exercised its holder gets the intrinsic value. It follows that an American call option must be worth at least its intrinsic value. A European call option can be worth less than its intrinsic value. Consider, for example, the situation where a stock is expected to provide a very high dividend during the life of an option.

The price of the stock will decline as a result of the dividend. Because the European option can be exercised only after the dividend has been paid, its value may be less than the intrinsic value today.

Problem 9.7.

In this case $c = 1$, $T = 0.25$, $S_0 = 19$, $K = 20$, and $r = 0.04$. From put–call parity

$$p = c + Ke^{-rT} - S_0$$

or

$$p = 1 + 20e^{-0.04 \times 0.25} - 19 = 1.80$$

so that the European put price is $1.80.

Problem 9.8.

When early exercise is not possible, we can argue that two portfolios that are worth the same at time T must be worth the same at earlier times. When early exercise is possible, the argument falls down. Suppose that $P + S > C + Ke^{-rT}$. This situation does not lead to an arbitrage opportunity. If we buy the call, short the put, and short the stock, we cannot be sure of the result because we do not know when the put will be exercised.

Problem 9.9.

The lower bound is

$$80 - 75e^{-0.1 \times 0.5} = \$8.66$$

Problem 9.10.

The lower bound is

$$65e^{-0.05 \times 2/12} - 58 = \$6.46$$

Problem 9.11.

The present value of the strike price is $60e^{-0.12 \times 4/12} = \$57.65$. The present value of the dividend is $0.80e^{-0.12 \times 1/12} = 0.79$. Because

$$5 < 64 - 57.65 - 0.79$$

the condition in equation (9.5) is violated. An arbitrageur should buy the option and short the stock. This generates $64 - 5 = \$59$. The arbitrageur invests $0.79 of this at 12% for one month to pay the dividend of $0.80 in one month. The remaining $58.21 is invested for four months at 12%. Regardless of what happens a profit will materialize.

   If the stock price declines below $60 in four months, the arbitrageur loses the $5 spent on the option but gains on the short position. The arbitrageur shorts when the stock price is $64, has to pay dividends with a present value of $0.79, and closes out the short position when the stock price is $60 or less. Because $57.65 is the present value of $60, the short position generates at least $64 - 57.65 - 0.79 = \$5.56$ in present value terms. The present value of the arbitrageur's gain is therefore at least $5.56 - 5.00 = \$0.56$.

If the stock price is above \$60 at the expiration of the option, the option is exercised. The arbitrageur buys the stock for \$60 in four months and closes out the short position. The present value of the \$60 paid for the stock is \$57.65 and as before the dividend has a present value of \$0.79. The gain from the short position and the exercise of the option is therefore exactly $64 - 57.65 - 0.79 = \$5.56$. The arbitrageur's gain in present value terms is exactly $5.56 - 5.00 = \$0.56$.

Problem 9.12.

In this case the present value of the strike price is $50e^{-0.06 \times 1/12} = 49.75$. Because

$$2.5 < 49.75 - 47.00$$

the condition in equation (9.2) is violated. An arbitrageur should borrow \$49.50 at 6% for one month, buy the stock, and buy the put option. This generates a profit in all circumstances.

If the stock price is above \$50 in one month, the option expires worthless, but the stock can be sold for at least \$50. A sum of \$50 received in one month has a present value of \$49.75 today. The strategy therefore generates profit with a present value of at least \$0.25.

If the stock price is below \$50 in one month the put option is exercised and the stock owned is sold for exactly \$50 (or \$49.75 in present value terms). The trading strategy therefore generates a profit of exactly \$0.25 in present value terms.

Problem 9.13.

The early exercise of an American put is attractive when the interest earned on the strike price is greater than the insurance element lost. When interest rates increase, the value of the interest earned on the strike price increases making early exercise more attractive. When volatility decreases, the insurance element is less valuable. Again this makes early exercise more attractive.

Problem 9.14.

Using the notation in the chapter, the put-call parity result in equation (9.7) gives

$$c + Ke^{-rT} + D = p + S_0$$

or

$$p = c + Ke^{-rT} + D - S_0$$

In this case

$$p = 2 + 30e^{-0.1 \times 6/12} + 0.5e^{-0.1 \times 2/12} + 0.5e^{-0.1 \times 5/12} - 29 = 2.51$$

In other words the put price is \$2.51.

Problem 9.15.

If the put price is $3.00, it is too high relative to the call price. An arbitrageur should buy the call, short the put and short the stock. This generates $-2+3+29 = \$30$ in cash which is invested at 10%. Regardless of what happens a profit with a present value of $3.00-2.51 = \$0.49$ is locked in.

If the stock price is above $30 in six months, the call option is exercised, and the put option expires worthless. The call option enables the stock to be bought for $30, or $30e^{-0.10\times6/12} = \$28.54$ in present value terms. The dividends on the short position cost $0.5e^{-0.1\times2/12} + 0.5e^{-0.1\times5/12} = \$0.97$ in present value terms so that there is a profit with a present value of $30-28.54-0.97 = \$0.49$.

If the stock price is below $30 in six months, the put option is exercised and the call option expires worthless. The short put option leads to the stock being bought for $30, or $30e^{-0.10\times6/12} = \$28.54$ in present value terms. The dividends on the short position cost $0.5e^{-0.1\times2/12} + 0.5e^{-0.1\times5/12} = \$0.97$ in present value terms so that there is a profit with a present value of $30-28.54-0.97 = \$0.49$.

Problem 9.16.

From equation (9.4)

$$S_0 - K \leq C - P \leq S_0 - Ke^{-rT}$$

In this case

$$31 - 30 \leq 4 - P \leq 31 - 30e^{-0.08\times0.25}$$

or

$$1.00 \leq 4.00 - P \leq 1.59$$

or

$$2.41 \leq P \leq 3.00$$

Upper and lower bounds for the price of an American put are therefore $2.41 and $3.00.

Problem 9.17.

If the American put price is greater than $3.00 an arbitrageur can sell the American put, short the stock, and buy the American call. This realizes at least $3+31-4 = \$30$ which can be invested at the risk-free interest rate. At some stage during the 3-month period either the American put or the American call will be exercised. The arbitrageur then pays $30, receives the stock and closes out the short position. The cash flows to the arbitrageur are +$30 at time zero and −$30 at some future time. These cash flows have a positive present value.

Problem 9.18.

As in the text we use c and p to denote the European call and put option price, and C and P to denote the American call and put option prices. Because $P \geq p$, it follows from put–call parity that

$$P \geq c + Ke^{-rT} - S_0$$

and since $c = C$,

$$P \geq C + Ke^{-rT} - S_0$$

or

$$C - P \geq S_0 - Ke^{-rT}$$

For a further relationship between C and P, consider

   Portfolio I: One European call option plus an amount of cash equal to K.
   Portfolio J: One American put option plus one share.

Both options have the same exercise price and expiration date. Assume that the cash in portfolio I is invested at the risk-free interest rate. If the put option is not exercised early portfolio J is worth

$$\max\left(S_T, K\right)$$

at time T. Portfolio I is worth

$$\max\left(S_T - K, 0\right) + Ke^{rT} = \max\left(S_T, K\right) - K + Ke^{rT}$$

at this time. Portfolio I is therefore worth more than portfolio J. Suppose next that the put option in portfolio J is exercised early, say, at time τ. This means that portfolio J is worth K at time τ. However, even if the call option were worthless, portfolio I would be worth $Ke^{r\tau}$ at time τ. It follows that portfolio I is worth at least as much as portfolio J in all circumstances. Hence

$$c + K \geq P + S_0$$

Since $c = C$,

$$C + K \geq P + S_0$$

or

$$C - P \geq S_0 - K$$

Combining this with the other inequality derived above for $C - P$, we obtain

$$S_0 - K \leq C - P \leq S_0 - Ke^{-rT}$$

Problem 9.19.

As in the text we use c and p to denote the European call and put option price, and C and P to denote the American call and put option prices. The present value of the dividends will be denoted by D. As shown in the answer to Problem 9.18, when there are no dividends

$$C - P \leq S_0 - Ke^{-rT}$$

Dividends reduce C and increase P. Hence this relationship must also be true when there are dividends.

For a further relationship between C and P, consider

> *Portfolio I:* One European call option plus an amount of cash equal to $D + K$.
> *Portfolio J:* One American put option plus one share.

Both options have the same exercise price and expiration date. Assume that the cash in portfolio I is invested at the risk-free interest rate. If the put option is not exercised early, portfolio J is worth

$$\max(S_T, K) + De^{rT}$$

at time T. Portfolio I is worth

$$\max(S_T - K, 0) + (D + K)e^{rT} = \max(S_T, K) + De^{rT} + Ke^{rT} - K$$

at this time. Portfolio I is therefore worth more than portfolio J. Suppose next that the put option in portfolio J is exercised early, say, at time τ. This means that portfolio J is worth at most $K + De^{r\tau}$ at time τ. However, even if the call option were worthless, portfolio I would be worth $(D + K)e^{r\tau}$ at time τ. It follows that portfolio I is worth more than portfolio J in all circumstances. Hence

$$c + D + K \geq P + S_0$$

Because $C \geq c$

$$C - P \geq S_0 - D - K$$

Problem 9.20.

Executive stock options may be exercised early because the executive needs the cash or because he or she is uncertain about the company's future prospects. Regular call options can be sold in the market in either of these two situations, but executive stock options cannot be sold. In theory an executive can short the company's stock as an alternative to exercising. In practice this is not usually encouraged and may even be illegal.

Problem 9.21.

The graphs can be produced from the first worksheet in DerivaGem. Select Equity as the Underlying Type. Select Analytic European as the Option Type. Input stock price as 50, volatility as 30%, risk-free rate as 5%, time to exercise as 1 year, and exercise price as 50. Leave the dividend table blank because we are assuming no dividends. Select the button corresponding to call. Do not select the implied volatility button. Hit the *Enter* key and click on calculate. DerivaGem will show the price of the option as 7.15562248. Move to the Graph Results on the right hand side of the worksheet. Enter Option Price for the vertical axis and Asset price for the horizontal axis. Choose the minimum strike price value as 10 (software will not accept 0) and the maximum strike price value as 100. Hit *Enter* and click on *Draw Graph*. This will produce Figure 9.1a. Figures 9.1c, 9.1e, 9.2a, and 9.2c can be produced similarly by changing the horizontal axis. By selecting put instead of call and recalculating the rest of the figures can be produced. You are encouraged to experiment with this worksheet. Try different parameter values and different types of options.

Chapter 10
Trading Strategies Involving Options

SOLUTIONS TO QUESTIONS AND PROBLEMS

Problem 10.1.

A protective put consists of a long position in a put option combined with a long position in the underlying shares. It is equivalent to a long position in a call option plus a certain amount of cash. This follows from put–call parity:

$$p + S_0 = c + Ke^{-rT} + D$$

Problem 10.2.

A bear spread can be created using two call options with the same maturity and different strike prices. The investor shorts the call option with the lower strike price and buys the call option with the higher strike price. A bear spread can also be created using two put options with the same maturity and different strike prices. In this case, the investor shorts the put option with the lower strike price and buys the put option with the higher strike price.

Problem 10.3.

A butterfly spread involves a position in options with three different strike prices (K_1, K_2, and K_3). A butterfly spread should be purchased when the investor considers that the price of the underlying stock is likely to stay close to the central strike price, K_2.

Problem 10.4.

An investor can create a butterfly spread by buying call options with strike prices of $15 and $20 and selling two call options with strike prices of $17\frac{1}{2}$. The initial investment is $4 + \frac{1}{2} - 2 \times 2 = \$\frac{1}{2}$. The following table shows the variation of profit with the final stock price:

Stock Price S_T	Profit
$S_T < 15$	$-\frac{1}{2}$
$15 < S_T < 17\frac{1}{2}$	$(S_T - 15) - \frac{1}{2}$
$17\frac{1}{2} < S_T < 20$	$(20 - S_T) - \frac{1}{2}$
$S_T > 20$	$-\frac{1}{2}$

Problem 10.5.

A reverse calendar spread is created by buying a short-maturity option and selling a long-maturity option, both with the same strike price.

Problem 10.6.

Both a straddle and a strangle are created by combining a long position in a call with a long position in a put. In a straddle the two have the same strike price and expiration date. In a strangle they have different strike prices and the same expiration date.

Problem 10.7.

A strangle is created by buying both options. The pattern of profits is as follows:

Stock Price S_T	Profit
$S_T < 45$	$(45 - S_T) - 5$
$45 < S_T < 50$	-5
$S_T > 50$	$(S_T - 50) - 5$

Problem 10.8.

A bull spread using calls provides a profit pattern with the same general shape as a bull spread using puts (see Figures 10.2 and 10.3 in the text). Define p_1 and c_1 as the prices of put and call with strike price K_1 and p_2 and c_2 as the prices of a put and call with strike price K_2. From put-call parity

$$p_1 + S = c_1 + K_1 e^{-rT}$$
$$p_2 + S = c_2 + K_2 e^{-rT}$$

Hence:

$$p_1 - p_2 = c_1 - c_2 - (K_2 - K_1)e^{-rT}$$

This shows that the initial investment when the spread is created from puts is less than the initial investment when it is created from calls by an amount $(K_2 - K_1)e^{-rT}$. In fact as mentioned in the text the initial investment when the bull spread is created from puts is negative, while the initial investment when it is created from calls is positive.

The profit when calls are used to create the bull spread is higher than when puts are used by $(K_2 - K_1)(1 - e^{-rT})$. This reflects the fact that the call strategy involves an additional risk-free investment of $(K_2 - K_1)e^{-rT}$ over the put strategy. This earns interest of $(K_2 - K_1)e^{-rT}(e^{rT} - 1) = (K_2 - K_1)(1 - e^{-rT})$.

Problem 10.9.

An aggressive bull spread using call options is discussed in the text. Both of the options used have relatively high strike prices. Similarly, an aggressive bear spread can be created using put options. Both of the options should be out of the money (that is, they should have relatively low strike prices). The spread then costs very little to set up because both of the puts are worth close to zero. In most circumstances the spread will provide zero payoff. However, there is a small chance that the stock price will fall fast so that on expiration both options will be in the money. The spread then provides a payoff equal to the difference between the two strike prices, $K_2 - K_1$.

Problem 10.10.

A bull spread is created by buying the $30 put and selling the $35 put. This strategy gives rise to an initial cash inflow of $3. The outcome is as follows:

Stock Price	Payoff	Profit
$S_T \geq 35$	0	3
$30 \leq S_T < 35$	$S_T - 35$	$S_T - 32$
$S_T < 30$	-5	-2

A bear spread is created by selling the $30 put and buying the $35 put. This strategy costs $3 initially. The outcome is as follows:

Stock Price	Payoff	Profit
$S_T \geq 35$	0	-3
$30 \leq S_T < 35$	$35 - S_T$	$32 - S_T$
$S_T < 30$	5	2

Problem 10.11.

Define c_1, c_2, and c_3 as the prices of calls with strike prices K_1, K_2 and K_3. Define p_1, p_2 and p_3 as the prices of puts with strike prices K_1, K_2 and K_3. With the usual notation

$$c_1 + K_1 e^{-rT} = p_1 + S$$
$$c_2 + K_2 e^{-rT} = p_2 + S$$
$$c_3 + K_3 e^{-rT} = p_3 + S$$

Hence

$$c_1 + c_3 - 2c_2 + (K_1 + K_3 - 2K_2)e^{-rT} = p_1 + p_3 - 2p_2$$

Because $K_2 - K_1 = K_3 - K_2$, it follows that $K_1 + K_3 - 2K_2 = 0$ and

$$c_1 + c_3 - 2c_2 = p_1 + p_3 - 2p_2$$

The cost of a butterfly spread created using European calls is therefore exactly the same as the cost of a butterfly spread created using European puts.

Problem 10.12.

A straddle is created by buying both the call and the put. This strategy costs $10. The profit/loss is shown in the following table:

Stock Price	Payoff	Profit
$S_T > 60$	$S_T - 60$	$S_T - 70$
$S_T \leq 60$	$60 - S_T$	$50 - S_T$

This shows that the straddle will lead to a loss if the final stock price is between $50 and $70.

Problem 10.13.

The bull spread is created by buying a put with strike price K_1 and selling a put with strike price K_2. The payoff is calculated as follows:

Stock Price Range	Payoff from Long Put Option	Payoff from Short Put Option	Total Payoff
$S_T \geq K_2$	0	0	0
$K_1 < S_T < K_2$	0	$S_T - K_2$	$-(K_2 - S_T)$
$S_T \leq K_1$	$K_1 - S_T$	$S_T - K_2$	$-(K_2 - K_1)$

Problem 10.14.

Possible strategies are:

    Strangle
    Straddle
    Strip
    Strap
    Reverse calendar spread
    Reverse butterfly spread

The strategies all provide positive profits when there are large stock price moves. A strangle is less expensive than a straddle, but requires a bigger move in the stock price in order to provide a positive profit. Strips and straps are more expensive than straddles but provide bigger profits in certain circumstances. A strip will provide a bigger profit when there is a large downward stock price move. A strap will provide a bigger profit when there is a large upward stock price move. In the case of strangles, straddles, strips and straps, the profit increases as the size of the stock price movement increases. By contrast in a reverse calendar spread and a reverse butterfly spread there is a maximum potential profit regardless of the size of the stock price movement.

Problem 10.15.

Suppose that the delivery price is K and the delivery date is T. The forward contract is created by buying a European call and selling a European put when both options have strike price K and exercise date T. This portfolio provides a payoff of $S_T - K$ under all circumstances where S_T is the stock price at time T. Suppose that F_0 is the forward price. If $K = F_0$, the forward contract that is created has zero value. This shows that the price of a call equals the price of a put when the strike price is F_0.

Figure S10.1: Profit Pattern in Problem 10.17

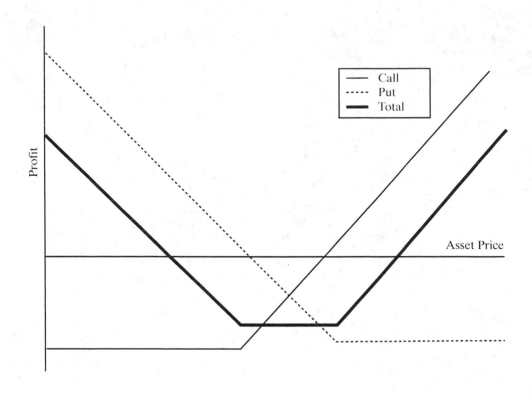

Problem 10.16.

A box spread is a bull spread created using calls and a bear spread created using puts. With the notation in the text it consists of a) a long call with strike K_1, b) a short call with strike K_2, c) a long put with strike K_2, and d) a short put with strike K_1. a) and d) give a long forward contract with delivery price K_1; b) and c) give a short forward contract with delivery price K_2. The two forward contracts taken together give the payoff of $K_2 - K_1$.

Problem 10.17.

The result is shown in Figure S10.1. The profit pattern from a long position in a call and a put when the put has a higher strike price than a call is much the same as when the call has a higher strike price than the put. Both the initial investment and the final payoff are much higher in the first case.

Problem 10.18.

To use DerivaGem select the first worksheet and choose Currency as the Underlying Type. Select Analytic European as the Option Type. Input exchange rate as 0.64, volatility as 15%, risk-free rate as 5%, foreign risk-free interest rate as 4%, time to exercise as 1 year, and exercise price as 0.60. Select the button corresponding to call. Do not select the implied volatility button. Hit the *Enter* key and click on calculate. DerivaGem will show the price of the option as 0.0618. Change the exercise price to 0.65, hit *Enter*, and click on calculate again. DerivaGem will show the value of the option as 0.0352. Change the exercise price to 0.70, hit *Enter*, and click on calculate. DerivaGem will show the value of the option as 0.0181.

Now select the button corresponding to put and repeat the procedure. DerivaGem shows the values of puts with strike prices 0.60, 0.65, and 0.70 to be 0.0176, 0.0386, and 0.0690, respectively.

The cost of setting up the butterfly spread when calls are used is therefore

$$0.0618 + 0.0181 - 2 \times 0.0352 = 0.0095$$

The cost of setting up the butterfly spread when puts are used is

$$0.0176 + 0.0690 - 2 \times 0.0386 = 0.0094$$

Allowing for rounding errors these two are the same.

Chapter 11
Binomial Trees

SOLUTIONS TO QUESTIONS AND PROBLEMS

Problem 11.1.

Consider a portfolio consisting of :

$$-1 \quad : \quad \text{call option}$$
$$+\Delta \quad : \quad \quad \text{shares}$$

If the stock price rises to \$42, the portfolio is worth $42\Delta - 3$. If the stock price falls to \$38, it is worth 38Δ. These are the same when

$$42\Delta - 3 = 38\Delta$$

or $\Delta = 0.75$. The value of the portfolio in one month is 28.5 for both stock prices. Its value today must be the present value of 28.5, or $28.5e^{-0.08\times0.08333} = 28.31$. This means that

$$-f + 40\Delta = 28.31$$

where f is the call price. Because $\Delta = 0.75$, the call price is $40 \times 0.75 - 28.31 = \$1.69$. As an alternative approach, we can calculate the probability, p, of an up movement in a risk-neutral world. This must satisfy:

$$42p + 38(1-p) = 40e^{0.08\times0.08333}$$

so that

$$4p = 40e^{0.08\times0.08333} - 38$$

or $p = 0.5669$. The value of the option is then its expected payoff discounted at the risk-free rate:

$$[3 \times 0.5669 + 0 \times 0.4331]e^{-0.08\times0.08333} = 1.69$$

or \$1.69. This agrees with the previous calculation.

Problem 11.2.

In the no-arbitrage approach, we set up a riskless portfolio consisting of a position in the option and a position in the stock. By setting the return on the portfolio equal to the risk-free interest rate, we are able to value the option. When we use risk-neutral valuation, we first choose probabilities for the branches of the tree so that the expected return on the stock equals the risk-free interest rate. We then value the option by calculating its expected payoff and discounting this expected payoff at the risk-free interest rate.

Problem 11.3.

The delta of a stock option measures the sensitivity of the option price to the price of the stock when small changes are considered. Specifically, it is the ratio of the change in the price of the stock option to the change in the price of the underlying stock.

Problem 11.4.

Consider a portfolio consisting of :

$$-1 \quad : \quad \text{put option}$$
$$+\Delta \quad : \quad \text{shares}$$

If the stock price rises to $55, this is worth 55Δ. If the stock price falls to $45, the portfolio is worth $45\Delta - 5$. These are the same when

$$45\Delta - 5 = 55\Delta$$

or $\Delta = -0.50$. The value of the portfolio in one month is -27.5 for both stock prices. Its value today must be the present value of -27.5, or $-27.5e^{-0.1 \times 0.5} = -26.16$. This means that

$$-f + 50\Delta = -26.16$$

where f is the put price. Because $\Delta = -0.50$, the put price is $1.16. As an alternative approach we can calculate the probability, p, of an up movement in a risk-neutral world. This must satisfy:
$$55p + 45(1 - p) = 50e^{0.1 \times 0.5}$$

so that
$$10p = 50e^{0.1 \times 0.5} - 45$$

or $p = 0.7564$. The value of the option is then its expected payoff discounted at the risk-free rate:
$$[0 \times 0.7564 + 5 \times 0.2436]e^{-0.1 \times 0.5} = 1.16$$

or $1.16. This agrees with the previous calculation.

Problem 11.5.

In this case $u = 1.10$, $d = 0.90$, $\Delta t = 0.5$, and $r = 0.08$, so that

$$p = \frac{e^{0.08 \times 0.5} - 0.90}{1.10 - 0.90} = 0.7041$$

Figure S11.1: Tree for Problem 11.5

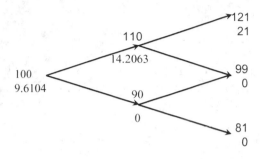

The tree for stock price movements is shown in Figure S11.1. We can work back from the end of the tree to the beginning, as indicated in the diagram, to give the value of the option as $9.61. The option value can also be calculated directly from equation (11.10):

$$[0.7041^2 \times 21 + 2 \times 0.7041 \times 0.2959 \times 0 + 0.2959^2 \times 0]e^{-2 \times 0.08 \times 0.5} = 9.61$$

or $9.61.

Problem 11.6.

Figure S11.2 shows how we can value the put option using the same tree as in Problem 11.5. The value of the option is $1.92. The option value can also be calculated directly from equation (11.10):

$$e^{-2 \times 0.08 \times 0.5}[0.7041^2 \times 0 + 2 \times 0.7041 \times 0.2959 \times 1 + 0.2959^2 \times 19] = 1.92$$

or $1.92. The stock price plus the put price is $100 + 1.92 = \$101.92$. The present value of the strike price plus the call price is $100e^{-0.08 \times 1} + 9.61 = \$101.92$. These are the same, verifying that put–call parity holds.

Problem 11.7.

$u = e^{\sigma\sqrt{\Delta t}}$ and $d = e^{-\sigma\sqrt{\Delta t}}$.

Problem 11.8.

The riskless portfolio consists of a short position in the option and a long position in Δ shares. Because Δ changes during the life of the option, this riskless portfolio must also change.

Problem 11.9.

At the end of two months the value of the option will be either $4 (if the stock price is $53) or $0 (if the stock price is $48). Consider a portfolio consisting of:

$$+\Delta \quad : \quad \text{shares}$$
$$-1 \quad : \quad \text{option}$$

Figure S11.2: Tree for Problem 11.6

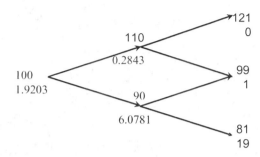

The value of the portfolio is either 48Δ or $53\Delta - 4$ in two months. If

$$48\Delta = 53\Delta - 4$$

i.e.,

$$\Delta = 0.8$$

the value of the portfolio is certain to be 38.4. For this value of Δ the portfolio is therefore riskless. The current value of the portfolio is:

$$0.8 \times 50 - f$$

where f is the value of the option. Since the portfolio must earn the risk-free rate of interest

$$(0.8 \times 50 - f)e^{0.10 \times 2/12} = 38.4$$

i.e.,

$$f = 2.23$$

The value of the option is therefore $2.23.

This can also be calculated directly from equations (11.2) and (11.3). $u = 1.06$, $d = 0.96$ so that

$$p = \frac{e^{0.10 \times 2/12} - 0.96}{1.06 - 0.96} = 0.5681$$

and

$$f = e^{-0.10 \times 2/12} \times 0.5681 \times 4 = 2.23$$

Problem 11.10.

At the end of four months the value of the option will be either $5 (if the stock price is $75) or $0 (if the stock price is $85). Consider a portfolio consisting of:

$$-\Delta \quad : \quad \text{shares}$$
$$+1 \quad : \quad \text{option}$$

(Note: The delta, Δ of a put option is negative. We have constructed the portfolio so that it is +1 option and $-\Delta$ shares rather than -1 option and $+\Delta$ shares so that the initial investment is positive.)

The value of the portfolio is either -85Δ or $-75\Delta + 5$ in four months. If

$$-85\Delta = -75\Delta + 5$$

i.e.,

$$\Delta = -0.5$$

the value of the portfolio is certain to be 42.5. For this value of Δ the portfolio is therefore riskless. The current value of the portfolio is:

$$0.5 \times 80 + f$$

where f is the value of the option. Since the portfolio is riskless

$$(0.5 \times 80 + f)e^{0.05 \times 4/12} = 42.5$$

i.e.,

$$f = 1.80$$

The value of the option is therefore \$1.80.

This can also be calculated directly from equations (11.2) and (11.3). $u = 1.0625$, $d = 0.9375$ so that

$$p = \frac{e^{0.05 \times 4/12} - 0.9375}{1.0625 - 0.9375} = 0.6345$$

$1 - p = 0.3655$ and

$$f = e^{-0.05 \times 4/12} \times 0.3655 \times 5 = 1.80$$

Problem 11.11.

At the end of three months the value of the option is either \$5 (if the stock price is \$35) or \$0 (if the stock price is \$45).

Consider a portfolio consisting of:

$$-\Delta \quad : \quad \text{shares}$$
$$+1 \quad : \quad \text{option}$$

(Note: The delta, Δ, of a put option is negative. We have constructed the portfolio so that it is +1 option and $-\Delta$ shares rather than -1 option and $+\Delta$ shares so that the initial investment is positive.)

The value of the portfolio is either $-35\Delta + 5$ or -45Δ. If:

$$-35\Delta + 5 = -45\Delta$$

i.e.,

$$\Delta = -0.5$$

the value of the portfolio is certain to be 22.5. For this value of Δ the portfolio is therefore riskless. The current value of the portfolio is

$$-40\Delta + f$$

where f is the value of the option. Since the portfolio must earn the risk-free rate of interest

$$(40 \times 0.5 + f) \times 1.02 = 22.5$$

Hence

$$f = 2.06$$

i.e., the value of the option is $2.06.

   This can also be calculated using risk-neutral valuation. Suppose that p is the probability of an upward stock price movement in a risk-neutral world. We must have

$$45p + 35(1-p) = 40 \times 1.02$$

i.e.,

$$10p = 5.8$$

or:

$$p = 0.58$$

The expected value of the option in a risk-neutral world is:

$$0 \times 0.58 + 5 \times 0.42 = 2.10$$

This has a present value of

$$\frac{2.10}{1.02} = 2.06$$

This is consistent with the no-arbitrage answer.

Problem 11.12.

A tree describing the behavior of the stock price is shown in Figure S11.3. The risk-neutral probability of an up move, p, is given by

$$p = \frac{e^{0.05 \times 3/12} - 0.95}{1.06 - 0.95} = 0.5689$$

There is a payoff from the option of $56.18 - 51 = 5.18$ for the highest final node (which corresponds to two up moves) zero in all other cases. The value of the option is therefore

$$5.18 \times 0.5689^2 \times e^{-0.05 \times 6/12} = 1.635$$

Figure S11.3: Tree for Problem 11.12

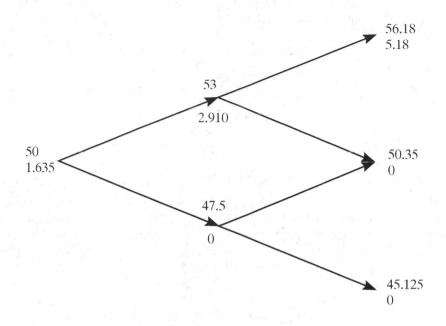

This can also be calculated by working back through the tree as indicated in Figure S11.1. The value of the call option is the lower number at each node in the figure.

Problem 11.13.

The tree for valuing the put option is shown in Figure S11.4. We get a payoff of $51 - 50.35 = 0.65$ if the middle final node is reached and a payoff of $51 - 45.125 = 5.875$ if the lowest final node is reached. The value of the option is therefore

$$(0.65 \times 2 \times 0.5689 \times 0.4311 + 5.875 \times 0.4311^2)e^{-0.05 \times 6/12} = 1.376$$

This can also be calculated by working back through the tree as indicated in Figure S11.2.
The value of the put plus the stock price is from Problem 11.12

$$1.376 + 50 = 51.376$$

The value of the call plus the present value of the strike price is

$$1.635 + 51e^{-0.05 \times 6/12} = 51.376$$

This verifies that put–call parity holds.

Figure S11.4: Tree for Problem 11.13

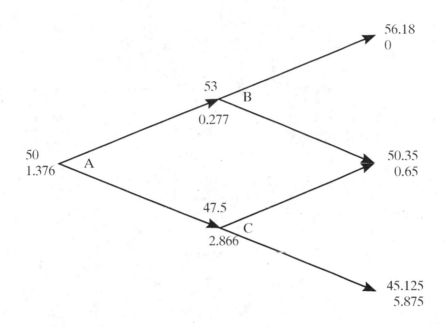

To test whether it worth exercising the option early we compare the value calculated for the option at each node with the payoff from immediate exercise. At node C the payoff from immediate exercise is $51 - 47.5 = 3.5$. Because this is greater than 2.8664, the option should be exercised at this node. The option should not be exercised at either node A or node B.

Problem 11.14.

At the end of two months the value of the derivative will be either 529 (if the stock price is 23) or 729 (if the stock price is 27). Consider a portfolio consisting of:

$$+\Delta \quad : \quad \text{shares}$$
$$-1 \quad : \quad \text{derivative}$$

The value of the portfolio is either $27\Delta - 729$ or $23\Delta - 529$ in two months. If

$$27\Delta - 729 = 23\Delta - 529$$

i.e.,

$$\Delta = 50$$

the value of the portfolio is certain to be 621. For this value of Δ the portfolio is therefore riskless. The current value of the portfolio is:

$$50 \times 25 - f$$

where f is the value of the derivative. Since the portfolio must earn the risk-free rate of interest

$$(50 \times 25 - f)e^{0.10 \times 2/12} = 621$$

i.e.,

$$f = 639.3$$

The value of the option is therefore $639.3.

This can also be calculated directly from equations (11.2) and (11.3). $u = 1.08$, $d = 0.92$ so that

$$p = \frac{e^{0.10 \times 2/12} - 0.92}{1.08 - 0.92} = 0.6050$$

and

$$f = e^{-0.10 \times 2/12}(0.6050 \times 729 + 0.3950 \times 529) = 639.3$$

Problem 11.15.

In this case

$$a = e^{(0.05 - 0.08) \times 1/12} = 0.9975$$

$$u = e^{0.12\sqrt{1/12}} = 1.0352$$

$$d = 1/u = 0.9660$$

$$p = \frac{0.9975 - 0.9660}{1.0352 - 0.9660} = 0.4553$$

Chapter 12
Wiener Processes and Itô's Lemma

SOLUTIONS TO QUESTIONS AND PROBLEMS

Problem 12.1.

Imagine that you have to forecast the future temperature from a) the current temperature, b) the history of the temperature in the last week, and c) a knowledge of seasonal averages and seasonal trends. If temperature followed a Markov process, the history of the temperature in the last week would be irrelevant.

To answer the second part of the question you might like to consider the following scenario for the first week in May:

(i) Monday to Thursday are warm days; today, Friday, is a very cold day.

(ii) Monday to Friday are all very cold days.

What is your forecast for the weekend? If you are more pessimistic in the case of the second scenario, temperatures do not follow a Markov process.

Problem 12.2.

The first point to make is that any trading strategy can, just because of good luck, produce above average returns. The key question is whether a trading strategy *consistently* outperforms the market when adjustments are made for risk. It is certainly possible that a trading strategy could do this. However, when enough investors know about the strategy and trade on the basis of the strategy, the profit will disappear.

As an illustration of this, consider a phenomenon known as the small firm effect. Portfolios of stocks in small firms appear to have outperformed portfolios of stocks in large firms when appropriate adjustments are made for risk. Papers were published about this in the early 1980s and mutual funds were set up to take advantage of the phenomenon. There is some evidence that this has resulted in the phenomenon disappearing.

Problem 12.3.

Suppose that the company's initial cash position is x. The probability distribution of the cash position at the end of one year is

$$\phi(x + 4 \times 0.5, \sqrt{4} \times \sqrt{4}) = \phi(x + 2.0, 4)$$

where $\phi(m,s)$ is a normal probability distribution with mean m and standard deviation s. The probability of a negative cash position at the end of one year is

$$N\left(-\frac{x+2.0}{4}\right)$$

where $N(x)$ is the cumulative probability that a standardized normal variable (with mean zero and standard deviation 1.0) is less than x. From normal distribution tables

$$N\left(-\frac{x+2.0}{4}\right) = 0.05$$

when:

$$-\frac{x+2.0}{4} = -1.6449$$

i.e., when $x = 4.5796$. The initial cash position must therefore be \$4.58 million.

Problem 12.4.

(a) Suppose that X_1 and X_2 equal a_1 and a_2 initially. After a time period of length T, X_1 has the probability distribution

$$\phi(a_1 + \mu_1 T, \sigma_1\sqrt{T})$$

and X_2 has a probability distribution

$$\phi(a_2 + \mu_2 T, \sigma_2\sqrt{T})$$

From the property of sums of independent normally distributed variables, $X_1 + X_2$ has the probability distribution

$$\phi\left(a_1 + \mu_1 T + a_2 + \mu_2 T, \sqrt{\sigma_1^2 T + \sigma_2^2 T}\right)$$

i.e.,

$$\phi\left[a_1 + a_2 + (\mu_1 + \mu_2)T, \sqrt{(\sigma_1^2 + \sigma_2^2)T}\right]$$

This shows that $X_1 + X_2$ follows a generalized Wiener process with drift rate $\mu_1 + \mu_2$ and variance rate $\sigma_1^2 + \sigma_2^2$.

(b) In this case the change in the value of $X_1 + X_2$ in a short interval of time Δt has the probability distribution:

$$\phi\left[(\mu_1 + \mu_2)\Delta t, \sqrt{(\sigma_1^2 + \sigma_2^2 + 2\rho\sigma_1\sigma_2)\Delta t}\right]$$

If μ_1, μ_2, σ_1, σ_2 and ρ are all constant, arguments similar to those in Section 12.2 show that the change in a longer period of time T is

$$\phi\left[(\mu_1 + \mu_2)T, \sqrt{(\sigma_1^2 + \sigma_2^2 + 2\rho\sigma_1\sigma_2)T}\right]$$

The variable, $X_1 + X_2$, therefore follows a generalized Wiener process with drift rate $\mu_1 + \mu_2$ and variance rate $\sigma_1^2 + \sigma_2^2 + 2\rho\sigma_1\sigma_2$.

Problem 12.5.

The change in S during the first three years has the probability distribution

$$\phi(2 \times 3, 3 \times \sqrt{3}) = \phi(6, 5.20)$$

The change during the next three years has the probability distribution

$$\phi(3 \times 3, 4 \times \sqrt{3}) = \phi(9, 6.93)$$

The change during the six years is the sum of a variable with probability distribution $\phi(6, 5.20)$ and a variable with probability distribution $\phi(9, 6.93)$. The probability distribution of the change is therefore

$$\phi(6+9, \sqrt{5.20^2 + 6.93^2})$$

$$= \phi(15, 8.66)$$

Since the initial value of the variable is 5, the probability distribution of the value of the variable at the end of year six is

$$\phi(20, 8.66)$$

Problem 12.6.

From Itô's lemma

$$\sigma_G G = \frac{\partial G}{\partial S} \sigma_S S$$

Also the drift of G is

$$\frac{\partial G}{\partial S} \mu S + \frac{\partial G}{\partial t} + \frac{1}{2} \frac{\partial^2 G}{\partial S^2} \sigma^2 S^2$$

where μ is the expected return on the stock. When μ increases by $\lambda \sigma_S$, the drift of G increases by

$$\frac{\partial G}{\partial S} \lambda \sigma_S S$$

or

$$\lambda \sigma_G G$$

The growth rate of G, therefore, increases by $\lambda \sigma_G$.

Problem 12.7.

Define S_A, μ_A and σ_A as the stock price, expected return and volatility for stock A. Define S_B, μ_B and σ_B as the stock price, expected return and volatility for stock B. Define ΔS_A and ΔS_B as the change in S_A and S_B in time Δt. Since each of the two stocks follows geometric Brownian motion,

$$\Delta S_A = \mu_A S_A \Delta t + \sigma_A S_A \varepsilon_A \sqrt{\Delta t}$$

$$\Delta S_B = \mu_B S_B \Delta t + \sigma_B S_B \varepsilon_B \sqrt{\Delta t}$$

where ε_A and ε_B are independent random samples from a normal distribution.

$$\Delta S_A + \Delta S_B = (\mu_A S_A + \mu_B S_B)\Delta t + (\sigma_A S_A \varepsilon_A + \sigma_B S_B \varepsilon_B)\sqrt{\Delta t}$$

This *cannot* be written as

$$\Delta S_A + \Delta S_B = \mu(S_A + S_B)\Delta t + \sigma(S_A + S_B)\varepsilon\sqrt{\Delta t}$$

for any constants μ and σ. (Neither the drift term nor the stochastic term correspond.) Hence the value of the portfolio does not follow geometric Brownian motion.

Problem 12.8.

In:

$$\Delta S = \mu S \Delta t + \sigma S \varepsilon \sqrt{\Delta t}$$

the expected increase in the stock price and the variability of the stock price are constant when both are expressed as a proportion (or as a percentage) of the stock price.

In:

$$\Delta S = \mu \Delta t + \sigma \varepsilon \sqrt{\Delta t}$$

the expected increase in the stock price and the variability of the stock price are constant in absolute terms. For example, if the expected growth rate is $5 per annum when the stock price is $25, it is also $5 per annum when it is $100. If the standard deviation of weekly stock price movements is $1 when the price is $25, it is also $1 when the price is $100.

In:

$$\Delta S = \mu S \Delta t + \sigma \varepsilon \sqrt{\Delta t}$$

the expected increase in the stock price is a constant proportion of the stock price while the variability is constant in absolute terms.

In:

$$\Delta S = \mu \Delta t + \sigma S \varepsilon \sqrt{\Delta t}$$

the expected increase in the stock price is constant in absolute terms while the variability of the proportional stock price change is constant.

The model:

$$\Delta S = \mu S \Delta t + \sigma S \varepsilon \sqrt{\Delta t}$$

is the most appropriate one since it is most realistic to assume that the expected *percentage return* and the variability of the *percentage return* in a short interval are constant.

Problem 12.9.

The drift rate is $a(b-r)$. Thus, when the interest rate is above b the drift rate is negative and, when the interest rate is below b, the drift rate is positive. The interest rate is therefore continually pulled towards the level b. The rate at which it is pulled toward this level is a. A volatility equal to c is superimposed upon the "pull" or the drift.

Suppose $a = 0.4$, $b = 0.1$ and $c = 0.15$ and the current interest rate is 20% per annum. The interest rate is pulled towards the level of 10% per annum. This can be regarded as a long run average. The current drift is -4% per annum so that the expected rate at the end of one year is about 16% per annum. (In fact it is slightly greater than this, because as the interest rate decreases, the "pull" decreases.) Superimposed upon the drift is a volatility of 15% per annum.

Problem 12.10.

If $G(S,t) = S^n$ then $\partial G/\partial t = 0$, $\partial G/\partial S = nS^{n-1}$, and $\partial^2 G/\partial S^2 = n(n-1)S^{n-2}$. Using Itô's lemma:

$$dG = [\mu nG + \frac{1}{2}n(n-1)\sigma^2 G]\,dt + \sigma nG\,dz$$

This shows that $G = S^n$ follows geometric Brownian motion where the expected return is

$$\mu n + \frac{1}{2}n(n-1)\sigma^2$$

and the volatility is $n\sigma$. The stock price S has an expected return of μ and the expected value of S_T is $S_0 e^{\mu T}$. The expected value of S_T^n is

$$S_0^n e^{[\mu n + \frac{1}{2}n(n-1)\sigma^2]T}$$

Problem 12.11.

The process followed by B, the bond price, is from Itô's lemma:

$$dB = \left[\frac{\partial B}{\partial x}a(x_0 - x) + \frac{\partial B}{\partial t} + \frac{1}{2}\frac{\partial^2 B}{\partial x^2}s^2 x^2 \right] dt + \frac{\partial B}{\partial x}sx\,dz$$

Since:

$$B = e^{-x(T-t)}$$

the required partial derivatives are

$$\frac{\partial B}{\partial t} = xe^{-x(T-t)} = xB$$

$$\frac{\partial B}{\partial x} = -(T-t)e^{-x(T-t)} = -(T-t)B$$

$$\frac{\partial^2 B}{\partial x^2} = (T-t)^2 e^{-x(T-t)} = (T-t)^2 B$$

Hence:

$$dB = \left[-a(x_0 - x)(T-t) + x + \frac{1}{2}s^2 x^2 (T-t)^2 \right] B\,dt - sx(T-t)B\,dz$$

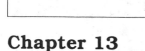

Chapter 13

The Black–Scholes–Merton Model

SOLUTIONS TO QUESTIONS AND PROBLEMS

Problem 13.1.

The Black–Scholes option pricing model assumes that the probability distribution of the stock price in 1 year (or at any other future time) is lognormal. It assumes that the continuously compounded rate of return on the stock during the year is normally distributed.

Problem 13.2.

The standard deviation of the percentage price change in time Δt is $\sigma\sqrt{\Delta t}$ where σ is the volatility. In this problem $\sigma = 0.3$ and, assuming 252 trading days in one year, $\Delta t = 1/252 = 0.004$ so that $\sigma\sqrt{\Delta t} = 0.3\sqrt{0.004} = 0.019$ or 1.9%.

Problem 13.3.

The price of an option or other derivative when expressed in terms of the price of the underlying stock is independent of risk preferences. Options therefore have the same value in a risk-neutral world as they do in the real world. We may therefore assume that the world is risk neutral for the purposes of valuing options. This simplifies the analysis. In a risk-neutral world all securities have an expected return equal to risk-free interest rate. Also, in a risk-neutral world, the appropriate discount rate to use for expected future cash flows is the risk-free interest rate.

Problem 13.4.

In this case $S_0 = 50$, $K = 50$, $r = 0.1$, $\sigma = 0.3$, $T = 0.25$, and

$$d_1 = \frac{\ln(50/50) + (0.1 + 0.09/2)0.25}{0.3\sqrt{0.25}} = 0.2417$$

$$d_2 = d_1 - 0.3\sqrt{0.25} = 0.0917$$

The European put price is

$$50N(-0.0917)e^{-0.1\times0.25} - 50N(-0.2417)$$
$$= 50 \times 0.4634e^{-0.1\times0.25} - 50 \times 0.4045 = 2.37$$

or \$2.37.

Problem 13.5.

In this case we must subtract the present value of the dividend from the stock price before using Black–Scholes. Hence the appropriate value of S_0 is

$$S_0 = 50 - 1.50e^{-0.1667 \times 0.1} = 48.52$$

As before $K = 50$, $r = 0.1$, $\sigma = 0.3$, and $T = 0.25$. In this case

$$d_1 = \frac{\ln(48.52/50) + (0.1 + 0.09/2)0.25}{0.3\sqrt{0.25}} = 0.0414$$

$$d_2 = d_1 - 0.3\sqrt{0.25} = -0.1086$$

The European put price is

$$50N(0.1086)e^{-0.1 \times 0.25} - 48.52N(-0.0414)$$

$$= 50 \times 0.5432e^{-0.1 \times 0.25} - 48.52 \times 0.4835 = 3.03$$

or $3.03.

Problem 13.6.

The implied volatility is the volatility that makes the Black–Scholes price of an option equal to its market price. It is calculated using an iterative procedure.

Problem 13.7.

In this case $\mu = 0.15$ and $\sigma = 0.25$. From equation (13.7) the probability distribution for the rate of return over a 2-year period with continuous compounding is:

$$\phi\left(0.15 - \frac{0.25^2}{2}, \frac{0.25}{\sqrt{2}}\right)$$

i.e.,

$$\phi(0.11875, 0.1768)$$

The expected value of the return is 11.875% per annum and the standard deviation is 17.68% per annum.

Problem 13.8.

(a) The required probability is the probability of the stock price being above $40 in six months' time. Suppose that the stock price in six months is S_T

$$\ln S_T \sim \phi\left(\ln 38 + (0.16 - \frac{0.35^2}{2})0.5, 0.35\sqrt{0.5}\right)$$

i.e.,

$$\ln S_T \sim \phi(3.687, 0.247)$$

Since $\ln 40 = 3.689$, the required probability is

$$1 - N\left(\frac{3.689 - 3.687}{0.247}\right) = 1 - N(0.008)$$

From normal distribution tables $N(0.008) = 0.5032$ so that the required probability is 0.4968. In general the required probability is $N(d_2)$. (See Problem 13.22).

(b) In this case the required probability is the probability of the stock price being less than \$40 in six months' time. It is

$$1 - 0.4968 = 0.5032$$

Problem 13.9.

From equation (13.3):

$$\ln S_T \sim \phi\left[\ln S_0 + (\mu - \frac{\sigma^2}{2})T, \sigma\sqrt{T}\right]$$

95% confidence intervals for $\ln S_T$ are therefore

$$\ln S_0 + (\mu - \frac{\sigma^2}{2})T - 1.96\sigma\sqrt{T}$$

and

$$\ln S_0 + (\mu - \frac{\sigma^2}{2})T + 1.96\sigma\sqrt{T}$$

95% confidence intervals for S_T are therefore

$$e^{\ln S_0 + (\mu - \sigma^2/2)T - 1.96\sigma\sqrt{T}}$$

and

$$e^{\ln S_0 + (\mu - \sigma^2/2)T + 1.96\sigma\sqrt{T}}$$

i.e.

$$S_0 e^{(\mu - \sigma^2/2)T - 1.96\sigma\sqrt{T}}$$

and

$$S_0 e^{(\mu - \sigma^2/2)T + 1.96\sigma\sqrt{T}}$$

Problem 13.10.

The statement is misleading in that a certain sum of money, say \$1000, when invested for 10 years in the fund would have realized a return (with annual compounding) of less than 20% per annum.

The average of the returns realized in each year is always greater than the return per annum (with annual compounding) realized over 10 years. The first is an arithmetic average of the returns in each year; the second is a geometric average of these returns.

Problem 13.11.

(a) At time t, the expected value of $\ln S_T$ is, from equation (13.3)

$$\ln S + (\mu - \frac{\sigma^2}{2})(T - t)$$

In a risk-neutral world the expected value of $\ln S_T$ is therefore:

$$\ln S + (r - \frac{\sigma^2}{2})(T - t)$$

Using risk-neutral valuation the value of the security at time t is:

$$e^{-r(T-t)}\left[\ln S + (r - \frac{\sigma^2}{2})(T - t)\right]$$

(b) If:

$$f = e^{-r(T-t)}\left[\ln S + (r - \frac{\sigma^2}{2})(T - t)\right]$$

$$\frac{\partial f}{\partial t} = re^{-r(T-t)}\left[\ln S + (r - \frac{\sigma^2}{2})(T - t)\right] - e^{-r(T-t)}(r - \frac{\sigma^2}{2})$$

$$\frac{\partial f}{\partial S} = \frac{e^{-r(T-t)}}{S}$$

$$\frac{\partial^2 f}{\partial S^2} = -\frac{e^{-r(T-t)}}{S^2}$$

The left-hand side of the Black Scholes differential equation is

$$e^{-r(T-t)}\left[r\ln S + r(r - \frac{\sigma^2}{2})(T - t) - (r - \frac{\sigma^2}{2}) + r - \frac{\sigma^2}{2}\right]$$

$$= re^{-r(T-t)}\left[\ln S + (r - \frac{\sigma^2}{2})(T - t)\right]$$

$$= rf$$

Hence equation (13.16) is satisfied.

Problem 13.12.

This problem is related to Problem 12.10.

(a) If $G(S,t) = h(t,T)S^n$ then $\partial G/\partial t = h_t S^n$, $\partial G/\partial S = hnS^{n-1}$, and $\partial^2 G/\partial S^2 = hn(n-1)S^{n-2}$ where $h_t = \partial h/\partial t$. Substituting into the Black–Scholes differential equation we obtain

$$h_t + rhn + \frac{1}{2}\sigma^2 hn(n-1) = rh$$

(b) The derivative is worth S^n when $t = T$. The boundary condition for this differential equation is therefore $h(T,T) = 1$

(c) The equation

$$h(t,T) = e^{[0.5\sigma^2 n(n-1)+r(n-1)](T-t)}$$

satisfies the boundary condition since it collapses to $h = 1$ when $t = T$. It can also be shown that it satisfies the differential equation in (a). Alternatively we can solve the differential equation in (a) directly. The differential equation can be written

$$\frac{h_t}{h} = -r(n-1) - \frac{1}{2}\sigma^2 n(n-1)$$

The solution to this is

$$\ln h = [-r(n-1) - \frac{1}{2}\sigma^2 n(n-1)]t + k$$

where k is a constant. Since $\ln h = 0$ when $t = T$ it follows that

$$k = [r(n-1) + \frac{1}{2}\sigma^2 n(n-1)]T$$

so that

$$\ln h = [r(n-1) + \frac{1}{2}\sigma^2 n(n-1)](T-t)$$

or

$$h(t,T) = e^{[0.5\sigma^2 n(n-1)+r(n-1)](T-t)}$$

Problem 13.13.

In this case $S_0 = 52$, $K = 50$, $r = 0.12$, $\sigma = 0.30$ and $T = 0.25$.

$$d_1 = \frac{\ln(52/50) + (0.12 + 0.3^2/2)0.25}{0.30\sqrt{0.25}} = 0.5365$$

$$d_2 = d_1 - 0.30\sqrt{0.25} = 0.3865$$

The price of the European call is

$$52N(0.5365) - 50e^{-0.12\times0.25}N(0.3865)$$
$$= 52 \times 0.7042 - 50e^{-0.03} \times 0.6504$$
$$= 5.06$$

or $5.06.

Problem 13.14.

In this case $S_0 = 69$, $K = 70$, $r = 0.05$, $\sigma = 0.35$ and $T = 0.5$.

$$d_1 = \frac{\ln(69/70) + (0.05 + 0.35^2/2) \times 0.5}{0.35\sqrt{0.5}} = 0.1666$$
$$d_2 = d_1 - 0.35\sqrt{0.5} = -0.0809$$

The price of the European put is

$$70e^{-0.05\times0.5}N(0.0809) - 69N(-0.1666)$$
$$= 70e^{-0.025} \times 0.5323 - 69 \times 0.4338$$
$$= 6.40$$

or $6.40.

Problem 13.15.

Using the notation of Section 13.12, $D_1 = D_2 = 1$, $K(1 - e^{-r(T-t_2)}) = 65(1 - e^{-0.1\times0.1667}) = 1.07$, and $K(1 - e^{-r(t_2-t_1)}) = 65(1 - e^{-0.1\times0.25}) = 1.60$. Since

$$D_1 < K(1 - e^{-r(T-t_2)})$$

and

$$D_2 < K(1 - e^{-r(t_2-t_1)})$$

It is never optimal to exercise the call option early. DerivaGem shows that the value of the option is 10.94.

Problem 13.16.

In the case $c = 2.5$, $S_0 = 15$, $K = 13$, $T = 0.25$, $r = 0.05$. The implied volatility must be calculated using an iterative procedure.

A volatility of 0.2 (or 20% per annum) gives $c = 2.20$. A volatility of 0.3 gives $c = 2.32$. A volatility of 0.4 gives $c = 2.507$. A volatility of 0.39 gives $c = 2.487$. By interpolation the implied volatility is about 0.397 or 39.7% per annum.

Problem 13.17.

(a) Since $N(x)$ is the cumulative probability that a variable with a standardized normal distribution will be less than x, $N'(x)$ is the probability density function for a standardized normal distribution, that is,

$$N'(x) = \frac{1}{\sqrt{2\pi}} e^{-\frac{x^2}{2}}$$

(b)
$$N'(d_1) = N'(d_2 + \sigma\sqrt{T-t})$$

$$= \frac{1}{\sqrt{2\pi}} \exp\left[-\frac{d_2^2}{2} - \sigma d_2\sqrt{T-t} - \frac{1}{2}\sigma^2(T-t)\right]$$

$$= N'(d_2)\exp\left[-\sigma d_2\sqrt{T-t} - \frac{1}{2}\sigma^2(T-t)\right]$$

Because

$$d_2 = \frac{\ln(S/K) + (r - \sigma^2/2)(T-t)}{\sigma\sqrt{T-t}}$$

it follows that

$$\exp\left[-\sigma d_2\sqrt{T-t} - \frac{1}{2}\sigma^2(T-t)\right] = \frac{Ke^{-r(T-t)}}{S}$$

As a result

$$SN'(d_1) = Ke^{-r(T-t)}N'(d_2)$$

which is the required result.

(c)
$$d_1 = \frac{\ln\frac{S}{K} + (r + \frac{\sigma^2}{2})(T-t)}{\sigma\sqrt{T-t}}$$

$$= \frac{\ln S - \ln K + (r + \frac{\sigma^2}{2})(T-t)}{\sigma\sqrt{T-t}}$$

Hence

$$\frac{\partial d_1}{\partial S} = \frac{1}{S\sigma\sqrt{T-t}}$$

Similarly

$$d_2 = \frac{\ln S - \ln K + (r - \frac{\sigma^2}{2})(T-t)}{\sigma\sqrt{T-t}}$$

and

$$\frac{\partial d_2}{\partial S} = \frac{1}{S\sigma\sqrt{T-t}}$$

Therefore:

$$\frac{\partial d_1}{\partial S} = \frac{\partial d_2}{\partial S}$$

(d)
$$c = SN(d_1) - Ke^{-r(T-t)}N(d_2)$$

$$\frac{\partial c}{\partial t} = SN'(d_1)\frac{\partial d_1}{\partial t} - rKe^{-r(T-t)}N(d_2) - Ke^{-r(T-t)}N'(d_2)\frac{\partial d_2}{\partial t}$$

From (b):
$$SN'(d_1) = Ke^{-r(T-t)}N'(d_2)$$

Hence
$$\frac{\partial c}{\partial t} = -rKe^{-r(T-t)}N(d_2) + SN'(d_1)\left(\frac{\partial d_1}{\partial t} - \frac{\partial d_2}{\partial t}\right)$$

Since
$$d_1 - d_2 = \sigma\sqrt{T-t}$$
$$\frac{\partial d_1}{\partial t} - \frac{\partial d_2}{\partial t} = \frac{\partial}{\partial t}(\sigma\sqrt{T-t})$$
$$= -\frac{\sigma}{2\sqrt{T-t}}$$

Hence
$$\frac{\partial c}{\partial t} = -rKe^{-r(T-t)}N(d_2) - SN'(d_1)\frac{\sigma}{2\sqrt{T-t}}$$

(e) From differentiating the Black–Scholes formula for a call price we obtain
$$\frac{\partial c}{\partial S} = N(d_1) + SN'(d_1)\frac{\partial d_1}{\partial S} - Ke^{-r(T-t)}N'(d_2)\frac{\partial d_2}{\partial S}$$

From the results in (b) and (c) it follows that
$$\frac{\partial c}{\partial S} = N(d_1)$$

(f) Differentiating the result in (e) and using the result in (c), we obtain
$$\frac{\partial^2 c}{\partial S^2} = N'(d_1)\frac{\partial d_1}{\partial S}$$
$$= N'(d_1)\frac{1}{S\sigma\sqrt{T-t}}$$

From the results in (d) and (e)
$$\frac{\partial c}{\partial t} + rS\frac{\partial c}{\partial S} + \frac{1}{2}\sigma^2 S^2\frac{\partial^2 c}{\partial S^2} = -rKe^{-r(T-t)}N(d_2) - SN'(d_1)\frac{\sigma}{2\sqrt{T-t}} +$$
$$+ rSN(d_1) + \frac{1}{2}\sigma^2 S^2 N'(d_1)\frac{1}{S\sigma\sqrt{T-t}}$$
$$= r[SN(d_1) - Ke^{-r(T-t)}N(d_2)]$$
$$= rc$$

This shows that the Black–Scholes formula for a call option does indeed satisfy the Black–Scholes differential equation.

(g) Consider what happens in the formula for c in part (d) as t approaches T. If $S > K$, d_1 and d_2 tend to infinity and $N(d_1)$ and $N(d_2)$ tend to 1. If $S < K$, d_1 and d_2 tend to zero. It follows that the formula for c tends to $\max(S - K, 0)$.

Problem 13.18.

From the Black–Scholes equations

$$p + S_0 = Ke^{-rT}N(-d_2) - S_0N(-d_1) + S_0$$

Because $1 - N(-d_1) = N(d_1)$ this is

$$Ke^{-rT}N(-d_2) + S_0N(d_1)$$

Also:

$$c + Ke^{-rT} = S_0N(d_1) - Ke^{-rT}N(d_2) + Ke^{-rT}$$

Because $1 - N(d_2) = N(-d_2)$, this is also

$$Ke^{-rT}N(-d_2) + S_0N(d_1)$$

The Black–Scholes equations are therefore consistent with put–call parity.

Problem 13.19.

This problem naturally leads on to the material in Chapter 16 on volatility smiles. Using DerivaGem we obtain the following table of implied volatilities:

Strike Price ($)	Maturity (months)		
	3	6	12
45	37.78	34.99	34.02
50	34.15	32.78	32.03
55	31.98	30.77	30.45

The option prices are not exactly consistent with Black–Scholes. If they were, the implied volatilities would be all the same. We usually find in practice that low strike price options on a stock have significantly higher implied volatilities than high strike price options on the same stock.

Problem 13.20.

Black's approach in effect assumes that the holder of option must decide at time zero whether it is a European option maturing at time t_n (the final ex-dividend date) or a European option maturing at time T. In fact the holder of the option has more flexibility than this. The holder can choose to exercise at time t_n if the stock price at that time is above some level but not otherwise. Furthermore, if the option is not exercised at time t_n, it can still be exercised at time T.

It appears from this argument that Black's approach understates the true option value. However, the way in which volatility is applied can lead to Black's approach overstating the option value. Black applies the volatility to the option price. The binomial model, as we will see in Chapter 17, applies the volatility to the stock price less the present value of the dividend. This issue is also discussed in Example 13.9.

Problem 13.21.

With the notation in the text

$$D_1 = D_2 = 1.50, \quad t_1 = 0.3333, \quad t_2 = 0.8333, \quad T = 1.25, \quad r = 0.08 \quad \text{and} \quad K = 55$$

$$K\left[1 - e^{-r(T-t_2)}\right] = 55(1 - e^{-0.08 \times 0.4167}) = 1.80$$

Hence

$$D_2 < K\left[1 - e^{-r(T-t_2)}\right]$$

Also:

$$K\left[1 - e^{-r(t_2-t_1)}\right] = 55(1 - e^{-0.08 \times 0.5}) = 2.16$$

Hence:

$$D_1 < K\left[1 - e^{-r(t_2-t_1)}\right]$$

It follows from the conditions established in Section 13.12 that the option should never be exercised early.

The present value of the dividends is

$$1.5e^{-0.3333 \times 0.08} + 1.5e^{-0.8333 \times 0.08} = 2.864$$

The option can be valued using the European pricing formula with:

$$S_0 = 50 - 2.864 = 47.136, \quad K = 55, \quad \sigma = 0.25, \quad r = 0.08, \quad T = 1.25$$

$$d_1 = \frac{\ln(47.136/55) + (0.08 + 0.25^2/2)1.25}{0.25\sqrt{1.25}} = -0.0545$$

$$d_2 = d_1 - 0.25\sqrt{1.25} = -0.3340$$

$$N(d_1) = 0.4783, \quad N(d_2) = 0.3692$$

and the call price is

$$47.136 \times 0.4783 - 55e^{-0.08 \times 1.25} \times 0.3692 = 4.17$$

or \$4.17.

Problem 13.22.

The probability that the call option will be exercised is the probability that $S_T > K$ where S_T is the stock price at time T. In a risk neutral world

$$\ln S_T \sim \phi\left[\ln S_0 + (r - \sigma^2/2)T, \sigma\sqrt{T}\right]$$

The probability that $S_T > K$ is the same as the probability that $\ln S_T > \ln K$. This is

$$1 - N\left[\frac{\ln K - \ln S_0 - (r - \sigma^2/2)T}{\sigma\sqrt{T}}\right]$$

$$= N\left[\frac{\ln(S_0/K) + (r - \sigma^2/2)T}{\sigma\sqrt{T}}\right]$$

$$= N(d_2)$$

The expected value at time T in a risk neutral world of a derivative security which pays off $100 when $S_T > K$ is therefore

$$100N(d_2)$$

From risk neutral valuation the value of the security at time t is

$$100e^{-rT}N(d_2)$$

Problem 13.23.

If $f = S^{-2r/\sigma^2}$ then

$$\frac{\partial f}{\partial S} = -\frac{2r}{\sigma^2}S^{-2r/\sigma^2 - 1}$$

$$\frac{\partial^2 f}{\partial S^2} = \left(\frac{2r}{\sigma^2}\right)\left(\frac{2r}{\sigma^2} + 1\right)S^{-2r/\sigma^2 - 2}$$

$$\frac{\partial f}{\partial t} = 0$$

$$\frac{\partial f}{\partial t} + rS\frac{\partial f}{\partial S} + \frac{1}{2}\sigma^2 S^2\frac{\partial^2 f}{\partial S^2} = rS^{-2r/\sigma^2} = rf$$

This shows that the Black–Scholes equation is satisfied. S^{-2r/σ^2} could therefore be the price of a traded security.

Problem 13.24.

The answer is no. If markets are efficient they have already taken potential dilution into account in determining the stock price. This argument is explained in Business Snapshot 13.3.

Problem 13.25.

The Black-Scholes price of the option is given by setting $S_0 = 50$, $K = 50$, $r = 0.05$, $\sigma = 0.25$, and $T = 5$. It is 16.252. From an analysis similar to that in Section 13.10 the cost to the company of the options is

$$\frac{10}{10+3} \times 16.252 = 12.5$$

or about $12.5 per option. The total cost is therefore 3 million times this or $37.5 million. If the market perceives no benefits from the options the stock price will fall by $3.75.

Chapter 14

Options on Stock Indices, Currencies, and Futures Contracts

SOLUTIONS TO QUESTIONS AND PROBLEMS

Problem 14.1.

When the S&P 100 goes down to 480, the value of the portfolio can be expected to be $10 \times (480/500) = \$9.6$ million. (This assumes that the dividend yield on the portfolio equals the dividend yield on the index.) Buying put options on $10{,}000{,}000/500 = 20{,}000$ times the index with a strike of 480 therefore provides protection against a drop in the value of the portfolio below \$9.6 million. Since each contract is on 100 times the index a total of 200 contracts would be required.

Problem 14.2.

A stock index is analogous to a stock paying a continuous dividend yield, the dividend yield being the dividend yield on the index. A currency is analogous to a stock paying a continuous dividend yield, the dividend yield being the foreign risk-free interest rate. A futures contract is analogous to a stock paying a continuous dividend yield, the dividend yield being the domestic risk-free interest rate.

Problem 14.3.

The lower bound is given by equation 14.1 as

$$300e^{-0.03 \times 0.5} - 290e^{-0.08 \times 0.5} = 16.90$$

Problem 14.4.

The tree of exchange-rate movements is shown in Figure S14.1. In this case $u = 1.02$ and $d = 0.98$. The probability of an up movement is

$$p = \frac{e^{(0.06-0.08) \times 0.08333} - 0.98}{1.02 - 0.98} = 0.4584$$

The tree shows that the value of an option to purchase one unit of the currency is \$0.0067.

Figure S14.1: Tree for Problem 14.4

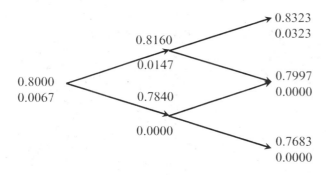

Problem 14.5.

A call option on yen gives the holder the right to buy yen in the spot market at an exchange rate equal to the strike price. A call option on yen futures gives the holder the right to receive the amount by which the futures price exceeds the strike price. If the yen futures option is exercised, the holder also obtains a long position in the yen futures contract.

Problem 14.6.

A company that knows it is due to receive a foreign currency at a certain time in the future can buy a put option. This guarantees that the price at which the currency will be sold will be at or above a certain level. A company that knows it is due to pay a foreign currency a certain time in the future can buy a call option. This guarantees that the price at which the currency will be purchased will be at or below a certain level.

Problem 14.7.

In this case, $S_0 = 250$, $K = 250$, $r = 0.10$, $\sigma = 0.18$, $T = 0.25$, $q = 0.03$ and

$$d_1 = \frac{\ln(250/250) + (0.10 - 0.03 + 0.18^2/2)0.25}{0.18\sqrt{0.25}} = 0.2394$$
$$d_2 = d_1 - 0.18\sqrt{0.25} = 0.1494$$

and the call price is

$$250N(0.2394)e^{-0.03\times0.25} - 250N(0.1494)e^{-0.10\times0.25}$$
$$= 250 \times 0.5946e^{-0.03\times0.25} - 250 \times 0.5594e^{-0.10\times0.25}$$

or 11.15.

Problem 14.8.

The American futures option is worth more than the corresponding American option on the underlying asset when the futures price is greater than the spot price prior to the maturity of the futures contract. This is the case when the cost of carry net of the convenience yield is positive.

Problem 14.9.

In this case $S_0 = 0.52$, $K = 0.50$, $r = 0.04$, $r_f = 0.08$, $\sigma = 0.12$, $T = 0.6667$, and

$$d_1 = \frac{\ln(0.52/0.50) + (0.04 - 0.08 + 0.12^2/2)0.6667}{0.12\sqrt{0.6667}} = 0.1771$$

$$d_2 = d_1 - 0.12\sqrt{0.6667} = 0.0791$$

and the put price is

$$0.50N(-0.0791)e^{-0.04\times0.6667} - 0.52N(-0.1771)e^{-0.08\times0.6667}$$
$$= 0.50 \times 0.4685e^{-0.04\times0.6667} - 0.52 \times 0.4297e^{-0.08\times0.6667}$$
$$= 0.0162$$

Problem 14.10.

The main reason is that a bond futures contract is a more liquid instrument than a bond. The price of a Treasury bond futures contract is known immediately from trading on CBOT. The price of a bond can be obtained only by contacting dealers.

Problem 14.11.

A futures price behaves like a stock paying a continuous dividend yield at the risk-free interest rate.

Problem 14.12.

In this case $u = 1.12$ and $d = 0.92$. The probability of an up movement in a risk-neutral world is

$$\frac{1 - 0.92}{1.12 - 0.92} = 0.4$$

From risk-neutral valuation, the value of the call is

$$e^{-0.06\times0.5}(0.4 \times 6 + 0.6 \times 0) = 2.33$$

Problem 14.13.

In this case $F_0 = 19$, $K = 20$, $r = 0.12$, $\sigma = 0.20$, and $T = 0.4167$. The value of the European put futures option is

$$20N(-d_2)e^{-0.12\times0.4167} - 19N(-d_1)e^{-0.12\times0.4167}$$

where

$$d_1 = \frac{\ln(19/20) + (0.04/2)0.4167}{0.2\sqrt{0.4167}} = -0.3327$$

$$d_2 = d_1 - 0.2\sqrt{0.4167} = -0.4618$$

This is

$$e^{-0.12 \times 0.4167}[20N(0.4618) - 19N(0.3327)]$$

$$= e^{-0.12 \times 0.4167}(20 \times 0.6778 - 19 \times 0.6303)$$

$$= 1.50$$

or $1.50.

Problem 14.14.

A total return index behaves like a stock paying no dividends. In a risk-neutral world it can be expected to grow on average at the risk-free rate. Forward contracts and options on total return indices should be valued in the same way as forward contracts and options on non-dividend-paying stocks.

Problem 14.15.

In this case $S_0 = 696$, $K = 700$, $r = 0.07$, $\sigma = 0.3$, $T = 0.25$ and $q = 0.04$. The option can be valued using equation (14.5).

$$d_1 = \frac{\ln(696/700) + (0.07 - 0.04 + 0.09/2) \times 0.25}{0.3\sqrt{0.25}} = 0.0868$$

$$d_2 = d_1 - 0.3\sqrt{0.25} = -0.0632$$

and

$$N(-d_1) = 0.4654, \quad N(-d_2) = 0.5252$$

The value of the put, p, is given by:

$$p = 700e^{-0.07 \times 0.25} \times 0.5252 - 696e^{-0.04 \times 0.25} \times 0.4654 = 40.6$$

i.e., it is $40.6.

Problem 14.16.

The put–call parity relationship for European currency options is

$$c + Ke^{-rT} = p + Se^{-r_fT}$$

To prove this result, the two portfolios to consider are:

Portfolio A: One call option plus one discount bond which will be worth K at time T.

Portfolio B: One put option plus e^{-r_fT} of foreign currency invested at the foreign risk-free interest rate.

Both portfolios are worth $\max(S_T, K)$ at time T. They must therefore be worth the same today. The result follows.

Problem 14.17.

Lower bound for European option is

$$S_0 e^{-r_f T} - K e^{-rT} = 1.5 e^{-0.09 \times 0.5} - 1.4 e^{-0.05 \times 0.5} = 0.069$$

Lower bound for American option is

$$S_0 - K = 0.10$$

Problem 14.18.

In this case $S_0 = 250$, $q = 0.04$, $r = 0.06$, $T = 0.25$, $K = 245$, and $c = 10$. Using put–call parity

$$c + K e^{-rT} = p + S_0 e^{-qT}$$

or

$$p = c + K e^{-rT} - S_0 e^{-qT}$$

Substituting:

$$p = 10 + 245 e^{-0.25 \times 0.06} - 250 e^{-0.25 \times 0.04} = 3.84$$

The put price is 3.84.

Problem 14.19.

The volatility of a stock index can be expected to be less than the volatility of a typical stock. This is because some risk (i.e., return uncertainty) is diversified away when a portfolio of stocks is created. In capital asset pricing model terminology, there exists systematic and unsystematic risk in the returns from an individual stock. However, in a stock index, unsystematic risk has been largely diversified away and only the systematic risk contributes to volatility.

Problem 14.20.

The cost of portfolio insurance increases as the beta of the portfolio increases. This is because portfolio insurance involves the purchase of a put option on a portfolio. As beta increases, the volatility of the portfolio increases and the strike price required also increases.

Problem 14.21.

If the value of the portfolio mirrors the value of the index, the index can be expected to have dropped by 10% when the value of the portfolio drops by 10%. Hence when the value of the portfolio drops to $54 million the value of the index can be expected to be 1080. This indicates that put options with an exercise price of 1080 should be purchased. The options should be on:

$$\frac{60,000,000}{1200} = \$50,000$$

times the index. Each option contract is for $100 times the index. Hence 500 contracts should be purchased.

Problem 14.22.

When the value of the portfolio falls to $54 million the holder of the portfolio makes a capital loss of 10%. After dividends are taken into account the loss is 7% during the year. This is 12% below the risk-free interest rate. According to the capital asset pricing model:

$$\text{Excess expected return of portfolio above riskless interest rate} = \beta \times \text{Excess return of market above riskless interest rate}$$

Therefore, when the portfolio provides a return 12% below the risk-free interest rate, the market's expected return is 6% below the risk-free interest rate. As the index can be assumed to have a beta of 1.0, this is also the excess expected return (including dividends) from the index. The expected return from the index is therefore -1% per annum. Since the index provides a 3% per annum dividend yield, the expected movement in the index is -4%. Thus when the portfolio's value is $54 million the expected value of the index $0.96 \times 1200 = 1152$. Hence European put options should be purchased with an exercise price of 1152. Their maturity date should be in one year.

The number of options required is twice the number required in Problem 14.21. This is because we wish to protect a portfolio which is twice as sensitive to changes in market conditions as the portfolio in Problem 14.21. Hence options on $100,000 (or 1,000 contracts) should be purchased.

To check that the answer is correct consider what happens when the value of the portfolio declines by 20% to $48 million. The return including dividends is -17%. This is 22% less than the risk-free interest rate. The index can be expected to provide a return (including dividends) which is 11% less than the risk-free interest rate, i.e. a return of -6%. The index can therefore be expected to drop by 9% to 1092. The payoff from the put options is $(1152 - 1092) \times 100,000 = \$6$ million. This is exactly what is required to restore the value of the portfolio to $54 million.

Problem 14.23.

An amount $(400 - 380) \times 100 = \$2,000$ is added to your margin account and you acquire a short futures position giving you the right to sell 100 ounces of gold in October. This position is marked to market at the end of each day in the usual way until you choose to close it out.

Problem 14.24.

In this case an amount $(0.75 - 0.70) \times 40,000 = \$2,000$ is subtracted from your margin account and you acquire a short position in a live cattle futures contract to sell 40,000 pounds of cattle in April. This position is marked to marked at the end of each day in the usual way until you choose to close it out.

Problem 14.25.

Lower bound if option is European is

$$(F_0 - K)e^{-rT} = (47 - 40)e^{-0.1 \times 0.1667} = 6.88$$

Lower bound if option is American is

$$F_0 - K = 7$$

Problem 14.26.

Lower bound if option is European is

$$(K - F_0)e^{-rT} = (50 - 47)e^{-0.1 \times 0.3333} = 2.90$$

Lower bound if option is American is

$$K - F_0 = 3$$

Problem 14.27

In this case the risk-neutral probability of an up move is

$$\frac{1 - 0.9}{1.1 - 0.9} = 0.5$$

In the tree shown in Figure S14.2 the middle number at each node is the price of the European option and the lower number is the price of the American option. The tree shows that the price of both the European and the American option is 3.0265. The American option should never be exercised early.

Problem 14.28.

In this case the risk-neutral probability of an up move is

$$\frac{1 - 0.9}{1.1 - 0.9} = 0.5$$

The tree in Figure S14.3 shows that the price of the European option is 3.0265 while the price of the American option is 3.0847.

Using the result in the previous problem

$$c + Ke^{-rT} = 3.0265 + 60e^{-0.04} = 60.6739$$

From this problem

$$p + F_0 e^{-rT} = 3.0265 + 60e^{-0.04} = 60.6739$$

Figure S14.2: Tree to evaluate European and American call options in Problem 14.27.

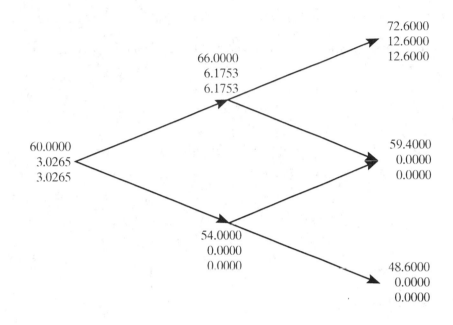

Figure S14.3: Tree to evaluate European and American call options in Problem 14.28.

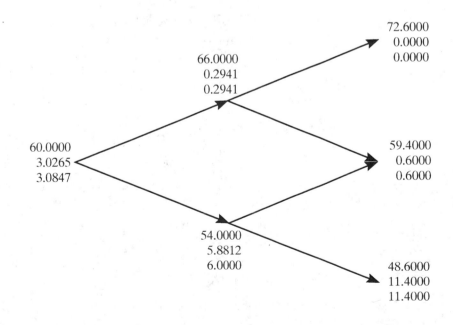

This verifies that the put–call parity relationship in equation (14.11) holds for the European option prices. For the American option prices we have:

$$C - P = -0.0582; \qquad F_0 e^{-rT} - K = -2.353; \qquad F_0 - Ke^{-rT} = 2.353$$

The put–call inequalities for American options are therefore satisfied.

Problem 14.29.

In this case $F_0 = 25$, $K = 26$, $\sigma = 0.3$, $r = 0.1$, $T = 0.75$

$$d_1 = \frac{\ln(F_0/K) + \sigma^2 T/2}{\sigma\sqrt{T}} = -0.0211$$

$$d_2 = \frac{\ln(F_0/K) - \sigma^2 T/2}{\sigma\sqrt{T}} = -0.2809$$

$$c = e^{-0.075}[25N(-0.0211) - 26N(-0.2809)]$$
$$= e^{-0.075}[25 \times 0.4916 - 26 \times 0.3894] = 2.01$$

Problem 14.30.

In this case $F_0 = 70$, $K = 65$, $\sigma = 0.2$, $r = 0.06$, $T = 0.4167$

$$d_1 = \frac{\ln(F_0/K) + \sigma^2 T/2}{\sigma\sqrt{T}} = 0.6386$$

$$d_2 = \frac{\ln(F_0/K) - \sigma^2 T/2}{\sigma\sqrt{T}} = 0.5095$$

$$p = e^{-0.025}[65N(-0.5095) - 70N(-0.6386)]$$
$$= e^{-0.025}[65 \times 0.3052 - 70 \times 0.2615] = 1.495$$

Problem 14.31.

In this case

$$c + Ke^{-rT} = 2 + 34e^{-0.1 \times 1} = 32.76$$
$$p + F_0 e^{-rT} = 2 + 35e^{-0.1 \times 1} = 33.67$$

Put-call parity shows that the put is overpriced relative to the call. We should buy one call, short one put and short $e^{-0.1} = 0.90$ of the stock.

Problem 14.32.

The put price is

$$e^{-rT}[KN(-d_2) - F_0 N(-d_1)]$$

Since $N(-x) = 1 - N(x)$ for all x the put price can also be written

$$e^{-rT}[K - KN(d_2) - F_0 + F_0 N(d_1)]$$

Since $F_0 = K$ this is the same as the call price:

$$e^{-rT}[F_0 N(d_1) - KN(d_2)]$$

This result can also be proved from put–call parity showing that it is not model dependent.

Problem 14.33.

From the result at the end of Section 14.5, $C - P$ must lie between

$$30e^{-0.05 \times 3/12} - 28 = 1.63$$

and

$$30 - 28e^{-0.05 \times 3/12} = 2.35$$

Since $C = 4$ we must have

$$1.65 < P < 2.37$$

Problem 14.34.

There is no way of doing this. A natural idea is to create an option to exchange K euros for one yen from an option to exchange Y dollars for 1 yen and an option to exchange K euros for Y dollars. The problem with this is that it assumes that either both options are exercised or that neither option is exercised. There are always some circumstances where the first option is in-the-money at expiration while the second is not and vice versa.

Problem 14.35.

The appropriate contract is a three-month Eurodollar call futures option contract with a strike price of 93.00. This provides protection against LIBOR falling below 7%, or LIBOR minus 50 basis points falling below 6.5%. If the 90-day rate in three months is X basis points below 7%, one contract will pay off $25X$ dollars. The corporation requires a payoff of $0.25 \times 5,000,000 \times 0.0001 \times X = 125X$ when the 90-day rate is X basis points below 7%. A total of 5 contracts should therefore be purchased.

Problem 14.36.

In portfolio A, the cash, if it is invested at the risk-free interest rate, will grow to K at time T. If $S_T > K$, the call option is exercised at time T and portfolio A is worth S_T. If $S_T < K$, the call option expires worthless and the portfolio is worth K. Hence, at time T, portfolio A is worth

$$\max(S_T, K)$$

Because of the reinvestment of dividends, portfolio B becomes one share at time T. It is, therefore, worth S_T at this time. It follows that portfolio A is always worth as much as, and is sometimes worth more than, portfolio B at time T. In the absence of arbitrage opportunities, this must also be true today. Hence,

$$c + Ke^{-rT} \geq S_0 e^{-qT}$$

or

$$c \geq S_0 e^{-qT} - Ke^{-rT}$$

This proves equation (14.1).

In portfolio C, the reinvestment of dividends means that the portfolio is one put option plus one share at time T. If $S_T < K$, the put option is exercised at time T and portfolio C is worth K. If $S_T > K$, the put option expires worthless and the portfolio is worth S_T. Hence, at time T, portfolio C is worth

$$\max(S_T, K)$$

Portfolio D is worth K at time T. It follows that portfolio C is always worth as much as, and is sometimes worth more than, portfolio D at time T. In the absence of arbitrage opportunities, this must also be true today. Hence,

$$p + S_0 e^{-qT} \geq Ke^{-rT}$$

or

$$p \geq Ke^{-rT} - S_0 e^{-qT}$$

This proves equation (14.2).

Portfolios A and C are both worth $\max(S_T, K)$ at time T. They must, therefore, be worth the same today, and the put–call parity result in equation (14.3) follows.

Problem 14.37.

Following the hint, we first consider

> *Portfolio A:* A European call option plus an amount K invested at the risk-free rate.
> *Portfolio B:* An American put option plus e^{-qT} of stock with dividends being reinvested in the stock.

Portfolio A is worth $c + K$ while portfolio B is worth $P + S_0 e^{-qT}$. If the put option is exercised at time $\tau (0 \leq \tau \leq T)$, portfolio B becomes:

$$K - S_\tau + S_\tau e^{-q(T-\tau)} \leq K$$

where S_τ is the stock price at time τ. Portfolio A is worth

$$c + Ke^{r\tau} > K$$

Hence portfolio A is worth more than portfolio B. If both portfolios are held to maturity (time T), portfolio A is worth

$$\max(S_T - K, 0) + Ke^{rT}$$
$$= \max(S_T, K) + K[e^{rT} - 1]$$

Portfolio B is worth $\max(S_T, K)$. Hence portfolio A is worth more than portfolio B.

Since portfolio A is worth more than portfolio B in all circumstances so that

$$P + S_0 e^{-qT} < c + K$$

Since $c \leq C$:

$$P + S_0 e^{-qT} < C + K$$

or

$$S_0 e^{-qT} - K < C - P$$

This proves the first part of the inequality.

For the second part consider:

> *Portfolio A:* An American call option plus an amount Ke^{-rT} invested at the risk-free rate.
>
> *Portfolio B:* A European put option plus one stock with dividends being reinvested in the stock.

Portfolio C is worth $C + Ke^{-rT}$ while portfolio D is worth $p + S_0$. If the call option is exercised at time $\tau (0 \leq \tau < T)$ portfolio C becomes:

$$S_\tau - K + Ke^{-r(T-\tau)} < S_\tau$$

while portfolio D is worth

$$p + S_\tau e^{q(\tau - t)} > S_\tau$$

Hence portfolio D is worth more than portfolio C. If both portfolios are held to maturity (time T), portfolio C is worth $\max(S_T, K)$ while portfolio D is worth

$$\max(K - S_T, 0) + S_T e^{qT}$$
$$= \max(S_T, K) + S_T [e^{qT} - 1]$$

Hence portfolio D is worth more than portfolio C.

Since portfolio D is worth more than portfolio C in all circumstances:

$$C + Ke^{-rT} < p + S_0$$

Since $p < P$:

$$C + Ke^{-rT} < P + S_0$$

or

$$C - P < S_0 - Ke^{-rT}$$

This proves the second part of the inequality. Hence:

$$S_0 e^{-qT} - K < C - P < S_0 - Ke^{-rT}$$

Problem 14.38.

In this case we consider

Portfolio A: A European call option on futures plus an amount K invested at the risk-free interest rate.

Portfolio B: An American put option on futures plus an amount $F_0 e^{-rT}$ invested at the risk-free interest rate plus a long futures contract maturing at time T.

Following the arguments in Chapter 5 we will treat all futures contracts as forward contracts. Portfolio A is worth $c + K$ while portfolio B is worth $P + F_0 e^{-rT}$. If the put option is exercised at time $\tau (0 \le \tau \le T)$, portfolio B becomes:

$$K - F_\tau + F_0 e^{-r(T-\tau)} + F_\tau - F_0$$
$$= K + F_0 e^{-r(T-\tau)} - F_0 < K$$

where F_τ is the futures price at time τ. Portfolio A is worth

$$c + K e^{r\tau} > K$$

Hence portfolio A is worth more than portfolio B. If both portfolios are held to maturity (time T) portfolio A is worth

$$\max(F_T - K, 0) + K e^{rT}$$
$$= \max(F_T, K) + K[e^{rT} - 1]$$

Portfolio B is worth

$$\max(K - F_T, 0) + F_0 + F_T - F_0 = \max(F_T, K)$$

Hence portfolio A is worth more than portfolio B.

Since portfolio A is worth more than portfolio B in all circumstances:

$$P + F_0 e^{-r(T-t)} < c + K$$

Since $c < C$ it follows that

$$P + F_0 e^{-rT} < C + K$$

or

$$F_0 e^{-rT} - K < C - P$$

This proves the first part of the inequality.

For the second part of the inequality consider:

Portfolio C: An American call futures option plus an amount $K e^{-rT}$ invested at the risk-free interest rate.

Portfolio D: A European put futures option plus an amount F_0 invested at the risk-free interest rate plus a long futures contract.

Portfolio C is worth $C + Ke^{-rT}$ while portfolio D is worth $p + F_0$. If the call option is exercised at time $\tau(0 \le \tau < T)$ portfolio C becomes:

$$F_\tau - K + Ke^{-r(T-\tau)} < F_\tau$$

while portfolio D is worth

$$p + F_0 e^{r\tau} + F_\tau - F_0$$
$$= p + F_0[e^{r\tau} - 1] + F_\tau > F_\tau$$

Hence portfolio D is worth more than portfolio C. If both portfolios are held to maturity (time T), portfolio C is worth $\max(F_T, K)$ while portfolio D is worth

$$\max(K - F_T, 0) + F_0 e^{rT} + F_T - F_0$$
$$= \max(K, F_T) + F_0[e^{rT} - 1]$$
$$> \max(K, F_T)$$

Hence portfolio D is worth more than portfolio C.

Since portfolio D is worth more than portfolio C in all circumstances

$$C + Ke^{-rT} < p + F_0$$

Since $p < P$ it follows that

$$C + Ke^{-rT} < P + F_0$$

or

$$C - P < F_0 - Ke^{-rT}$$

This proves the second part of the inequality. The result:

$$F_0 e^{-rT} - K < C - P < F_0 - Ke^{-rT}$$

has therefore been proved.

Problem 14.39.

The risk-neutral process for the price of currency A in terms of the price of currency B is

$$dS = (r_B - r_A)S dt + \sigma S dz$$

The price of currency B expressed in terms of currency A is $1/S$. Define

$$G = \frac{1}{S}$$

then:

$$\frac{\partial G}{\partial t} = 0; \quad \frac{\partial G}{\partial S} = -\frac{1}{S^2}; \quad \frac{\partial^2 G}{\partial S^2} = \frac{2}{S^3}$$

Applying Itô's lemma:

$$dG = \left(-\frac{1}{S^2}\mu S + \frac{1}{2}\frac{2}{S^3}\sigma^2 S^2 \right) dt - \frac{1}{S^2}\sigma S dz$$

$$= \frac{1}{S}\left(-\mu + \sigma^2 \right) dt - \frac{1}{S}\sigma dz$$

$$= (-\mu + \sigma^2)G dt - \sigma G dz$$

We can define a process dz^* by:

$$dz^* = -dz$$

This is also a Wiener process and:

$$dG = (r_A - r_B + \sigma^2)G dt + \sigma G dz^*$$

This shows that $G = 1/S$ follows geometric Brownian motion. The expected growth rate might be expected to be $r_A - r_B$ rather than $r_A - r_B + \sigma^2$. This result is sometimes referred to as Siegel's paradox and is discussed in Chapter 27.

Chapter 15

The Greek Letters

SOLUTIONS TO QUESTIONS AND PROBLEMS

Problem 15.1.

Suppose the strike price is 10.00. The option writer aims to be fully covered whenever the option is in the money and naked whenever it is out of the money. The option writer attempts to achieve this by buying the assets underlying the option as soon as the asset price reaches 10.00 from below and selling as soon as the asset price reaches 10.00 from above. The trouble with this scheme is that it assumes that when the asset price moves from 9.99 to 10.00, the next move will be to a price above 10.00. (In practice the next move might back to 9.99.) Similarly it assumes that when the asset price moves from 10.01 to 10.00, the next move will be to a price below 10.00. (In practice the next move might be back to 10.01.) The scheme can be implemented by buying at 10.01 and selling at 9.99. However, it is not a good hedge. The cost of the trading strategy is zero if the asset price never reaches 10.00 and can be quite high if it reaches 10.00 many times. A good hedge has the property that its cost is always very close the value of the option.

Problem 15.2.

A delta of 0.7 means that, when the price of the stock increases by a small amount, the price of the option increases by 70% of this amount. Similarly, when the price of the stock decreases by a small amount, the price of the option decreases by 70% of this amount. A short position in 1,000 options has a delta of -700 and can be made delta neutral with the purchase of 700 shares.

Problem 15.3.

In this case $S_0 = K$, $r = 0.1$, $\sigma = 0.25$, and $T = 0.5$. Also,

$$d_1 = \frac{\ln(S_0/K) + (0.1 + 0.25^2/2)0.5}{0.25\sqrt{0.5}} = 0.3712$$

The delta of the option is $N(d_1)$ or 0.64.

Problem 15.4.

A theta of -0.1 means that if Δt years pass with no change in either the stock price or its volatility, the value of the option declines by $0.1\Delta t$. If a trader feels that neither the stock price nor its implied volatility will change, he or she should write an option with as high a theta as possible. Relatively short-life at-the-money options have the highest theta.

Problem 15.5.

The gamma of an option position is the rate of change of the delta of the position with respect to the asset price. For example, a gamma of 0.1 would indicate that when the asset price increases by a certain small amount delta increases by 0.1 of this amount. When the gamma of an option writer's position is large and negative and the delta is zero, the option writer will lose significant amounts of money if there is a large movement (either an increase or a decrease) in the asset price.

Problem 15.6.

To hedge an option position it is necessary to create the opposite option position synthetically. For example, to hedge a long position in a put it is necessary to create a short position in a put synthetically. It follows that the procedure for creating an option position synthetically is the reverse of the procedure for hedging the option position.

Problem 15.7.

Portfolio insurance involves creating a put option synthetically. It assumes that as soon as a portfolio's value declines by a small amount the portfolio manager's position is rebalanced by either (a) selling part of the portfolio, or (b) selling index futures. On October 19, 1987, the market declined so quickly that the sort of rebalancing anticipated in portfolio insurance schemes could not be accomplished.

Problem 15.8.

The strategy costs the trader $0.20 each time the stock is bought and sold. The total expected cost of the strategy, in present value terms, must be $4. This means that the expected number of times the stock will be bought and sold is approximately 20. The expected number of times it will be bought is approximately 20 and the expected number of times it will be sold is also approximately 20. The buy and sell transactions can take place at any time during the life of the option. The above numbers are therefore only approximately correct because of the effects of discounting. Also they assume a risk-neutral world.

Problem 15.9.

The holding of the stock at any given time must be $N(d_1)$. Hence the stock is bought just after the price has risen and sold just after the price has fallen. (This is the buy high sell low strategy referred to in the text.) In the first scenario the stock is continually bought. In second scenario the stock is bought, sold, bought again, sold again, etc. The final holding is the same in both scenarios. The buy, sell, buy, sell... situation clearly leads to higher costs than the buy, buy, buy... situation. This problem emphasizes one disadvantage of creating options synthetically. Whereas the cost of an option that is purchased is known up front and depends on the forecasted volatility, the cost of an option that is created synthetically is not known up front and depends on the volatility actually encountered.

Problem 15.10.

The delta of a European futures option is usually defined as the rate of change of the option price with respect to the futures price (not the spot price). It is

$$e^{-rT}N(d_1)$$

In this case $F_0 = 8$, $K = 8$, $r = 0.12$, $\sigma = 0.18$, $T = 0.6667$

$$d_1 = \frac{\ln(8/8) + (0.18^2/2) \times 0.6667}{0.18\sqrt{0.6667}} = 0.0735$$

$N(d_1) = 0.5293$ and the delta of the option is

$$e^{-0.12 \times 0.6667} \times 0.5293 = 0.4886$$

The delta of a short position in 1000 futures options is therefore -488.6.

Problem 15.11.

In order to answer this problem it is important to distinguish between the rate of change of the price of a derivative security with respect to the futures price and the rate of change of the price of the derivative security with respect to the spot price.

The former will be referred to as the futures delta; the latter will be referred to as the spot delta. The futures delta of a nine-month futures contract to buy one ounce of silver is by definition 1.0. Hence, from the answer to Problem 15.10, a long position in nine-month futures on 488.6 ounces is necessary to hedge the option position.

The spot delta of a nine-month futures contract is $e^{0.12 \times 0.75} = 1.094$ assuming no storage costs. (This is because silver can be treated in the same way as a non-dividend-paying stock when there are no storage costs.) Hence the spot delta of the option position is $-488.6 \times 1.094 = -534.6$. Thus a long position in 534.6 ounces of silver is necessary to hedge the option position.

The spot delta of a one-year silver futures contract to buy one ounce of silver is $e^{0.12} = 1.1275$. Hence a long position in $e^{-0.12} \times 534.6 = 474.1$ ounces of one-year silver futures is necessary to hedge the option position.

Problem 15.12.

A long position in either a put or a call option has a positive gamma. From Figure 15.8, when gamma is positive the hedger gains from a large change in the stock price and loses from a small change in the stock price. Hence the hedger will fare better in case (b).

Problem 15.13.

A short position in either a put or a call option has a negative gamma. From Figure 15.8, when gamma is negative the hedger gains from a small change in the stock price and loses from a large change in the stock price. Hence the hedger will fare better in case (a).

Problem 15.14.

In this case $S_0 = 0.80$, $K = 0.81$, $r = 0.08$, $r_f = 0.05$, $\sigma = 0.15$, $T = 0.5833$

$$d_1 = \frac{\ln(0.80/0.81) + (0.08 - 0.05 + 0.15^2/2) \times 0.5833}{0.15\sqrt{0.5833}} = 0.1016$$

$$d_2 = d_1 - 0.15\sqrt{0.5833} = -0.0130$$

$$N(d_1) = 0.5405; \quad N(d_2) = 0.4998$$

The delta of one call option is $e^{-r_f T} N(d_1) = e^{-0.05 \times 0.5833} \times 0.5405 = 0.5250$.

$$N'(d_1) = \frac{1}{\sqrt{2\pi}} e^{-d_1^2/2} = \frac{1}{\sqrt{2\pi}} e^{-0.00516} = 0.3969$$

so that the gamma of one call option is

$$\frac{N'(d_1)e^{-r_f T}}{S_0 \sigma \sqrt{T}} = \frac{0.3969 \times 0.9713}{0.80 \times 0.15 \times \sqrt{0.5833}} = 4.206$$

The vega of one call option is

$$S_0 \sqrt{T} N'(d_1) e^{-r_f T} = 0.80\sqrt{0.5833} \times 0.3969 \times 0.9713 = 0.2355$$

The theta of one call option is

$$-\frac{S_0 N'(d_1)\sigma e^{-r_f T}}{2\sqrt{T}} + r_f S_0 N(d_1) e^{-r_f T} - rKe^{-rT} N(d_2)$$

$$= -\frac{0.8 \times 0.3969 \times 0.15 \times 0.9713}{2\sqrt{0.5833}}$$

$$+ 0.05 \times 0.8 \times 0.5405 \times 0.9713 - 0.08 \times 0.81 \times 0.9544 \times 0.4948$$

$$= -0.0399$$

The rho of one call option is

$$KTe^{-rT} N(d_2)$$

$$= 0.81 \times 0.5833 \times 0.9544 \times 0.4948$$

$$= 0.2231$$

Delta can be interpreted as meaning that, when the spot price increases by a small amount (measured in cents), the value of an option to buy one yen increases by 0.525 times that amount. Gamma can be interpreted as meaning that, when the spot price increases by a small amount (measured in cents), the delta increases by 4.206 times that amount. Vega can be interpreted as meaning that, when the volatility (measured in decimal form) increases by a small amount, the option's value increases by 0.2355 times that amount. Theta can be interpreted as meaning that, when a small amount of time (measured in years) passes, the option's value decreases by 0.0399 times that amount. Finally, rho can be interpreted as meaning that, when the interest rate (measured in decimal form) increases by a small amount the option's value increases by 0.2231 times that amount.

Problem 15.15.

Assume that S_0, K, r, σ, T, q are the parameters for the over-the-counter option and S_0, K^*, r, σ, T^*, q are the parameters for the traded option. Suppose that d_1 has its usual meaning and is calculated on the basis of the first set of parameters while d_1^* is the value of d_1 calculated on the basis of the second set of parameters. Suppose further that w traded options are held for each over-the-counter option. The gamma of the portfolio is:

$$\alpha \left[\frac{N'(d_1)e^{-qT}}{S_0\sigma\sqrt{T}} + w\frac{N'(d_1^*)e^{-qT^*}}{S_0\sigma\sqrt{T^*}} \right]$$

where α is the number of over-the-counter options held.
Since we require gamma to be zero:

$$w = -\frac{N'(d_1)e^{-q(T-T^*)}}{N'(d_1^*)}\sqrt{\frac{T^*}{T}}$$

The vega of the portfolio is:

$$\alpha \left[S_0\sqrt{T}N'(d_1)e^{-q(T)} + wS_0\sqrt{T^*}N'(d_1^*)e^{-q(T^*)} \right]$$

Since we require vega to be zero:

$$w = -\sqrt{\frac{T}{T^*}}\frac{N'(d_1)e^{-q(T-T^*)}}{N'(d_1^*)}$$

Equating the two expressions for w
$$T^* = T$$

Hence the maturity of the option used for hedging must equal the maturity of the option being hedged.

Problem 15.16.

The fund is worth $300,000 times the value of the index. When the value of the portfolio falls by 5% (to $342 million), the value of the S&P 500 also falls by 5% to 1140. The fund manager therefore requires European put options on 300,000 times the S&P 500 with exercise price 1140.

(a) $S_0 = 1200$, $K = 1140$, $r = 0.06$, $\sigma = 0.30$, $T = 0.50$ and $q = 0.03$. Hence:

$$d_1 = \frac{\ln(1200/1140) + (0.06 - 0.03 + 0.3^2/2) \times 0.5}{0.3\sqrt{0.5}} = 0.4186$$

$$d_2 = d_1 - 0.3\sqrt{0.5} = 0.2064$$

$$N(d_1) = 0.6622; \quad N(d_2) = 0.5818$$

$$N(-d_1) = 0.3378; \quad N(-d_2) = 0.4182$$

The value of one put option is

$$1140e^{-rT}N(-d_2) - 1200e^{-qT}N(-d_1)$$
$$= 1140e^{-0.06\times0.5} \times 0.4182 - 1200e^{-0.03\times0.5} \times 0.3378$$
$$= 63.40$$

The total cost of the insurance is therefore

$$300,000 \times 63.40 = \$19,020,000$$

(b) From put–call parity

$$S_0 e^{-qT} + p = c + Ke^{-rT}$$

or:

$$p = c - S_0 e^{-qT} + Ke^{-rT}$$

This shows that a put option can be created by selling (or shorting) e^{-qT} of the index, buying a call option and investing the remainder at the risk-free rate of interest. Applying this to the situation under consideration, the fund manager should:

1) Sell $360e^{-0.03\times0.5} = \$354.64$ million of stock
2) Buy call options on 300,000 times the S&P 500 with exercise price 1140 and maturity in six months.
3) Invest the remaining cash at the risk-free interest rate of 6% per annum.

This strategy gives the same result as buying put options directly.

(c) The delta of one put option is

$$e^{-qT}[N(d_1) - 1]$$
$$= e^{-0.03\times0.5}(0.6622 - 1)$$
$$-0.3327$$

This indicates that 33.27% of the portfolio (i.e., \$119.77 million) should be initially sold and invested in risk-free securities.

(d) The delta of a nine-month index futures contract is

$$e^{(r-q)T} = e^{0.03 \times 0.75} = 1.023$$

The spot short position required is

$$\frac{119,770,000}{1200} = 99,808$$

times the index. Hence a short position in

$$\frac{99,808}{1.023 \times 250} = 390$$

futures contracts is required.

Problem 15.17.

When the value of the portfolio goes down 5% in six months, the total return from the portfolio, including dividends, in the six months is

$$-5 + 2 = -3\%$$

i.e., -6% per annum. This is 12% per annum less than the risk-free interest rate. Since the portfolio has a beta of 1.5 we would expect the market to provide a return of 8% per annum less than the risk-free interest rate, i.e., we would expect the market to provide a return of -2% per annum. Since dividends on the market index are 3% per annum, we would expect the market index to have dropped at the rate of 5% per annum or 2.5% per six months; i.e., we would expect the market to have dropped to 1170. A total of $450,000 = (1.5 \times 300,000)$ put options on the S&P 500 with exercise price 1170 and exercise date in six months are therefore required.

(a) $S_0 = 1200$, $K = 1170$, $r = 0.06$, $\sigma = 0.3$, $T = 0.5$ and $q = 0.03$. Hence

$$d_1 = \frac{\ln(1200/1170) + (0.06 - 0.03 + 0.09/2) \times 0.5}{0.3\sqrt{0.5}} = 0.2961$$

$$d_2 = d_1 - 0.3\sqrt{0.5} = 0.0840$$

$$N(d_1) = 0.6164; \quad N(d_2) = 0.5335$$

$$N(-d_1) = 0.3836; \quad N(-d_2) = 0.4665$$

The value of one put option is

$$Ke^{-rT}N(-d_2) - S_0 e^{-qT}N(-d_1)$$
$$= 1170e^{-0.06 \times 0.5} \times 0.4665 - 1200e^{-0.03 \times 0.5} \times 0.3836$$
$$= 76.28$$

The total cost of the insurance is therefore

$$450,000 \times 76.28 = \$34,326,000$$

Note that this is significantly greater than the cost of the insurance in Problem 15.16.

(b) As in Problem 15.16 the fund manager can 1) sell \$354.64 million of stock, 2) buy call options on 450,000 times the S&P 500 with exercise price 1170 and exercise date in six months and 3) invest the remaining cash at the risk-free interest rate.

(c) The portfolio is 50% more volatile than the S&P 500. When the insurance is considered as an option on the portfolio the parameters are as follows: $S_0 = 360$, $K = 342$, $r = 0.06$, $\sigma = 0.45$, $T = 0.5$ and $q = 0.04$

$$d_1 = \frac{\ln(360/342) + \left(0.06 - 0.04 + 0.45^2/2\right) \times 0.5}{0.45\sqrt{0.5}} = 0.3516$$

$$N(d_1) = 0.6374$$

The delta of the option is

$$e^{-qT}[N(d_1) - 1]$$
$$= e^{-0.03 \times 0.5}(0.6474 - 1)$$
$$= -0.355$$

This indicates that 35.5% of the portfolio (i.e., \$127.8 million) should be sold and invested in riskless securities.

(d) We now return to the situation considered in (a) where put options on the index are required. The delta of each put option is

$$e^{-qT}(N(d_1) - 1)$$
$$= e^{-0.03 \times 0.5}(0.6164 - 1)$$
$$= -0.3779$$

The delta of the total position required in put options is $-450,000 \times 0.3779 = -170,000$. The delta of a nine month index futures is (see Problem 15.16) 1.023. Hence a short position in

$$\frac{170,000}{1.023 \times 250} = 665$$

index futures contracts.

Problem 15.18.

(a) For a call option on a non-dividend-paying stock

$$\Delta = N(d_1)$$
$$\Gamma = \frac{N'(d_1)}{S_0 \sigma \sqrt{T}}$$
$$\Theta = -\frac{S_0 N'(d_1)\sigma}{2\sqrt{T}} - rKe^{-rT}N(d_2)$$

Hence the left-hand side of equation (15.7) is:

$$= -\frac{S_0 N'(d_1)\sigma}{2\sqrt{T}} - rKe^{-rT}N(d_2) + rS_0 N(d_1) + \frac{1}{2}\sigma S_0 \frac{N'(d_1)}{\sqrt{T}}$$

$$= r[S_0 N(d_1) - Ke^{-rT}N(d_2)]$$

$$= r\Pi$$

(b) For a put option on a non-dividend-paying stock

$$\Delta = N(d_1) - 1 = -N(-d_1)$$

$$\Gamma = \frac{N'(d_1)}{S_0 \sigma \sqrt{T}}$$

$$\Theta = -\frac{S_0 N'(d_1)\sigma}{2\sqrt{T}} + rKe^{-rT}N(-d_2)$$

Hence the left-hand side of equation (15.7) is:

$$-\frac{S_0 N'(d_1)\sigma}{2\sqrt{T}} + rKe^{-rT}N(-d_2) - rS_0 N(-d_1) + \frac{1}{2}\sigma S_0 \frac{N'(d_1)}{\sqrt{T}}$$

$$= r[Ke^{-rT}N(-d_2) - S_0 N(-d_1)]$$

$$= r\Pi$$

(c) For a portfolio of options, Π, Δ, Θ and Γ are the sums of their values for the individual options in the portfolio. It follows that equation (15.7) is true for any portfolio of European put and call options.

Problem 15.19.

A currency is analogous to a stock paying a continuous dividend yield at rate r_f. The differential equation for a portfolio of derivatives dependent on a currency is (see equation 14.6)

$$\frac{\partial \Pi}{\partial t} + (r - r_f)S\frac{\partial \Pi}{\partial S} + \frac{1}{2}\sigma^2 S^2 \frac{\partial^2 \Pi}{\partial S^2} = r\Pi$$

Hence

$$\Theta + (r - r_f)S\Delta + \frac{1}{2}\sigma^2 S^2 \Gamma = r\Pi$$

Similarly, for a portfolio of derivatives dependent on a futures price (see equation 14.15)

$$\Theta + \frac{1}{2}\sigma^2 S^2 \Gamma = r\Pi$$

Problem 15.20.

We can regard the position of all portfolio insurers taken together as a single put option. The three known parameters of the option, before the 23% decline, are $S_0 = 70$, $K = 66.5$, $T = 1$. Other parameters can be estimated as $r = 0.06$, $\sigma = 0.25$ and $q = 0.03$. Then:

$$d_1 = \frac{\ln(70/66.5) + (0.06 - 0.03 + 0.25^2/2)}{0.25} = 0.4502$$

$$N(d_1) = 0.6737$$

The delta of the option is

$$e^{-qT}[N(d_1) - 1]$$
$$= e^{-0.03}(0.6737 - 1)$$
$$= -0.3167$$

This shows that 31.67% or $22.17 billion of assets should have been sold before the decline. After the decline, $S_0 = 53.9$, $K = 66.5$, $T = 1$, $r = 0.06$, $\sigma = 0.25$ and $q = 0.03$.

$$d_1 = \frac{\ln(53.9/66.5) + (0.06 - 0.03 + 0.25^2/2)}{0.25} = -0.5953$$
$$N(d_1) = 0.2758$$

The delta of the option has dropped to

$$e^{-0.03 \times 0.5}(0.2758 - 1)$$
$$= -0.7028$$

This shows that cumulatively 70.28% or $49.20 billion of assets (measured at their pre-crash prices) should be sold. In other words about $27 billion of additional assets should be sold as a result of the decline.

Problem 15.21.

With our usual notation the value of a forward contract on the asset is $S_0e^{-qT} - Ke^{-rT}$. When there is a small change, ΔS, in S_0 the value of the forward contract changes by $e^{-qT}\Delta S$. The delta of the forward contract is therefore e^{-qT}. The futures price is $S_0e^{(r-q)T}$. When there is a small change, ΔS, in S_0 the futures price changes by $\Delta Se^{(r-q)T}$. Given the daily settlement procedures in futures contracts, this is also the immediate change in the wealth of the holder of the futures contract. The delta of the futures contract is therefore $e^{(r-q)T}$. We conclude that the deltas of a futures and forward contract are not the same. The delta of the futures is greater than the delta of the corresponding forward by a factor of e^{rT}.

Problem 15.22.

The delta indicates that when the value of the euro exchange rate increases by \$0.01, the value of the bank's position increases by $0.01 \times 30,000 = \$300$. The gamma indicates that when the euro exchange rate increases by \$0.01 the delta of the portfolio decreases by $0.01 \times 80,000 = 800$. For delta neutrality 30,000 euros should be shorted. When the exchange rate moves up to 0.93, we expect the delta of the portfolio to decrease by $(0.93 - 0.90) \times 80,000 = 2,400$ so that it becomes 27,600. To maintain delta neutrality, it is therefore necessary for the bank to unwind its short position 2,400 euros so that a net 27,600 have been shorted. As shown in the text (see Figure 15.8), when a portfolio is delta neutral and has a negative gamma, a loss is experienced when there is a large movement in the underlying asset price. We can conclude that the bank is likely to have lost money.

Problem 15.23.

For a non-dividend paying stock, put-call parity gives at a general time t:

$$p + S = c + Ke^{-r(T-t)}$$

(a) Differentiating with respect to S:

$$\frac{\partial p}{\partial S} + 1 = \frac{\partial c}{\partial S}$$

or

$$\frac{\partial p}{\partial S} = \frac{\partial c}{\partial S} - 1$$

This shows that the delta of a European put equals the delta of the corresponding European call less 1.0.

(b) Differentiating with respect to S again

$$\frac{\partial^2 p}{\partial S^2} = \frac{\partial^2 c}{\partial S^2}$$

Hence the gamma of a European put equals the gamma of a European call.

(c) Differentiating the put-call parity relationship with respect to σ

$$\frac{\partial p}{\partial \sigma} = \frac{\partial c}{\partial \sigma}$$

showing that the vega of a European put equals the vega of a European call.

(d) Differentiating the put-call parity relationship with respect to T

$$\frac{\partial p}{\partial t} = rKe^{-r(T-t)} + \frac{\partial c}{\partial t}$$

This is in agreement with the thetas of European calls and puts given in Section 15.5 since $N(d_2) = 1 - N(-d_2)$.

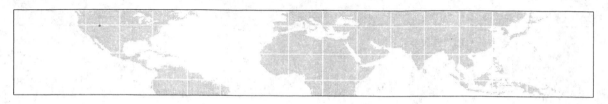

Chapter 16
Volatility Smiles

SOLUTIONS TO QUESTIONS AND PROBLEMS

Problem 16.1.

When both tails of the stock price distribution are less heavy than those of the lognormal distribution, Black–Scholes will tend to produce relatively high prices for options when they are either significantly out of the money or significantly in the money. This leads to an implied volatility pattern similar to that in Figure 16.7. When the right tail is heavier and the left tail is less heavy, Black–Scholes will tend to produce relatively low prices for out-of-the-money calls and in-the-money puts. It will tend to produce relatively high prices for out-of-the-money puts and in-the-money calls. This leads to implied volatility being an increasing function of strike price.

Problem 16.2.

A downward sloping volatility smile is usually observed for equities.

Problem 16.3.

Jumps tend to make both tails of the stock price distribution heavier than those of the lognormal distribution. This creates a volatility smile similar to that in Figure 16.1. The volatility smile is likely to be more pronounced for the three-month option.

Problem 16.4.

The put is has a price that is too low relative to the call's price. The correct trading strategy is to buy the put, buy the stock and sell the call.

Problem 16.5.

The heavier left tail should lead to high prices, and therefore high implied volatilities, for out-of-the-money (low-strike-price) puts. Similarly the less heavy right tail should lead to low prices, and therefore low volatilities for out-of-the-money (high-strike-price) calls. A volatility smile where volatility is a decreasing function of strike price results.

Problem 16.6.

With the notation in the text

$$c_{\mathrm{bs}} + Ke^{-rT} = p_{\mathrm{bs}} + Se^{-qT}$$

$$c_{\text{mkt}} + Ke^{-rT} = p_{\text{mkt}} + Se^{-qT}$$

It follows that

$$c_{\text{bs}} - c_{\text{mkt}} = p_{\text{bs}} - p_{\text{mkt}}$$

In this case $c_{\text{mkt}} = 3.00$; $c_{\text{bs}} = 3.50$; and $p_{\text{bs}} = 1.00$. It follows that p_{mkt} should be 0.50.

Problem 16.7.

The crashophobia argument is an attempt to explain the pronounced volatility skew in equity markets since 1987. (This was the year equity markets shocked everyone by crashing more than 20% in one day). The argument is that traders are concerned about another crash and as a result increase the price of out-of-the-money puts. This creates the volatility skew.

Problem 16.8.

The probability distribution of the stock price in one month is not lognormal. Possibly it consists of two lognormal distributions superimposed upon each other and is bimodal. Black–Scholes is clearly inappropriate, because it assumes that the stock price at any future time is lognormal.

Problem 16.9.

When the asset price is positively correlated with volatility, the volatility tends to increase as the asset price increases, producing thin left tails and fat right tails. Implied volatility then increases with the strike price.

Problem 16.10.

There are a number of problems in testing an option pricing model empirically. These include the problem of obtaining synchronous data on stock prices and option prices, the problem of estimating the dividends that will be paid on the stock during the option's life, the problem of distinguishing between situations where the market is inefficient and situations where the option pricing model is incorrect, and the problems of estimating stock price volatility.

Problem 16.11.

In this case the probability distribution of the exchange rate has a thin left tail and a thin right tail relative to the lognormal distribution. We are in the opposite situation to that described for foreign currencies in Section 16.2. Both out-of-the-money and in-the-money calls and puts can be expected to have lower implied volatilities than at-the-money calls and puts. The pattern of implied volatilities is likely to be similar to Figure 16.7.

Problem 16.12.

A deep-out-of-the-money option has a low value. Decreases in its volatility reduce its value. However, this reduction is small because the value can never go below zero. Increases in its volatility, on the other hand, can lead to significant percentage increases in the value of the option. The option does, therefore, have some of the same attributes as an option on volatility.

Problem 16.13.

As explained in the chapter, put–call parity implies that European put and call options have the same implied volatility. If a call option has an implied volatility of 30% and a put option has an implied volatility of 33%, the call is priced too low relative to the put. The correct trading strategy is to buy the call, sell the put and short the stock. This does not depend on the lognormal assumption underlying Black–Scholes. Put–call parity is true for any set of assumptions.

Problem 16.14.

Suppose that p is the probability of a favorable ruling. The expected price of Microsoft tomorrow is

$$75p + 50(1 - p) = 50 + 25p$$

This must be the price of Microsoft today. (We ignore the expected return to an investor over one day.) Hence

$$50 + 25p = 60$$

or $p = 0.4$.

If the ruling is favorable, the volatility, σ, will be 25%. Other option parameters are $S_0 = 75$, $r = 0.06$, and $T = 0.5$. For a value of K equal to 50, DerivaGem gives the value of a European call option price as 26.502.

If the ruling is unfavorable, the volatility, σ will be 40% Other option parameters are $S_0 = 50$, $r = 0.06$, and $T = 0.5$. For a value of K equal to 50, DerivaGem gives the value of a European call option price as 6.310.

The value today of a European call option with a strike price today is the weighted average of 26.502 and 6.310 or:

$$0.4 \times 26.502 + 0.6 \times 6.310 = 14.387$$

DerivaGem can be used to calculate the implied volatility when the option has this price. The parameter values are $S_0 = 60$, $K = 50$, $T = 0.5$, $r = 0.06$ and $c = 14.387$. The implied volatility is 47.76%.

These calculations can be repeated for other strike prices. The results are shown in the table below. The pattern of implied volatilities is shown in Figure S16.1.

Strike Price	Call Option Price Favorable Outcome	Call Option Price Unfavorable Outcome	Weighted Price	Implied Volatility (%)
30	45.887	21.001	30.955	46.67
40	36.182	12.437	21.935	47.78
50	26.502	6.310	14.387	47.76
60	17.171	2.826	8.564	46.05
70	9.334	1.161	4.430	43.22
80	4.159	0.451	1.934	40.36

Figure S16.1: Implied volatilities in Problem 16.14

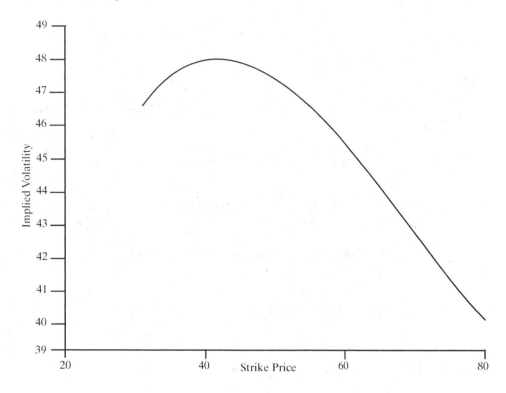

Problem 16.15.

As pointed out in Chapters 5 and 14 an exchange rate behaves like a stock that provides a dividend yield equal to the foreign risk-free rate. Whereas the growth rate in a non-dividend-paying stock in a risk-neutral world is r, the growth rate in the exchange rate in a risk-neutral world is $r - r_f$. Exchange rates have low systematic risks and so we can reasonably assume that this is also the growth rate in the real world. In this case the foreign risk-free rate equals the domestic risk-free rate ($r = r_f$). The expected growth rate in the exchange rate is therefore zero. If S_T is the exchange rate at time T its probability distribution is given by equation (13.3) with $\mu = 0$:

$$\ln S_T \sim \phi(\ln S_0 - \sigma^2 T/2, \sigma\sqrt{T})$$

where S_0 is the exchange rate at time zero and σ is the volatility of the exchange rate. In this case $S_0 = 0.8000$ and $\sigma = 0.12$, and $T = 0.25$ so that

$$\ln S_T \sim \phi(\ln 0.8 - 0.12^2 \times 0.25/2, 0.12\sqrt{0.25})$$

or

$$\ln S_T \sim \phi(-0.2249, 0.06)$$

(a) ln $0.70 = -0.3567$. The probability that $S_T < 0.70$ is the same as the probability that $\ln S_T < -0.3567$. It is

$$N\left(\frac{-0.3567 + 0.2249}{0.06}\right) = N(-2.1955)$$

This is 1.41%.

(b) ln $0.75 = -0.2877$. The probability that $S_T < 0.75$ is the same as the probability that $\ln S_T < -0.2877$. It is

$$N\left(\frac{-0.2877 + 0.2249}{0.06}\right) = N(-1.0456)$$

This is 14.79%. The probability that the exchange rate is between 0.70 and 0.75 is therefore $14.79 - 1.41 = 13.38\%$.

(c) ln $0.80 = -0.2231$. The probability that $S_T < 0.80$ is the same as the probability that $\ln S_T < -0.2231$. It is

$$N\left(\frac{-0.2231 + 0.2249}{0.06}\right) = N(0.0300)$$

This is 51.20%. The probability that the exchange rate is between 0.75 and 0.80 is therefore $51.20 - 14.79 = 36.41\%$.

(d) ln $0.85 = -0.1625$. The probability that $S_T < 0.85$ is the same as the probability that $\ln S_T < -0.1625$. It is

$$N\left(\frac{-0.1625 + 0.2249}{0.06}\right) = N(1.0404)$$

This is 85.09%. The probability that the exchange rate is between 0.80 and 0.85 is therefore $85.09 - 51.20 = 33.89\%$.

(e) ln $0.90 = -0.1054$. The probability that $S_T < 0.90$ is the same as the probability that $\ln S_T < -0.1054$. It is

$$N\left(\frac{-0.1054 + 0.2249}{0.06}\right) = N(1.9931)$$

This is 97.69%. The probability that the exchange rate is between 0.85 and 0.90 is therefore $97.69 - 85.09 = 12.60\%$.

(f) The probability that the exchange rate is greater than 0.90 is $100 - 97.69 = 2.31\%$

The volatility smile encountered for foreign exchange options is shown in Figure 16.1 of the text and implies the probability distribution in Figure 16.2. Figure 16.2 suggests that we would expect the probabilities in (a), (c), (d), and (f) to be too low and the probabilities in (b) and (e) to be too high.

Problem 16.16.

The difference between the two implied volatilities is consistent with Figure 16.3 in the text. For equities the volatility smile is downward sloping. A high strike price option has a lower implied volatility than a low strike price option. The reason is that traders consider that the probability of a large downward movement in the stock price is higher than that predicted by the lognormal probability distribution. The implied distribution assumed by traders is shown in Figure 16.4.

To use DerivaGem to calculate the price of the first option, proceed as follows. Select Equity as the Underlying Type in the first worksheet. Select Analytic European as the Option Type. Input the stock price as 40, volatility as 35%, risk-free rate as 5%, time to exercise as 0.5 year, and exercise price as 30. Leave the dividend table blank because we are assuming no dividends. Select the button corresponding to call. Do not select the implied volatility button. Hit the *Enter* key and click on calculate. DerivaGem will show the price of the option as 11.155. Change the volatility to 28% and the strike price to 50. Hit the *Enter* key and click on calculate. DerivaGem will show the price of the option as 0.725.

Put–call parity is

$$c + Ke^{-rT} = p + S_0$$

so that

$$p = c + Ke^{-rT} - S_0$$

For the first option, $c = 11.155$, $S_0 = 40$, $r = 0.054$, $K = 30$, and $T = 0.5$ so that

$$p = 11.155 + 30e^{-0.05 \times 0.5} - 40 = 0.414$$

For the second option, $c = 0.725$, $S_0 = 40$, $r = 0.06$, $K = 50$, and $T = 0.5$ so that

$$p = 0.725 + 50e^{-0.05 \times 0.5} - 40 = 9.490$$

To use DerivaGem to calculate the implied volatility of the first put option, input the stock price as 40, the risk-free rate as 5%, time to exercise as 0.5 year, and the exercise price as 30. Input the price as 0.414 in the second half of the Option Data table. Select the buttons for a put option and implied volatility. Hit the *Enter* key and click on calculate. DerivaGem will show the implied volatility as 34.99%.

Similarly, to use DerivaGem to calculate the implied volatility of the first put option, input the stock price as 40, the risk-free rate as 5%, time to exercise as 0.5 year, and the exercise price as 50. Input the price as 9.490 in the second half of the Option Data table. Select the buttons for a put option and implied volatility. Hit the *Enter* key and click on calculate. DerivaGem will show the implied volatility as 27.99%.

These results are what we would expect. DerivaGem gives the implied volatility of a put with strike price 30 to be almost exactly the same as the implied volatility of a call with a strike price of 30. Similarly, it gives the implied volatility of a put with strike price 50 to be almost exactly the same as the implied volatility of a call with a strike price of 50.

Problem 16.17.

When plain vanilla call and put options are being priced, traders do use the Black–Scholes model as an interpolation tool. They calculate implied volatilities for the options whose prices they can observe in the market. By interpolating between strike prices and between times to maturity, they estimate implied volatilities for other options. These implied volatilities are then substituted into Black–Scholes to calculate prices for these options. In practice much of the work in producing a table such as Table 16.2 in the over-the-counter market is done by brokers. Brokers often act as intermediaries between participants in the over-the-counter market and usually have more information on the trades taking place than any individual financial institution. The brokers provide a table such as Table 16.2 to their clients as a service.

Chapter 17

Basic Numerical Procedures

SOLUTIONS TO QUESTIONS AND PROBLEMS

Problem 17.1.

Delta, gamma, and theta can be determined from a single binomial tree. Vega is determined by making a small change to the volatility and recomputing the option price using a new tree. Rho is calculated by making a small change to the interest rate and recomputing the option price using a new tree.

Problem 17.2.

In this case, $S_0 = 60$, $K = 60$, $r = 0.1$, $\sigma = 0.45$, $T = 0.25$, and $\Delta t = 0.0833$. Also

$$u = e^{\sigma\sqrt{\Delta t}} = e^{0.45\sqrt{0.0833}} = 1.1387$$
$$d = \frac{1}{u} = 0.8782$$
$$a = e^{r\Delta t} = e^{0.1\times 0.0833} = 1.0084$$
$$p = \frac{a-u}{u-d} = 0.4998$$
$$1 - p = 0.5002$$

The output from DerivaGem for this example is shown in the Figure S17.1. The calculated price of the option is $5.16.

Problem 17.3.

The control variate technique is implemented by

(a) valuing an American option using a binomial tree in the usual way $(= f_A)$.

(b) valuing the European option with the same parameters as the American option using the same tree $(= f_E)$.

(c) valuing the European option using Black–Scholes $(= f_{BS})$.

The price of the American option is estimated as $f_A + f_{BS} - f_E$.

Figure S17.1: Tree for Problem 17.2

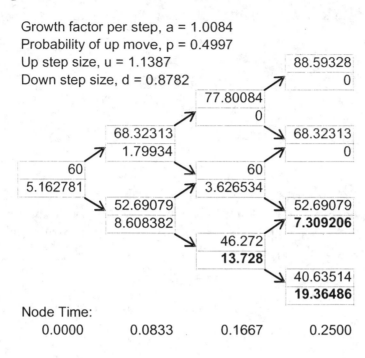

Growth factor per step, a = 1.0084
Probability of up move, p = 0.4997
Up step size, u = 1.1387
Down step size, d = 0.8782

Node Time:
0.0000   0.0833   0.1667   0.2500

Problem 17.4.

In this case $F_0 = 198$, $K = 200$, $r = 0.08$, $\sigma = 0.3$, $T = 0.75$, and $\Delta t = 0.25$. Also

$$u = e^{0.3\sqrt{0.25}} = 1.1618$$
$$d = \frac{1}{u} = 0.8607$$
$$a = 1$$
$$p = \frac{a - d}{u - d} = 0.4626$$
$$1 - p = 0.5373$$

The output from DerivaGem for this example is shown in the Figure S17.2. The calculated price of the option is 20.34 cents.

Problem 17.5.

A binomial tree cannot be used in the way described in this chapter. This is an example of what is known as a history-dependent option. The payoff depends on the path followed by the stock price as well as its final value. The option cannot be valued by starting at the end of the tree and working backward since the payoff at the final branches is not known unambiguously.

Figure S17.2: Tree for Problem 17.4

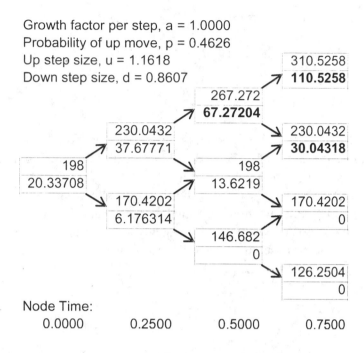

Growth factor per step, a = 1.0000
Probability of up move, p = 0.4626
Up step size, u = 1.1618
Down step size, d = 0.8607

Node Time:

| 0.0000 | 0.2500 | 0.5000 | 0.7500 |

Chapter 24 describes an extension of the binomial tree approach that can be used to handle options where the payoff depends on the average value of the stock price.

Problem 17.6.

Suppose a dividend equal to D is paid during a certain time interval. If S is the stock price at the beginning of the time interval, it will be either $Su - D$ or $Sd - D$ at the end of the time interval. At the end of the next time interval, it will be one of $(Su - D)u$, $(Su - D)d$, $(Sd - D)u$ and $(Sd - D)d$. Since $(Su - D)d$ does not equal $(Sd - D)u$ the tree does not recombine. If S is equal to the stock price less the present value of future dividends, this problem is avoided.

Problem 17.7.

With the usual notation

$$p = \frac{a - d}{u - d}$$

$$1 - p = \frac{u - a}{u - d}$$

If $a < d$ or $a > u$, one of the two probabilities is negative. This happens when

$$e^{(r-q)\Delta t} < e^{-\sigma\sqrt{\Delta t}}$$

or

$$e^{(r-q)\Delta t} > e^{\sigma \sqrt{\Delta t}}$$

This in turn happens when $(q-r)\sqrt{\Delta t} > \sigma$ or $(r-q)\sqrt{\Delta t} > \sigma$ Hence negative probabilities occur when

$$\sigma < |(r-q)\sqrt{\Delta t}|$$

This is the condition in footnote 9.

Problem 17.8.

In Table 17.1 cells A1, A2, A3,..., A100 are random numbers between 0 and 1 defining how far to the right in the square the dart lands. Cells B1, B2, B3,...,B100 are random numbers between 0 and 1 defining how high up in the square the dart lands. For stratified sampling we could choose equally spaced values for the A's and the B's and consider every possible combination. To generate 100 samples we need ten equally spaced values for the A's and the B's so that there are $10 \times 10 = 100$ combinations. The equally spaced values should be 0.05, 0.15, 0.25,..., 0.95. We could therefore set the A's and B's as follows:

$$A1 = A2 = A3 = ... = A10 = 0.05$$

$$A11 = A12 = A13 = ... = A20 = 0.15$$

...

...

$$A91 = A92 = A93 = ... = A100 = 0.95$$

and

$$B1 = B11 = B21 = ... = B91 = 0.05$$

$$B2 = B12 = B22 = ... = B92 = 0.15$$

...

...

$$B10 = B20 = B30 = ... = B100 = 0.95$$

We get a value for π equal to 3.2, which is closer to the true value than the value of 3.04 obtained with random sampling in Table 17.1. Because samples are not random we cannot easily calculate a standard error of the estimate.

Problem 17.9.

In Monte Carlo simulation sample values for the derivative security in a risk-neutral world are obtained by simulating paths for the underlying variables. On each simulation run, values for the underlying variables are first determined at time Δt, then at time $2\Delta t$, then at time $3\Delta t$, etc. At time $i\Delta t$ ($i = 0, 1, 2...$) it is not possible to determine whether early exercise is optimal since the range of paths which might occur after time $i\Delta t$ have not been investigated. In short,

Figure S17.3: Tree for Problem 17.10

Growth factor per step, a = 1.0126
Probability of up move, p = 0.5043
Up step size, u = 1.1618
Down step size, d = 0.8607

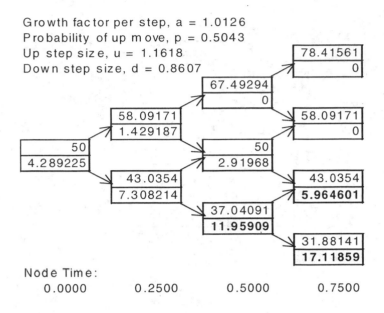

Node Time:
0.0000   0.2500   0.5000   0.7500

Monte Carlo simulation works by moving forward from time t to time T. Other numerical procedures which accommodate early exercise work by moving backwards from time T to time t.

Problem 17.10.

In this case, $S_0 = 50$, $K = 49$, $r = 0.05$, $\sigma = 0.30$, $T = 0.75$, and $\Delta t = 0.25$. Also

$$u = e^{\sigma\sqrt{\Delta t}} = e^{0.30\sqrt{0.25}} = 1.0126$$
$$d = \frac{1}{u} = 0.8607$$
$$a = e^{r\Delta t} = e^{0.1\times0.0833} = 1.0084$$
$$p = \frac{a-d}{u-d} = 0.5043$$
$$1 - p = 0.4957$$

The output from DerivaGem for this example is shown in the Figure S17.3. The calculated price of the option is \$4.29. Using 100 steps the price obtained is \$3.91.

Problem 17.11.

In this case $F_0 = 400$, $K = 420$, $r = 0.06$, $\sigma = 0.35$, $T = 0.75$, and $\Delta t = 0.25$. Also

$$u = e^{0.35\sqrt{0.25}} = 1.1912$$

Figure S17.4: Tree for Problem 17.11

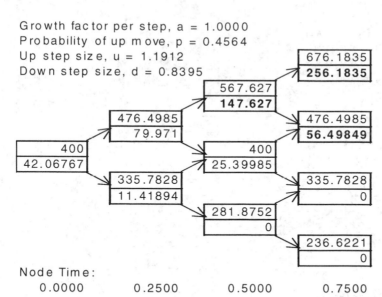

Growth factor per step, a = 1.0000
Probability of up move, p = 0.4564
Up step size, u = 1.1912
Down step size, d = 0.8395

Node Time:
0.0000   0.2500   0.5000   0.7500

$$d = \frac{1}{u} = 0.8395$$
$$a = 1$$
$$p = \frac{a-d}{u-d} = 0.4564$$
$$1-p = 0.5436$$

The output from DerivaGem for this example is shown in the Figure S17.4. The calculated price of the option is 42.07 cents. Using 100 time steps the price obtained is 38.64. The options delta is calculated from the tree is

$$(79.971 - 11.419)/(476.498 - 335.783) = 0.487$$

When 100 steps are used the estimate of the option's delta is 0.483.

Problem 17.12.

In this case the present value of the dividend is $2e^{-0.03 \times 0.125} = 1.9925$. We first build a tree for $S_0 = 20 - 1.9925 = 18.0075$, $K = 20$, $r = 0.03$, $\sigma = 0.25$, and $T = 0.25$ with $\Delta t = 0.08333$. This gives Figure S17.5. For nodes between times 0 and 1.5 months we then add the present value of the dividend to the stock price. The result is the tree in Figure S17.6. The price of the option calculated from the tree is 0.674. When 100 steps are used the price obtained is 0.690.

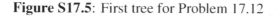

Figure S17.5: First tree for Problem 17.12

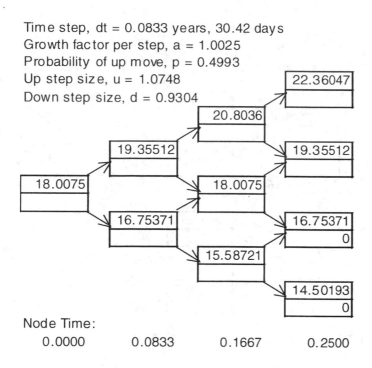

Time step, dt = 0.0833 years, 30.42 days
Growth factor per step, a = 1.0025
Probability of up move, p = 0.4993
Up step size, u = 1.0748
Down step size, d = 0.9304

22.36047

20.8036

19.35512   19.35512

18.0075   18.0075

16.75371   16.75371
                   0

15.58721

14.50193
     0

Node Time:
  0.0000   0.0833   0.1667   0.2500

Problem 17.13.

In this case $S_0 = 20$, $K = 18$, $r = 0.15$, $\sigma = 0.40$, $T = 1$, and $\Delta t = 0.25$. The parameters for the tree are

$$u = e^{\sigma\sqrt{\Delta t}} = e^{0.4\sqrt{0.25}} = 1.2214$$

$$d = 1/u = 0.8187$$

$$a = e^{r\Delta t} = 1.0382$$

$$p = \frac{a - d}{u - d} = \frac{1.0382 - 0.8187}{1.2214 - 0.8187} = 0.545$$

The tree produced by DerivaGem for the American option is shown in Figure S17.7. The estimated value of the American option is $1.29.

As shown in Figure S17.8, the same tree can be used to value a European put option with the same parameters. The estimated value of the European option is $1.14. The option parameters are $S = 20$, $K = 18$, $r = 0.15$, $\sigma = 0.40$ and $T = 1$

$$d_1 = \frac{\ln(20/18) + 0.15 + 0.40^2/2}{0.40} = 0.8384$$

$$d_2 = d_1 - 0.40 = 0.4384$$

Figure S17.6: Final tree for Problem 17.12

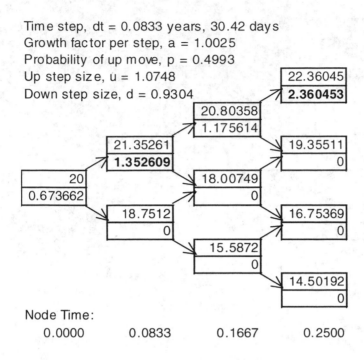

Time step, dt = 0.0833 years, 30.42 days
Growth factor per step, a = 1.0025
Probability of up move, p = 0.4993
Up step size, u = 1.0748
Down step size, d = 0.9304

Node Time:
  0.0000   0.0833   0.1667   0.2500

$$N(-d_1) = 0.2009; \quad N(-d_2) = 0.3306$$

The true European put price is therefore

$$18e^{-0.15} \times 0.3306 - 20 \times 0.2009 = 1.10$$

The control variate estimate of the American put price is therefore $1.29 + 1.10 - 1.14 = \$1.25$.

Problem 17.14.

In this case $S_0 = 484$, $K = 480$, $r = 0.10$, $\sigma = 0.25$ $q = 0.03$, $T = 0.1667$, and $\Delta t = 0.04167$

$$u = e^{\sigma\sqrt{\Delta t}} = e^{0.25\sqrt{0.04167}} = 1.0524$$
$$d = \frac{1}{u} = 0.9502$$
$$a = e^{(r-q)\Delta t} = 1.00292$$
$$p = \frac{a-d}{u-d} = \frac{1.0029 - 0.9502}{1.0524 - 0.9502} = 0.516$$

The tree produced by DerivaGem is shown in the Figure S17.9. The estimated price of the option is $14.93.

Figure S17.7: Tree to evaluate American option for Problem 17.13

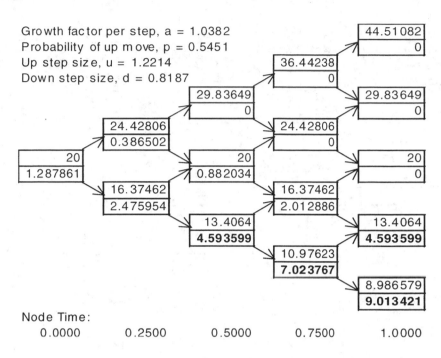

Growth factor per step, a = 1.0382
Probability of up move, p = 0.5451
Up step size, u = 1.2214
Down step size, d = 0.8187

Node Time:
0.0000   0.2500   0.5000   0.7500   1.0000

Problem 17.15.

First the delta of the American option is estimated in the usual way from the tree. Denote this by Δ_A^*. Then the delta of a European option which has the same parameters as the American option is calculated in the same way using the same tree. Denote this by Δ_B^*. Finally the true European delta, Δ_B, is calculated using the formulas in Chapter 15. The control variate estimate of delta is then:

$$\Delta_A^* - \Delta_B^* + \Delta_B$$

Problem 17.16.

In this case a simulation requires two sets of samples from standardized normal distributions. The first is to generate the volatility movements. The second is to generate the stock price movements once the volatility movements are known. The control variate technique involves carrying out a second simulation on the assumption that the volatility is constant. The same random number stream is used to generate stock price movements as in the first simulation. An improved estimate of the option price is

$$f_A^* - f_B^* + f_B$$

Figure S17.8: Tree to evaluate European option in Problem 17.13

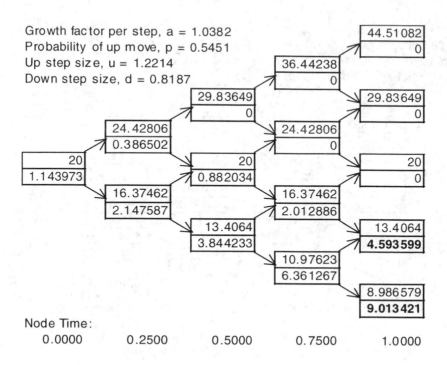

Growth factor per step, a = 1.0382
Probability of up move, p = 0.5451
Up step size, u = 1.2214
Down step size, d = 0.8187

Node Time:
0.0000   0.2500   0.5000   0.7500   1.0000

where f_A^* is the option value from the first simulation (when the volatility is stochastic), f_B^* is the option value from the second simulation (when the volatility is constant) and f_B is the true Black-Scholes value when the volatility is constant.

To use the antithetic variable technique, two sets of samples from standardized normal distributions must be used for each of volatility and stock price. Denote the volatility samples by $\{V_1\}$ and $\{V_2\}$ and the stock price samples by $\{S_1\}$ and $\{S_2\}$.

$\{V_1\}$ is antithetic to $\{V_2\}$ and $\{S_1\}$ is antithetic to $\{S_2\}$. Thus if

$$\{V_1\} = +0.83, +0.41, -0.21\ldots$$

then

$$\{V_2\} = -0.83, -0.41, +0.21\ldots$$

Similarly for $\{S_1\}$ and $\{S_2\}$.
An efficient way of proceeding is to carry out six simulations in parallel:

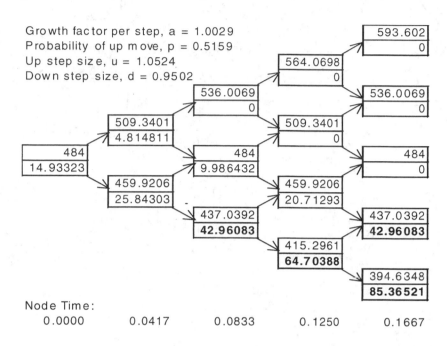

Figure S17.9: Tree to evaluate option in Problem 17.14

Growth factor per step, a = 1.0029
Probability of up move, p = 0.5159
Up step size, u = 1.0524
Down step size, d = 0.9502

Node Time:
0.0000   0.0417   0.0833   0.1250   0.1667

Simulation 1: Use $\{S_1\}$ with volatility constant
Simulation 2: Use $\{S_2\}$ with volatility constant
Simulation 3: Use $\{S_1\}$ and $\{V_1\}$
Simulation 4: Use $\{S_1\}$ and $\{V_2\}$
Simulation 5: Use $\{S_2\}$ and $\{V_1\}$
Simulation 6: Use $\{S_2\}$ and $\{V_2\}$

If f_i is the option price from simulation i, simulations 3 and 4 provide an estimate $0.5(f_3 + f_4)$ for the option price. When the control variate technique is used we combine this estimate with the result of simulation 1 to obtain $0.5(f_3 + f_4) - f_1 + f_B$ as an estimate of the price where f_B is, as above, the Black-Scholes option price. Similarly simulations 2, 5 and 6 provide an estimate $0.5(f_5 + f_6) - f_2 + f_B$. Overall the best estimate is:

$$0.5[0.5(f_3 + f_4) - f_1 + f_B + 0.5(f_5 + f_6) - f_2 + f_B]$$

Problem 17.17.

For an American call option on a currency

$$\frac{\partial f}{\partial t} + (r - r_f)S\frac{\partial f}{\partial S} + \frac{1}{2}\sigma^2 S^2\frac{\partial^2 f}{\partial S^2} = rf$$

With the notation in the text this becomes

$$\frac{f_{i+1,j} - f_{ij}}{\Delta t} + (r - r_f)j\Delta S\frac{f_{i,j+1} - f_{i,j-1}}{2\Delta S} + \frac{1}{2}\sigma^2 j^2 \Delta S^2\frac{f_{i,j+1} - 2f_{i,j} + f_{i,j-1}}{\Delta S^2} = rf_{ij}$$

for $j = 1, 2 \ldots M - 1$ and $i = 0, 1 \ldots N - 1$. Rearranging terms we obtain

$$a_j f_{i,j-1} + b_j f_{ij} + c_j f_{i,j+1} = f_{i+1,j}$$

where

$$a_j = \frac{1}{2}(r - r_f)j\Delta t - \frac{1}{2}\sigma^2 j^2 \Delta t$$

$$b_j = 1 + \sigma^2 j^2 \Delta t + r\Delta t$$

$$c_j = -\frac{1}{2}(r - r_f)j\Delta t - \frac{1}{2}\sigma^2 j^2 \Delta t$$

Equations (17.28), (17.29) and (17.30) become

$$f_{Nj} = \max\left[j\Delta S - K, 0\right] \quad j = 0, 1 \ldots M$$

$$f_{i0} = 0 \quad i = 0, 1 \ldots N$$

$$f_{iM} = M\Delta S - K \quad i = 0, 1 \ldots N$$

Problem 17.18.

We consider stock prices of $0, $4, $8, $12, $16, $20, $24, $28, $32, $36 and $40. Using equation (17.34) with $r = 0.10$, $\Delta t = 0.0833$, $\Delta S = 4$, $\sigma = 0.30$, $K = 21$, $T = 0.3333$ we obtain the table shown below. The option price is $1.56.

Stock Price	Time To Maturity (Months)				
($)	4	3	2	1	0
40	0.00	0.00	0.00	0.00	0.00
36	0.00	0.00	0.00	0.00	0.00
32	0.01	0.00	0.00	0.00	0.00
28	0.07	0.04	0.02	0.00	0.00
24	0.38	0.30	0.21	0.11	0.00
20	1.56	1.44	1.31	1.17	1.00
16	5.00	5.00	5.00	5.00	5.00
12	9.00	9.00	9.00	9.00	9.00
8	13.00	13.00	13.00	13.00	13.00
4	17.00	17.00	17.00	17.00	17.00
0	21.00	21.00	21.00	21.00	21.00

Problem 17.19.

In this case $\Delta t = 0.25$ and $\sigma = 0.4$ so that

$$u = e^{0.4\sqrt{0.25}} = 1.2214$$

$$d = \frac{1}{u} = 0.8187$$

The futures prices provide estimates of the growth rate in copper in a risk-neutral world. During the first three months this growth rate (with continuous compounding) is

$$4 \ln \frac{0.59}{0.60} = -6.72\% \text{ per annum}$$

The parameter p for the first three months is therefore

$$\frac{e^{-0.0672 \times 0.25} - 0.8187}{1.2214 - 0.8187} = 0.4088$$

The growth rate in copper is equal to -13.79%, -21.63% and -30.78% in the following three quarters. Therefore, the parameter p for the second three months is

$$\frac{e^{-0.1379 \times 0.25} - 0.8187}{1.2214 - 0.8187} = 0.3660$$

For the third quarter it is

$$\frac{e^{-0.2163 \times 0.25} - 0.8187}{1.2214 - 0.8187} = 0.3195$$

For the final quarter, it is

$$\frac{e^{-0.3078 \times 0.25} - 0.8187}{1.2214 - 0.8187} = 0.2663$$

The tree for the movements in copper prices in a risk-neutral world is shown in Figure S17.10. The value of the option is $0.062.

Problem 17.20.

In this problem we use exactly the same tree for copper prices as in Problem 17.19. However, the values of the derivative are different. On the final nodes the values of the derivative equal the square of the price of copper. On other nodes they are calculated in the usual way. The current value of the security is $0.275 (see Figure S17.11).

Problem 17.21.

Define S_t as the current asset price, S_{max} as the highest asset price considered and S_{min} as the lowest asset price considered. (In the example in the text $S_{min} = 0$). Let

$$Q_1 = \frac{S_{max} - S_t}{\Delta S} \quad \text{and} \quad Q_2 = \frac{S_t - S_{min}}{\Delta S}$$

and let N be the number of time intervals considered. From the structure of the calculations in the explicit version of the finite difference method, we can see that the values assumed for the derivative security at $S = S_{min}$ and $S = S_{max}$ affect the derivative security's value at time t if

$$N \geq \max{(Q_1, Q_2)}$$

Figure S17.10: Tree to value option in Problem 17.19: At each node, upper number is price of copper and lower number is option price.

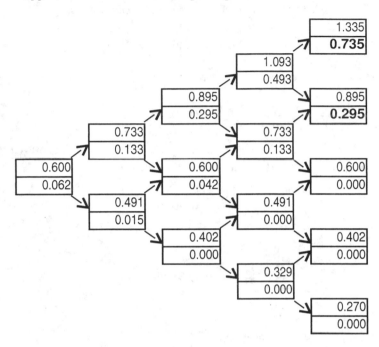

Problem 17.22.

To use the antithetic variable technique we would create three extra columns (e.g., H, I, and J) in the spread sheet. We would set H1 equal to the same expression as A1 with NORM-SINV(RAND()) replaced by –NORMSINV(RAND()) and I1 equal to the same expression as B1 with A1 replaced by H1. J1 would be set equal to the average of B1 and I1. Other entries in the H, I, and J columns would be defined similarly (using a select and drag operation in Excel). Our estimate of the value of the option is the average of the numbers in the J column.

Problem 17.23.

The basic approach is similar to that described in Section 17.8. The only difference is the boundary conditions. For a sufficiently small value of the stock price, S_{min}, it can be assumed that conversion will never take place and the convertible can be valued as a straight bond. The highest stock price which needs to be considered, S_{max}, is $18. When this is reached the value of the convertible bond is $36. At maturity the convertible is worth the greater of $2S_T$ and $25 where S_T is the stock price.

   The convertible can be valued by working backwards through the grid using either the explicit or the implicit finite difference method in conjunction with the boundary conditions. In formulas (17.25) and (17.32) the present value of the income on the convertible between

Figure S17.11: Tree to value derivative in Problem 17.20. At each node, upper number is price of copper and lower number is derivative security price.

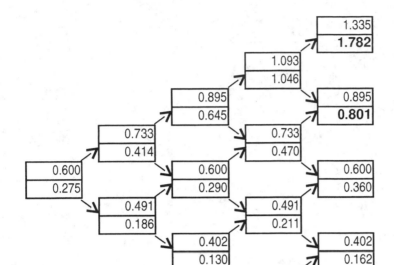

time $t+i\Delta t$ and $t+(i+1)\Delta t$ discounted to time $t+i\Delta t$ must be added to the right-hand side. Chapter 21 considers the pricing of convertibles in more detail.

Problem 17.24.

Suppose x_1, x_2, and x_3 are random samples from three independent normal distributions. Random samples with the required correlation structure are ε_1, ε_2, ε_3 where

$$\varepsilon_1 = x_1$$

$$\varepsilon_2 = \rho_{12}x_1 + x_2\sqrt{1-\rho_{12}^2}$$

and

$$\varepsilon_3 = \alpha_1 x_1 + \alpha_2 x_2 + \alpha_3 x_3$$

where

$$\alpha_1 = \rho_{13}$$

$$\alpha_1\rho_{12} + \alpha_2\sqrt{1-\rho_{12}^2} = \rho_{23}$$

and

$$\alpha_1^2 + \alpha_2^2 + \alpha_3^2 = 1$$

This means that

$$\alpha_1 = \rho_{13}$$

$$\alpha_2 = \frac{\rho_{23} - \rho_{13}\rho_{12}}{\sqrt{1 - \rho_{12}^2}}$$

$$\alpha_3 = \sqrt{1 - \alpha_1^2 - \alpha_2^2}$$

Chapter 18

Value at Risk

SOLUTIONS TO QUESTIONS AND PROBLEMS

Problem 18.1.

The standard deviation of the daily change in the investment in each asset is $1,000. The variance of the portfolio's daily change is

$$1,000^2 + 1,000^2 + 2 \times 0.3 \times 1,000 \times 1,000 = 2,600,000$$

The standard deviation of the portfolio's daily change is the square root of this or $1,612.45. The standard deviation of the 5-day change is

$$1,612.45 \times \sqrt{5} = \$3,605.55$$

From the tables of $N(x)$ we see that $N(-2.33) = 0.01$. This means that 1% of a normal distribution lies more than 2.33 standard deviations below the mean. The 5-day 99 percent value at risk is therefore $2.33 \times 3,605.55 = \$8,401$.

Problem 18.2.

The three alternative procedures mentioned in the chapter for handling interest rates when the model building approach is used to calculate VaR involve (a) the use of the duration model, (b) the use of cash flow mapping, and (c) the use of principal components analysis. When historical simulation is used we need to assume that the change in the zero-coupon yield curve between Day m and Day $m+1$ is the same as that between Day i and Day $i+1$ for different values of i. In the case of a LIBOR, the zero curve is usually calculated from deposit rates, Eurodollar futures quotes, and swap rates. We can assume that the percentage change in each of these between Day m and Day $m+1$ is the same as that between Day i and Day $i+1$. In the case of a Treasury curve it is usually calculated from the yields on Treasury instruments. Again we can assume that the percentage change in each of these between Day m and Day $m+1$ is the same as that between Day i and Day $i+1$.

Problem 18.3.

The approximate relationship between the daily change in the portfolio value, ΔP, and the daily change in the exchange rate, ΔS, is

$$\Delta P = 56\Delta S$$

The percentage daily change in the exchange rate, Δx, equals $\Delta S/1.5$. It follows that

$$\Delta P = 56 \times 1.5 \Delta x$$

or

$$\Delta P = 84 \Delta x$$

The standard deviation of Δx equals the daily volatility of the exchange rate, or 0.7 percent. The standard deviation of ΔP is therefore $84 \times 0.007 = 0.588$. It follows that the 10-day 99 percent VaR for the portfolio is

$$0.588 \times 2.33 \times \sqrt{10} = 4.33$$

Problem 18.4.

The relationship is

$$\Delta P = 56 \times 1.5 \Delta x + \frac{1}{2} \times 1.5^2 \times 16.2 \times \Delta x^2$$

or

$$\Delta P = 84 \Delta x + 18.225 \Delta x^2$$

Problem 18.5.

The factors calculated from a principal components analysis are uncorrelated. The daily variance of the portfolio is
$$6^2 \times 20^2 + 4^2 \times 8^2 = 15,424$$

and the daily standard deviation is $\sqrt{15,424} = \$124.19$. Since $N(-1.282) = 0.9$, the 5-day 90% value at risk is
$$124.19 \times \sqrt{5} \times 1.282 = \$356.01$$

Problem 18.6.

The linear model assumes that the percentage daily change in each market variable has a normal probability distribution. The historical simulation model assumes that the probability distribution observed for the percentage daily changes in the market variables in the past is the probability distribution that will apply over the next day.

Problem 18.7.

When a final exchange of principal is added in, the floating side is equivalent a zero coupon bond with a maturity date equal to the date of the next payment. The fixed side is a coupon-bearing bond, which is equivalent to a portfolio of zero-coupon bonds. The swap can therefore be mapped into a portfolio of zero-coupon bonds with maturity dates corresponding to the payment dates. Each of the zero-coupon bonds can then be mapped into positions in the adjacent standard-maturity zero-coupon bonds.

Problem 18.8.

Value at risk is the loss that is expected to be exceeded $(100 - X)\%$ of the time in N days for specified parameter values, X and N. Conditional Value at Risk is the expected loss conditional that the loss is greater than the Value at Risk.

Problem 18.9.

The change in the value of an option is not linearly related to the change in the value of the underlying variables. When the change in the values of underlying variables is normal, the change in the value of the option is non-normal. The linear model assumes that it is normal and is, therefore, only an approximation.

Problem 18.10.

The 0.3-year cash flow is mapped into a 3-month zero-coupon bond and a 6-month zero-coupon bond. The 0.25 and 0.50 year rates are 5.50 and 6.00 respectively. Linear interpolation gives the 0.30-year rate as 5.60%. The present value of $50,000 received at time 0.3 years is

$$\frac{50,000}{1.056^{0.30}} = 49,189.32$$

The volatility of 0.25-year and 0.50-year zero-coupon bonds are 0.06% and 0.10% per day respectively. The interpolated volatility of a 0.30-year zero-coupon bond is therefore 0.068% per day.

Assume that α of the value of the 0.30-year cash flow gets allocated to a 3-month zero-coupon bond and $1 - \alpha$ to a six-month zero coupon bond. To match variances we must have

$$0.00068^2 = 0.0006^2 \alpha^2 + 0.001^2 (1-\alpha)^2 + 2 \times 0.9 \times 0.0006 \times 0.001 \alpha (1-\alpha)$$

or

$$0.28\alpha^2 - 0.92\alpha + 0.5376 = 0$$

Using the formula for the solution to a quadratic equation

$$\alpha = \frac{-0.92 + \sqrt{0.92^2 - 4 \times 0.28 \times 0.5376}}{2 \times 0.28} = 0.760259$$

this means that a value of $0.760259 \times 49,189.32 = \$37,397$ is allocated to the three-month bond and a value of $0.239741 \times 49,189.32 = \$11,793$ is allocated to the six-month bond. The 0.3-year cash flow is therefore equivalent to a position of $37,397 in a 3-month zero-coupon bond and a position of $11,793 in a 6-month zero-coupon bond. This is consistent with the results in Table 18.7 of the appendix to Chapter 18.

Problem 18.11.

The 6.5-year cash flow is mapped into a 5-year zero-coupon bond and a 7-year zero-coupon bond. The 5-year and 7-year rates are 6% and 7% respectively. Linear interpolation gives the 6.5-year rate as 6.75%. The present value of $1,000 received at time 6.5 years is

$$\frac{1,000}{1.0675^{6.5}} = 654.05$$

The volatility of 5-year and 7-year zero-coupon bonds are 0.50% and 0.58% per day respectively. The interpolated volatility of a 6.5-year zero-coupon bond is therefore 0.056% per day.

Assume that α of the value of the 6.5-year cash flow gets allocated to a 5-year zero-coupon bond and $1 - \alpha$ to a 7-year zero coupon bond. To match variances we must have

$$.56^2 = .50^2\alpha^2 + .58^2(1 - \alpha)^2 + 2 \times 0.6 \times .50 \times .58\alpha(1 - \alpha)$$

or

$$.2384\alpha^2 - .3248\alpha + .0228 = 0$$

Using the formula for the solution to a quadratic equation

$$\alpha = \frac{.3248 - \sqrt{.3248^2 - 4 \times .2384 \times .0228}}{2 \times .2384} = 0.074243$$

this means that a value of $0.074243 \times 654.05 = \$48.56$ is allocated to the 5-year bond and a value of $0.925757 \times 654.05 = \$605.49$ is allocated to the 7-year bond. The 6.5-year cash flow is therefore equivalent to a position of $48.56 in a 5-year zero-coupon bond and a position of $605.49 in a 7-year zero-coupon bond.

The equivalent 5-year and 7-year cash flows are $48.56 \times 1.06^5 = 64.98$ and $605.49 \times 1.07^7 = 972.28$.

Problem 18.12.

The contract is a long position in a sterling bond combined with a short position in a dollar bond. The value of the sterling bond is $1.53e^{-0.05 \times 0.5}$ or $1.492 million. The value of the dollar bond is $1.5e^{-0.05 \times 0.5}$ or $1.463 million. The variance of the change in the value of the contract in one day is

$$1.492^2 \times 0.0006^2 + 1.463^2 \times 0.0005^2 - 2 \times 0.8 \times 1.492 \times 0.0006 \times 1.463 \times 0.0005$$

$$= 0.000000288$$

The standard deviation is therefore $0.000537 million. The 10-day 99% VaR is $0.000537 \times \sqrt{10} \times 2.33 = \$0.00396$ million.

Problem 18.13.

If we assume only one factor, the model is

$$\Delta P = -0.08 f_1$$

The standard deviation of f_1 is 17.49. The standard deviation of ΔP is therefore $0.08 \times 17.49 = 1.40$ and the 1-day 99 percent value at risk is $1.40 \times 2.33 = 3.26$. If we assume three factors, our exposure to the third factor is

$$10 \times (-0.37) + 4 \times (-0.38) - 8 \times (-0.30) - 7 \times (-0.12) + 2 \times (-0.04) = -2.06$$

The model is therefore

$$\Delta P = -0.08 f_1 - 4.40 f_2 - 2.06 f_3$$

The variance of ΔP is

$$0.08^2 \times 17.49^2 + 4.40^2 \times 6.05^2 + 2.06^2 \times 3.10^2 = 751.36$$

The standard deviation of ΔP is $\sqrt{751.36} = 27.41$ and the 1-day 99% value at risk is $27.41 \times 2.33 = \$63.87$.

The example illustrates that the relative importance of different factors depends on the portfolio being considered. Normally the second factor is less important than the first, but in this case it is much more important.

Problem 18.14.

The delta of the options is the rate if change of the value of the options with respect to the price of the asset. When the asset price increases by a small amount the value of the options decrease by 30 times this amount. The gamma of the options is the rate of change of their delta with respect to the price of the asset. When the asset price increases by a small amount, the delta of the portfolio decreases by five times this amount.

By entering 20 for S, 1% for the volatility per day, -30 for delta, -5 for gamma, and re-computing we see that $E(\Delta P) = -0.10$, $E(\Delta P^2) = 36.03$, and $E(\Delta P^3) = -32.415$. The 1-day, 99% VaR given by the software for the quadratic approximation is 14.5. This is a 99% 1-day VaR. The VaR is calculated using the formulas in footnote 9 and the results in Technical Note 10.

Problem 18.15.

Define σ as the volatility per year, $\Delta\sigma$ as the change in σ in one day, and Δw and the proportional change in σ in one day. We measure in σ as a multiple of 1% so that the current value of σ is $1 \times \sqrt{252} = 15.87$. The delta-gamma-vega model is

$$\Delta P = -30\Delta S - .5 \times 5 \times (\Delta S)^2 - 2\Delta\sigma$$

or

$$\Delta P = -30 \times 20\Delta x - 0.5 \times 5 \times 20^2 (\Delta x)^2 - 2 \times 15.87\Delta w$$

which simplifies to

$$\Delta P = -600\Delta x - 1,000(\Delta x)^2 - 31.74\Delta w$$

The change in the portfolio value now depends on two market variables. Once the daily volatility of σ and the correlation between σ and S have been estimated we can estimate moments of ΔP and use a Cornish–Fisher expansion.

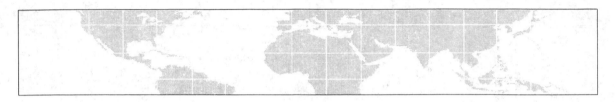

Chapter 19

Estimating Volatilities and Correlations

SOLUTIONS TO QUESTIONS AND PROBLEMS

Problem 19.1.

Define u_i as $(S_i - S_{i-1})/S_{i-1}$, where S_i is value of a market variable on day i. In the EWMA model, the variance rate of the market variable (i.e., the square of its volatility) calculated for day n is a weighted average of the u_{n-i}^2's ($i = 1, 2, 3, \ldots$). For some constant λ ($0 < \lambda < 1$) the weight given to u_{n-i-1}^2 is λ times the weight given to u_{n-i}^2. The volatility estimated for day n, σ_n, is related to the volatility estimated for day $n-1$, σ_{n-1}, by

$$\sigma_n^2 = \lambda \sigma_{n-1}^2 + (1-\lambda)u_{n-1}^2$$

This formula shows that the EWMA model has one very attractive property. To calculate the volatility estimate for day n, it is sufficient to know the volatility estimate for day $n-1$ and u_{n-1}.

Problem 19.2.

The EWMA model produces a forecast of the daily variance rate for day n which is a weighted average of (i) the forecast for day $n-1$, and (ii) the square of the proportional change on day $n-1$. The GARCH (1,1) model produces a forecast of the daily variance for day n which is a weighted average of (i) the forecast for day $n-1$, (ii) the square of the proportional change on day $n-1$. and (iii) a long run average variance rate. GARCH (1,1) adapts the EWMA model by giving some weight to a long run average variance rate. Whereas the EWMA has no mean reversion, GARCH (1,1) is consistent with a mean-reverting variance rate model.

Problem 19.3.

In this case $\sigma_{n-1} = 0.015$ and $u_n = 0.5/30 = 0.01667$, so that equation (19.7) gives

$$\sigma_n^2 = 0.94 \times 0.015^2 + 0.06 \times 0.01667^2 = 0.0002281$$

The volatility estimate on day n is therefore $\sqrt{0.0002281} = 0.015103$ or 1.5103%.

Problem 19.4.

Reducing λ from 0.95 to 0.85 means that more weight is put on recent observations of u_i^2 and less weight is given to older observations. Volatilities calculated with $\lambda = 0.85$ will react more quickly to new information and will "bounce around" much more than volatilities calculated with $\lambda = 0.95$.

Problem 19.5.

The volatility per day is $30/\sqrt{252} = 1.89\%$. There is a 99% chance that a normally distributed variable will lie within 2.57 standard deviations. We are therefore 99% confident that the daily change will be less than $2.57 \times 1.89 = 4.86\%$.

Problem 19.6.

The weight given to the long-run average variance rate is $1 - \alpha - \beta$ and the long-run average variance rate is $\omega/(1 - \alpha - \beta)$. Increasing ω increases the long-run average variance rate; Increasing α increases the weight given to the most recent data item, reduces the weight given to the long-run average variance rate, and increases the level of the long-run average variance rate. Increasing β increases the weight given to the previous variance estimate, reduces the weight given to the long-run average variance rate, and increases the level of the long-run average variance rate.

Problem 19.7.

The proportional daily change is $-0.005/1.5000 = -0.003333$. The current daily variance estimate is $0.006^2 = 0.000036$. The new daily variance estimate is

$$0.9 \times 0.000036 + 0.1 \times 0.003333^2 = 0.000033511$$

The new volatility is the square root of this. It is 0.00579 or 0.579%.

Problem 19.8.

With the usual notation $u_{n-1} = 20/1040 = 0.01923$ so that

$$\sigma_n^2 = 0.000002 + 0.06 \times 0.01923^2 + 0.92 \times 0.01^2 = 0.0001162$$

so that $\sigma_n = 0.01078$. The new volatility estimate is therefore 1.078% per day.

Problem 19.9.

(a) The volatilities and correlation imply that the current estimate of the covariance is $0.25 \times 0.016 \times 0.025 = 0.0001$.

(b) If the prices of the assets at close of trading are \$20.5 and \$40.5, the proportional changes are $0.5/20 = 0.025$ and $0.5/40 = 0.0125$. The new covariance estimate is

$$0.95 \times 0.0001 + 0.05 \times 0.025 \times 0.0125 = 0.0001106$$

The new variance estimate for asset A is

$$0.95 \times 0.016^2 + 0.05 \times 0.025^2 = 0.00027445$$

so that the new volatility is 0.0166. The new variance estimate for asset B is

$$0.95 \times 0.025^2 + 0.05 \times 0.0125^2 = 0.000601562$$

so that the new volatility is 0.0245. The new correlation estimate is

$$\frac{0.0001106}{0.0166 \times 0.0245} = 0.272$$

Problem 19.10.

The long-run average variance rate is $\omega/(1 - \alpha - \beta)$ or $0.000004/0.03 = 0.0001333$. The long-run average volatility is $\sqrt{0.0001333}$ or 1.155%. The equation describing the way the variance rate reverts to its long-run average is equation (19.13)

$$E[\sigma_{n+k}^2] = V_L + (\alpha + \beta)^k (\sigma_n^2 - V_L)$$

In this case

$$E[\sigma_{n+k}^2] = 0.0001333 + 0.97^k (\sigma_n^2 - 0.0001333)$$

If the current volatility is 20% per year, $\sigma_n = 0.2/\sqrt{252} = 0.0126$. The expected variance rate in 20 days is

$$0.0001333 + 0.97^{20}(0.0126^2 - 0.0001333) = 0.0001471$$

The expected volatility in 20 days is therefore $\sqrt{0.0001471} = 0.0121$ or 1.21% per day.

Problem 19.11.

Using the notation in the text $\sigma_{u,n-1} = 0.01$ and $\sigma_{v,n-1} = 0.012$ and the most recent estimate of the covariance between the asset returns is $\text{cov}_{n-1} = 0.01 \times 0.012 \times 0.50 = 0.00006$. The variable $u_{n-1} = 1/30 = 0.03333$ and the variable $v_{n-1} = 1/50 = 0.02$. The new estimate of the covariance, cov_n, is

$$0.000001 + 0.04 \times 0.03333 \times 0.02 + 0.94 \times 0.00006 = 0.0000841$$

The new estimate of the variance of the first asset, $\sigma_{u,n}^2$ is

$$0.000003 + 0.04 \times 0.03333^2 + 0.94 \times 0.01^2 = 0.0001414$$

so that $\sigma_{u,n} = \sqrt{0.0001414} = 0.01189$ or 1.189%. The new estimate of the variance of the second asset, $\sigma_{v,n}^2$ is

$$0.000003 + 0.04 \times 0.02^2 + 0.94 \times 0.012^2 = 0.0001544$$

so that $\sigma_{v,n} = \sqrt{0.0001544} = 0.01242$ or 1.242%. The new estimate of the correlation between the assets is therefore $0.0000841/(0.01189 \times 0.01242) = 0.569$.

Problem 19.12.

The FT-SE expressed in dollars is XY where X is the FT-SE expressed in sterling and Y is the exchange rate (value of one pound in dollars). Define x_i as the proportional change in X on day i and y_i as the proportional change in Y on day i. The proportional change in XY is approximately $x_i + y_i$. The standard deviation of x_i is 0.018 and the standard deviation of y_i is 0.009. The correlation between the two is 0.4. The variance of $x_i + y_i$ is therefore

$$0.018^2 + 0.009^2 + 2 \times 0.018 \times 0.009 \times 0.4 = 0.0005346$$

so that the volatility of $x_i + y_i$ is 0.0231 or 2.31%. This is the volatility of the FT-SE expressed in dollars. Note that it is greater than the volatility of the FT-SE expressed in sterling. This is the impact of the positive correlation. When the FT-SE increases the value of sterling measured in dollars also tends to increase. This creates an even bigger increase in the value of FT-SE measured in dollars. Similarly for a decrease in the FT-SE.

Problem 19.13.

Continuing with the notation in Problem 19.12, define z_i as the proportional change in the value of the S&P 500 on day i. The covariance between x_i and z_i is $0.7 \times 0.018 \times 0.016 = 0.0002016$. The covariance between y_i and z_i is $0.3 \times 0.009 \times 0.016 = 0.0000432$. The covariance between $x_i + y_i$ and z_i equals the covariance between x_i and z_i plus the covariance between y_i and z_i. It is

$$0.0002016 + 0.0000432 = 0.0002448$$

The correlation between $x_i + y_i$ and z_i is

$$\frac{0.0002448}{0.016 \times 0.0231} = 0.662$$

Note that the volatility of the S&P 500 drops out in this calculation.

Problem 19.14.

$$\sigma_n^2 = \omega + \alpha u_{n-1}^2 + \beta \sigma_{n-1}^2$$

so that

$$\sigma_n^2 - \sigma_{n-1}^2 = \omega + (\beta - 1)\sigma_{n-1}^2 + \alpha u_{n-1}^2$$

The variable u_{n-1}^2 has a mean of σ_{n-1}^2 and a variance of

$$E(u_{n-1})^4 - [E(u_{n-1}^2)]^2 = 2\sigma_{n-1}^4$$

The standard deviation of u_{n-1}^2 is $\sqrt{2}\sigma_{n-1}^2$. Assuming the u_i are generated by a Wiener process, dz, we can therefore write

$$u_{n-1}^2 = \sigma_{n-1}^2 + \sqrt{2}\sigma_{n-1}^2 \varepsilon$$

where ε is a random sample from a standard normal distribution. Substituting this into the equation for $\sigma_n^2 - \sigma_{n-1}^2$ we get

$$\sigma_n^2 - \sigma_{n-1}^2 = \omega + (\alpha + \beta - 1)\sigma_{n-1}^2 + \alpha\sqrt{2}\sigma_{n-1}^2\,\varepsilon$$

We can write $\Delta V = \sigma_n^2 - \sigma_{n-1}^2$ and $V = \sigma_{n-1}^2$. Also $a = 1 - \alpha - \beta$, $aV_L = \omega$, and $\xi = \alpha\sqrt{2}$ so that

$$\Delta V = a(V_L - V) + \xi \varepsilon V$$

Because time is measured in days, $\Delta t = 1$ and

$$\Delta V = a(V_L - V)\Delta t + \xi V \varepsilon \sqrt{\Delta t}$$

The result follows.

When time is measured in years $\Delta t = 1/252$ so that

$$\Delta V = a(V_L - V)252\Delta t + \xi V \varepsilon \sqrt{252}\sqrt{\Delta t}$$

and the process for V is

$$dV = 252a(V_L - V)\,dt + \xi V \sqrt{252}\,dz$$

Chapter 20
Credit Risk

SOLUTIONS TO QUESTIONS AND PROBLEMS

Problem 20.1.

From equation (20.2) the average default intensity over the three years is $0.0050/(1-0.3) = 0.0071$ or 0.71% per year.

Problem 20.2.

From equation (20.2) the average default intensity over the five years is $0.0060/(1-0.3) = 0.0086$ or 0.86% per year. Using the results in the previous question, the default intensity is 0.71% per year for the first three years and

$$\frac{0.86 \times 5 - 0.71 \times 3}{2} = 0.0107$$

or 1.07% per year in years 4 and 5.

Problem 20.3.

Real-world probabilities of default should be used for calculating credit value at risk. Risk-neutral probabilities of default should be used for adjusting the price of a derivative for default.

Problem 20.4.

The recovery rate for a bond is the value of the bond immediately after the issuer defaults as a percent of its face value.

Problem 20.5.

The default intensity, $h(t)$ at time t is defined so that $h(t)\Delta t$ is the probability of default between times t and $t + \Delta t$ conditional on no default prior to time t. The unconditional default probability density $q(t)$ is defined so that $q(t)\Delta t$ is the probability of default between times t and $t + \Delta t$ as seen at time zero.

Problem 20.6.

The first number in the second column of Table 20.4 is calculated as

$$-\frac{1}{7} \ln(1 - 0.0029) = 0.0004$$

or 0.04% per year. Other numbers in the column are calculated similarly. The numbers in the fourth column of Table 20.5 are the numbers in the second column of Table 20.4 multiplied by one minus the expected recovery rate. In this case the expected recovery rate is 0.4.

Problem 20.7.

Suppose company A goes bankrupt when it has a number of outstanding contracts with company B. Netting means that the contracts with a positive value to A are netted against those with a negative value in order to determine how much, if anything, company A owes company B. Company A is not allowed to "cherry pick" by keeping the positive-value contracts and defaulting on the negative-value contracts.

   The new transaction will increase the bank's exposure to the counterparty if the contract tends to have a positive value whenever the existing contract has a positive value and a negative value whenever the existing contract has a negative value. However, if the new transaction tends to offset the existing transaction, it is likely to have the incremental effect of reducing credit risk.

Problem 20.8.

Equation (20.10) gives the relationship between $\beta_{AB}(T)$ and ρ_{AB}. This involves $Q_A(T)$ and $Q_B(T)$. These change as we move from the real world to the risk-neutral world. It follows that the relationship between $\beta_{AB}(T)$ and ρ_{AB} in the real world is not the same as in the risk-neutral world. If $\beta_{AB}(T)$ is the same in the two worlds, ρ_{AB} is not.

Problem 20.9.

When securities are pledged as collateral the haircut is the discount applied to their market value for margin calculations. A company's own equity would not be good collateral. When the company defaults on its contracts its equity is likely to be worth very little.

Problem 20.10.

  (a) In the Gaussian copula model for time to default a credit loss is recognized only when a default occurs. In CreditMetrics it is recognized when there is a credit downgrade as well as when there is a default.

  (b) In the Gaussian copula model of time to default, the default correlation arises because the value of the factor M. This defines the default environment or average default rate in the economy. In CreditMetrics a copula model is applied to credit ratings migration and this determines the joint probability of particular changes in the credit ratings of two companies.

Problem 20.11.

   In equation (20.10), $Q_A(2) = 0.2$, $Q_B(2) = 0.15$, and $\rho_{AB} = 0.3$. Also

$$x_A(2) = N^{-1}(0.2) = -0.84162$$

$$x_B(2) = N^{-1}(0.15) = -1.03643$$

$$M(-0.84162, -1.03643, 0.3) = 0.0522$$

$$\beta_{AB}(2) = \frac{0.0522 - 0.2 \times 0.15}{\sqrt{(0.2 - 0.2^2)(0.15 - 0.15^2)}} = 0.156$$

Problem 20.12.

Suppose that the principal is $100. The asset swap is structured so that the $10 is paid initially. After that $2.50 is paid every six months. In return LIBOR plus a spread is received on the principal of $100. The present value of the fixed payments is

$$10 + 2.5e^{-0.06 \times 0.5} + 2.5e^{-0.06 \times 1} + \ldots + 2.5e^{-0.06 \times 5} + 100e^{-0.06 \times 5} = 105.3579$$

The spread over LIBOR must therefore have a present value of 5.3579. The present value of $1 received every six months for five years is 8.5105. The spread received every six months must therefore be $5.3579/8.5105 = \$0.6296$. The asset swap spread is therefore $2 \times 0.6296 = 1.2592\%$ per annum.

Problem 20.13.

When the claim amount is the no-default value, the loss for a corporate bond arising from a default at time t is

$$v(t)(1 - \hat{R})B^*$$

where $v(t)$ is the discount factor for time t and B^* is the no-default value of the bond at time t. Suppose that the zero-coupon bonds comprising the corporate bond have no-default values at time t of $Z_1, Z_2, \ldots, Z_n$, respectively. The loss from the ith zero-coupon bond arising from a default at time t is

$$v(t)(1 - \hat{R})Z_i$$

The total loss from all the zero-coupon bonds is

$$v(t)(1 - \hat{R})\sum_{i}^{n} Z_i = v(t)(1 - \hat{R})B^*$$

This shows that the loss arising from a default at time t is the same for the corporate bond as for the portfolio of its constituent zero-coupon bonds. It follows that the value of the corporate bond is the same as the value of its constituent zero-coupon bonds.

When the claim amount is the face value plus accrued interest, the loss for a corporate bond arising from a default at time t is

$$v(t)B^* - v(t)\hat{R}[L + a(t)]$$

where L is the face value and $a(t)$ is the accrued interest at time t. In general this is not the same as the loss from the sum of the losses on the constituent zero-coupon bonds.

Problem 20.14.

Define Q as the risk-free rate. The calculations are as follows

Time (yrs)	Def. Prob.	Recovery Amount ($)	Risk-free Value ($)	Loss Given Default ($)	Discount Factor	PV of Expected Loss ($)
1.0	Q	30	104.78	74.78	0.9704	72.57Q
2.0	Q	30	103.88	73.88	0.9418	69.58Q
3.0	Q	30	102.96	72.96	0.9139	66.68Q
4.0	Q	30	102.00	72.00	0.8869	63.86Q
Total						272.69Q

The bond pays a coupon of 2 every six months and has a continuously compounded yield of 5% per year. Its market price is 96.19. The risk-free value of the bond is obtained by discounting the promised cash flows at 3%. It is 103.66. The total loss from defaults should therefore be equated to $103.66 - 96.19 = 7.46$. The value of Q implied by the bond price is therefore given by $272.69Q = 7.46$, or $Q = 0.0274$. The implied probability of default is 2.74% per year.

Problem 20.15.

The table for the first bond is

Time (yrs)	Def. Prob.	Recovery Amount ($)	Risk-free Value ($)	Loss Given Default ($)	Discount Factor	PV of Expected Loss ($)
0.5	Q_1	40	103.01	63.01	0.9827	61.92Q_1
1.5	Q_1	40	102.61	62.61	0.9489	59.41Q_1
2.5	Q_1	40	102.20	62.20	0.9162	56.98Q_1
Total						178.31Q_1

The market price of the bond is 98.35 and the risk-free value is 101.23. It follows that Q_1 is given by

$$178.31Q_1 = 101.23 - 98.35$$

so that $Q_1 = 0.0161$.

The table for the second bond is

Time (yrs)	Def. Prob.	Recovery Amount ($)	Risk-free Value ($)	Loss Given Default ($)	Discount Factor	PV of Expected Loss ($)
0.5	Q_1	40	103.77	63.77	0.9827	62.67Q_1
1.5	Q_1	40	103.40	63.40	0.9489	60.16Q_1
2.5	Q_1	40	103.01	63.01	0.9162	57.73Q_1
3.5	Q_2	40	102.61	62.61	0.8847	55.39Q_2
4.5	Q_2	40	102.20	62.20	0.8543	53.13Q_2
Total						180.56$Q_1 + 108.53Q_2$

The market price of the bond is 96.24 is and the risk-free value is 101.97. It follows that

$$180.56Q_1 + 108.53Q_2 = 101.97 - 96.24$$

From which we get $Q_2 = 0.0260$ The bond prices therefore imply a probability of default of 1.61% per year for the first three years and 2.60% for the next two years.

Problem 20.16.

The statements in (a) and (b) are true. The statement in (c) is not. Suppose that v_X and v_Y are the exposures to X and Y. The expected value of $v_X + v_Y$ is the expected value of v_X plus the expected value of v_Y. The same is not true of 95% confidence limits.

Problem 20.17.

The cost of defaults is uv where u is percentage loss from defaults during the life of the contract and v is the value of an option that pays off $\max(150S_T - 100, 0)$ in one year and S_T is the value in dollars of one AUD. The value of u is

$$u = 1 - e^{-(0.06-0.05)\times 1} = 0.009950$$

The variable v is 150 times a call option to buy one AUD for 0.6667. The formula for the call option in terms of forward prices is

$$[FN(d_1) - KN(d_2)]e^{-rT}$$

where

$$d_1 = \frac{\log(F/K) + \sigma^2 T/2}{\sigma\sqrt{T}}$$

$$d_2 = d_1 - \sigma\sqrt{T}$$

In this case $F = 0.6667$, $K = 0.6667$, $\sigma = 0.12$, $T = 1$, and $r = 0.05$ so that $d_1 = 0.06, d_2 = -0.06$ and the value of the call option is 0.0303. It follows that $v = 150 \times 0.0303 = 4.545$ so that the cost of defaults is

$$4.545 \times 0.009950 = 0.04522$$

Problem 20.18.

In this case the costs of defaults is $u_1 v_1 + u_2 v_2$ where

$$u_1 = 1 - e^{-(0.055-0.05)\times 0.5} = 0.002497$$

$$u_2 = e^{-(0.055-0.05)\times 0.5} - e^{-(0.06-0.05)\times 1} = 0.007453$$

v_1 is the value of an option that pays off $\max(150S_T - 100, 0)$ in six months and v_2 is the value of a option that pays off $\max(150S_T - 100, 0)$ in one year. The calculations in Problem 20.17 show that v_2 is 4.545. Similarly $v_1 = 3.300$ so that the cost of defaults is

$$0.002497 \times 3.300 + 0.007453 \times 4.545 = 0.04211$$

Problem 20.19.

Assume that defaults happen only at the end of the life of the forward contract. In a default-free world the forward contract is the combination of a long European call and a short European put where the strike price of the options equals the delivery price and the maturity of the options equals the maturity of the forward contract. If the no-default value of the contract is positive at maturity, the call has a positive value and the put is worth zero. The impact of defaults on the forward contract is the same as that on the call. If the no-default value of the contract is negative at maturity, the call has a zero value and the put has a positive value. In this case defaults have no effect. Again the impact of defaults on the forward contract is the same as that on the call. It follows that the contract has a value equal to a long position in a call that is subject to default risk and short position in a default-free put.

Problem 20.20.

Suppose that the forward contract provides a payoff at time T. With our usual notation, the value of a long forward contract is $S_T - Ke^{-rT}$. The credit exposure on a long forward contract is therefore $\max(S_T - Ke^{-rT}, 0)$; that is, it is a call on the asset price with strike price Ke^{-rT}. Similarly the credit exposure on a short forward contract is $\max(Ke^{-rT} - S_T, 0)$; that is, it is a put on the asset price with strike price Ke^{-rT}. The total credit exposure is, therefore, a straddle with strike price Ke^{-rT}.

Problem 20.21.

The credit risk on a matched pair of interest rate swaps is $|B_{\text{fixed}} - B_{\text{floating}}|$. As maturity is approached all bond prices tend to par and this tends to zero. The credit risk on a matched pair of currency swaps is $|SB_{\text{foreign}} - B_{\text{fixed}}|$ where S is the exchange rate. The expected value of this tends to increase as the swap maturity is approached because of the uncertainty in S.

Problem 20.22.

As time passes there is a tendency for the currency which has the lower interest rate to strengthen. This means that a swap where we are receiving this currency will tend to move in the money (i.e., have a positive value). Similarly a swap where we are paying the currency will tend to move out of the money (i.e., have a negative value). From this it follows that our expected exposure on the swap where we are receiving the low-interest currency is much greater than our expected exposure on the swap where we are receiving the high-interest currency. We should therefore look for counterparties with a low credit risk on the side of the swap where we are receiving the low-interest currency. On the other side of the swap we are far less concerned about the creditworthiness of the counterparty.

Problem 20.23.

No, put–call parity does not hold when there is default risk. Suppose c^* and p^* are the no-default prices of a European call and put with strike price K and maturity T on a non-dividend-paying stock whose price is S, and that c and p are the corresponding values when there is default risk. The text shows that when we make the independence assumption (that is, we assume that the variables determining the no-default value of the option are independent of the variables determining default probabilities and recovery rates), $c = c^* e^{-[y(T)-y^*(T)]T}$ and $p = p^* e^{-[y(T)-y^*(T)]T}$. The relationship

$$c^* + Ke^{-y^*(T)T} = p^* + S$$

which holds in a no-default world therefore becomes

$$c + Ke^{-y(T)T} = p + Se^{-[y(T)-y^*(T)]T}$$

when there is default risk. This is not the same a regular put–call parity. What is more, the relationship depends on the independence assumption and cannot be deduced from the same sort of simple no-arbitrage arguments that we used in Chapter 9 for the put–call parity relationship in a no-default world.

Problem 20.24.

We can assume that the principal is paid and received at the end of the life of the swap without changing the swap's value. If the spread were zero the present value of the floating payments per dollar of principal would be 1. The payment of LIBOR plus the spread therefore has a present value of $1 + V$. The payment of the bond cash flows has a present value per dollar of principal of B^*. The inital payment required from the payer of the bond cash flows per dollar of principal is $1 - B$. (This may be negative; an initial amount of $B - 1$ is then paid by the payer of the floating rate). Because the asset swap is initially worth zero we have

$$1 + V = B^* + 1 - B$$

so that

$$V = B^* - B$$

Problem 20.25.

The value of the debt in Merton's model is $V_0 - E_0$ or

$$De^{-rT}N(d_2) - V_0N(d_1) + V_0 = De^{-rT}N(d_2) + V_0N(-d_1)$$

If the credit spread is s this should equal $De^{-(r+s)T}$ so that

$$De^{-(r+s)T} = De^{-rT}N(d_2) + V_0N(-d_1)$$

Substituting $De^{-rT} = LV_0$

$$LV_0e^{-sT} = LV_0N(d_2) + V_0N(-d_1)$$

or

$$Le^{-sT} = LN(d_2) + N(-d_1)$$

so that

$$s = \ln[N(d_2) + N(-d_1)/L]/T$$

Chapter 21

Credit Derivatives

SOLUTIONS TO QUESTIONS AND PROBLEMS

Problem 21.1.

Both provide insurance against a particular company defaulting during a period of time. In a credit default swap the payoff is the notional principal amount multiplied by one minus the recovery rate. In a binary swap the payoff is the notional principal.

Problem 21.2.

The seller receives

$$300,000,000 \times 0.0060 \times 0.5 = \$900,000$$

at times 0.5, 1.0, 1.5, 2.0, 2.5, 3.0, 3.5, and 4.0 years. The seller also receives a final accrual payment of about \$300,000 (= \$300,000,000 \times 0.060 \times 2/12) at the time of the default (4 years and two months). The seller pays

$$300,000,000 \times 0.6 = \$180,000,000$$

at the time of the default.

Problem 21.3.

Sometimes there is physical settlement and sometimes there is cash settlement. In the event of a default when there is physical settlement the buyer of protection sells bonds issued by the reference entity for their face value. Bonds with a total face value equal to the notional principal can be sold. In the event of a default when there is cash settlement a calculation agent estimates the value of the cheapest-to-deliver bonds issued by the reference entity a specified number of days after the default event. The cash payoff is then based on the excess of the face value of these bonds over the estimated value.

Problem 21.4.

A CDO is created from a bond portfolio. The returns from the bond portfolio flow to a number of tranches (i.e., different categories of investors). The tranches differ as far as the credit risk they assume. The first tranche might have an investment in 5% of the bond portfolio and be responsible for the first 5% of losses. The next tranche might have an investment in 10% of the portfolio and be responsible for the next 10% of the losses, and so on. In a synthetic CDO there is no bond portfolio. Instead a portfolio of credit default swaps is sold and the resulting credit risks are allocated to tranches in a similar way to that just described.

Problem 21.5.

In a first-to-default basket CDS there are a number of reference entities. When the first one defaults there is a payoff (calculated in the usual way for a CDS) and basket CDS terminates. The value of a first-to-default basket CDS decreases as the correlation between the reference entities in the basket increases. This is because the probability of a default is high when the correlation is zero and decreases as the correlation increases. In the limit when the correlation is one there is in effect only one company and the probability of a default is quite low.

Problem 21.6.

Risk-neutral default probabilities are backed out from credit default swaps or bond prices. Real-world default probabilities are calculated from historical data.

Problem 21.7.

Suppose a company wants to buy some assets. If a total return swap is used, a financial institution buys the assets and enters into a swap with the company where it pays the company the return on the assets and receives from the company LIBOR plus a spread. The financial institution has less risk than it would have if it lent the company money and used the assets as collateral. This is because, in the event of a default by the company it owns the assets.

Problem 21.8.

The table corresponding to Tables 21.1, giving unconditional default probabilities, is

Time (years)	Default Probability	Survival Probability
1	0.0300	0.9700
2	0.0291	0.9409
3	0.0282	0.9127
4	0.0274	0.8853
5	0.0266	0.8587

The table corresponding to Table 21.2, giving the present value of the expected regular payments (payment rate is s per year), is

Time (years)	Probability of Survival	Expected Payment	Discount Factor	PV of Expected Payment
1	0.9700	$0.9700s$	0.9324	$0.9044s$
2	0.9409	$0.9409s$	0.8694	$0.8180s$
3	0.9127	$0.9127s$	0.8106	$0.7398s$
4	0.8853	$0.8853s$	0.7558	$0.6691s$
5	0.8587	$0.8587s$	0.7047	$0.6051s$
Total				$3.7364s$

161

The table corresponding to Table 21.3, giving the present value of the expected payoffs (notional principal =$1), is

Time (years)	Probability of Default	Recovery Rate	Expected Payoff	Discount Factor	PV of Expected Payoff
0.5	0.0300	0.3	0.0210	0.9656	0.0203
1.5	0.0291	0.3	0.0204	0.9003	0.0183
2.5	0.0282	0.3	0.0198	0.8395	0.0166
3.5	0.0274	0.3	0.0192	0.7827	0.0150
4.5	0.0266	0.3	0.0186	0.7298	0.0136
Total					0.0838

The table corresponding to Table 21.4, giving the present value of accrual payments, is

Time (years)	Probability of Default	Expected Accrual Payment	Discount Factor	PV of Expected Accrual Payment
0.5	0.0300	$0.0150s$	0.9656	$0.0145s$
1.5	0.0291	$0.0146s$	0.9003	$0.0131s$
2.5	0.0282	$0.0141s$	0.8395	$0.0118s$
3.5	0.0274	$0.0137s$	0.7827	$0.0107s$
4.5	0.0266	$0.0133s$	0.7298	$0.0097s$
Total				$0.0598s$

The credit default swap spread s is given by:

$$3.7364s + 0.0598s = 0.0838$$

It is 0.0221 or 221 basis points.

Problem 21.9.

If the credit default swap spread is 150 basis points, the value of the swap to the buyer of protection is:

$$0.0838 - (3.7364 + 0.0598) \times 0.0150 = 0.0269$$

per dollar of notional principal.

Problem 21.10.

If the swap is a binary CDS, the present value of expected payoffs is calculated as follows

Time (years)	Probability of Default	Expected Payoff	Discount Factor	PV of Expected Payoff
0.5	0.0300	0.0300	0.9656	0.0290
1.5	0.0291	0.0291	0.9003	0.0262
2.5	0.0282	0.0282	0.8395	0.0237
3.5	0.0274	0.0274	0.7827	0.0214
4.5	0.0266	0.0266	0.7298	0.0194
Total				0.1197

The credit default swap spread s is given by:

$$3.7364s + 0.0598s = 0.1197$$

It is 0.0315 or 315 basis points.

Problem 21.11.

A five-year nth to default credit default swap works in the same way as a regular credit default swap except that there is a basket of companies. The payoff occurs when the nth default from the companies in the basket occurs. After the nth default has occurred the swap ceases to exist. When $n = 1$ (so that the swap is a "first to default") an increase in the default correlation lowers the value of the swap. When the default correlation is zero there are 100 independent events that can lead to a payoff. As the correlation increases the probability of a payoff decreases. In the limit when the correlation is perfect there is in effect only one company and therefore only one event that can lead to a payoff.

When $n = 25$ (so that the swap is a 25th to default) an increase in the default correlation increases the value of the swap. When the default correlation is zero there is virtually no chance that there will be 25 defaults and the value of the swap is very close to zero. As the correlation increases the probability of multiple defaults increases. In the limit when the correlation is perfect there is in effect only one company and the value of a 25th-to-default credit default swap is the same as the value of a first-to-default swap.

Problem 21.12.

The recovery rate of a bond is usually defined as the value of the bond a few days after a default occurs as a percentage of the bond's face value.

Problem 21.13.

The payoff from a plain vanilla CDS is $1 - R$ times the payoff from a binary CDS with the same principal. The payoff always occurs at the same time on the two instruments. It follows that the regular payments on a new plain vanilla CDS must be $1 - R$ times the payments on a new binary CDS. Otherwise there would be an arbitrage opportunity.

Problem 21.14.

The 1.61% implied default probability can be calculated by setting up a worksheet in Excel and using Solver. To verify that 1.61% is correct we note that, with a conditional default probability of 1.61%, the unconditional probabilities are:

Time (years)	Default Probability	Survival Probability
1	0.0161	0.9839
2	0.0158	0.9681
3	0.0156	0.9525
4	0.0153	0.9371
5	0.0151	0.9221

The present value of the regular payments becomes $4.1170s$, the present value of the expected payoffs becomes 0.0415, and the present value of the expected accrual payments becomes $0.0346s$. When $s = 0.01$ the present value of the expected payments equals the present value of the expected payoffs.

When the recovery rate is 20% the implied default probability (calculated using Solver) is 1.21% per year. Note that 1.21/1.61 is approximately equal to $(1 - 0.4)/(1 - 0.2)$ showing that the implied default probability is approximately proportional to $1/(1 - R)$.

In passing we note that if the CDS spread is used to imply an unconditional default probability (assumed to be the same each year) then this implied unconditional default probability is exactly proportional to $1/(1 - R)$. When we use the CDS spread to imply a conditional default probability (assumed to be the same each year) it is only approximately proportional to $1/(1 - R)$.

Problem 21.15.

In the case of a total return swap a company receives (pays) the increase (decrease) in the value of the bond. In the regular swap this does not happen.

Problem 21.16.

When a company enters into a long (short) forward contract it is obligated to buy (sell) the protection given by a specified credit default swap with a specified spread at a specified future time. When a company buys a call (put) option contract it has the option to buy (sell) the protection given by a specified credit default swap with a specified spread at a specified future time. Both contracts are normally structured so that they cease to exist if a default occurs during the life of the contract.

Problem 21.17.

A credit default swap insures a corporate bond issued by the reference entity against default. Its approximate effect is to convert the corporate bond into a risk-free bond. The buyer of a credit default swap has therefore chosen to exchange a corporate bond for a risk-free bond. This means that the buyer is long a risk-free bond and short a similar corporate bond.

Problem 21.18.

Payoffs from credit default swaps depend on whether a particular company defaults. Arguably some market participants have more information about this that other market participants. (See Business Snapshot 21.2.)

Problem 21.19.

Real world default probabilities are less than risk-neutral default probabilities. It follows that the use of actuarial default probabilities will tend to understate the value of a CDS.

Figure S21.1: Tree for Problem 21.21

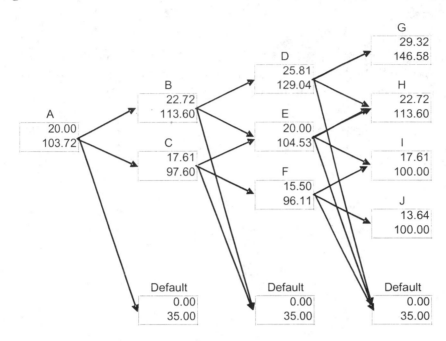

Problem 21.20.

In an asset swap the bond's promised payments are swapped for LIBOR plus a spread. In a total return swap the bond's actual payments are swapped for LIBOR plus a spread.

Problem 21.21.

In this case $\Delta t = 0.5$, $\lambda = 0.03$, $\sigma = 0.25$, $r = 0.06$ and $q = 0$ so that $u = 1.1360$, $d = 0.8803$, $a = 1.0305$, $p_u = 0.6386$, $p_d = 0.3465$, and the probability on default branches is 0.0149. This leads to the tree shown in Figure S21.1. The bond is called at nodes B and D and this forces exercise. Without the call the value at node D would be 129.55, the value at node B would be 115.94, and the value at node A would be 105.18. The value of the call option to the bond issuer is therefore $105.18 - 103.72 = 1.46$.

Problem 21.22.

Using equation (21.2) the probability of default conditional on a factor value of M is

$$N\left(\frac{N^{-1}(0.03) - \sqrt{0.2}M}{\sqrt{1 - 0.2}}\right)$$

For M equal to -2, -1, 0, 1, and 2 the probabilities of default are 0.135, 0.054, 0.018, 0.005, and 0.001 respectively. To six decimal places the probability of more that 10 defaults for these values of M can be calculated using the BINOMDIST function in Excel. They are 0.959284, 0.79851, 0.000016, 0, and 0, respectively.

Problem 21.23.

For a CDO squared we form a portfolio of CDO tranches and tranche the default losses in a similar way to Figure 21.3. For a CDO cubed we form a portfolio of CDO squared tranches and tranche the default losses in a similar way to Figure 21.3.

Chapter 22
Exotic Options

SOLUTIONS TO QUESTIONS AND PROBLEMS

Problem 22.1.

A forward start option is an option that is paid for now but will start at some time in the future. The strike price is usually equal to the price of the asset at the time the option starts. A chooser option is an option where, at some time in the future, the holder chooses whether the option is a call or a put.

Problem 22.2.

A lookback call provides a payoff of $S_T - S_{\min}$. A lookback put provides a payoff of $S_{\max} - S_T$. A combination of a lookback call and a lookback put therefore provides a payoff of $S_{\max} - S_{\min}$.

Problem 22.3.

No, it is never optimal to choose early. The resulting cash flows are the same regardless of when the choice is made. There is no point in the holder making a commitment earlier than necessary. This argument applies when the holder chooses between two American options providing the options cannot be exercised before the 2-year point. If the early exercise period starts as soon as the choice is made, the argument does not hold. For example, if the stock price fell to almost nothing in the first six months, the holder would choose a put option at this time and exercise it immediately.

Problem 22.4.

The payoffs are as follows:

$$c_1 : \ \max(\overline{S} - K, 0)$$
$$c_2 : \ \max(S_T - \overline{S}, 0)$$
$$c_3 : \ \max(S_T - K, 0)$$
$$p_1 : \ \max(K - \overline{S}, 0)$$
$$p_2 : \ \max(\overline{S} - S_T, 0)$$
$$p_3 : \ \max(K - S_T, 0)$$

The payoff from $c_1 - p_1$ is always $\overline{S} - K$; The payoff from $c_2 - p_2$ is always $S_T - \overline{S}$; The payoff from $c_3 - p_3$ is always $S_T - K$; It follows that

$$c_1 - p_1 + c_2 - p_2 = c_3 - p_3$$

or

$$c_1 + c_2 - c_3 = p_1 + p_2 - p_3$$

Problem 22.5.

Substituting for c, put-call parity gives

$$\max(c, p) = \max\left[p,\ p + S_1 e^{-q(T_2 - T_1)} - K e^{-r(T_2 - T_1)}\right]$$

$$= p + \max\left[0,\ S_1 e^{-q(T_2 - T_1)} - K e^{-r(T_2 - T_1)}\right]$$

This shows that the chooser option can be decomposed into

1. A put option with strike price K and maturity T_2; and
2. $e^{-q(T_2 - T_1)}$ call options with strike price $K e^{-(r-q)(T_2 - T_1)}$ and maturity T_1.

Problem 22.6.

Consider the formula for c_{do} when $H \geq K$

$$c_{do} = S_0 N(x_1) e^{-qT} - K e^{-rT} N(x_1 - \sigma\sqrt{T}) - S_0 e^{-qT} (H/S_0)^{2\lambda} N(y_1)$$

$$+ K e^{-rT} (H/S_0)^{2\lambda - 2} N(y_1 - \sigma\sqrt{T})$$

Substituting $H = K$ and noting that

$$\lambda = \frac{r - q + \sigma^2/2}{\sigma^2}$$

we obtain $x_1 = d_1$ so that

$$c_{do} = c - S_0 e^{-qT} (H/S_0)^{2\lambda} N(y_1) + K e^{-rT} (H/S_0)^{2\lambda - 2} N(y_1 - \sigma\sqrt{T})$$

The formula for c_{di} when $H \leq K$ is

$$c_{di} = S_0 e^{-qT} (H/S_0)^{2\lambda} N(y) - K e^{-rT} (H/S_0)^{2\lambda - 2} N(y - \sigma\sqrt{T})$$

Since $c_{do} = c - c_{di}$

$$c_{do} = c - S_0 e^{-qT} (H/S_0)^{2\lambda} N(y) + K e^{-rT} (H/S_0)^{2\lambda - 2} N(y - \sigma\sqrt{T})$$

From the formulas in the text $y_1 = y$ when $H = K$. The two expression for c_{do} are therefore equivalent when $H = K$.

Problem 22.7.

The option is in the money only when the asset price is less than the strike price. However, in these circumstances the barrier has been hit and the option has ceased to exist.

Problem 22.8.

The argument is similar to that given in Chapter 9 for a regular option on a non-dividend-paying stock. Consider a portfolio consisting of the option and cash equal to the present value of the terminal strike price. The initial cash position is

$$Ke^{gT-rT}$$

By time τ $(0 \le \tau \le T)$, the cash grows to

$$Ke^{-r(T-\tau)+gT} = Ke^{g\tau}e^{-(r-g)(T-\tau)}$$

Since $r > g$, this is less than $Ke^{g\tau}$ and therefore is less than the amount required to exercise the option. It follows that, if the option is exercised early, the terminal value of the portfolio is less than S_T. At time T the cash balance is Ke^{gT}. This is exactly what is required to exercise the option. If the early exercise decision is delayed until time T, the terminal value of the portfolio is therefore

$$\max[S_T, Ke^{gT}]$$

This is at least as great as S_T. It follows that early exercise cannot be optimal.

Problem 22.9.

When the strike price of an option on a non-dividend-paying stock is defined as 10% greater that the stock price, the value of the option is proportional to the stock price. The same argument as that given in the text for forward start options shows that if t_1 is the time when the option starts and t_2 is the time when it finishes, the option has the same value as an option starting today with a life of $t_2 - t_1$ and a strike price of 1.1 times the current stock price.

Problem 22.10.

Assume that we start calculating averages from time zero. The relationship between $A(t + \Delta t)$ and $A(t)$ is

$$A(t+\Delta t) \times (t+\Delta t) = A(t) \times t + S(t) \times \Delta t$$

where $S(t)$ is the stock price at time t and terms of higher order than Δt are ignored. If we continue to ignore terms of higher order than Δt, it follows that

$$A(t+\Delta t) = A(t)\left[1 - \frac{\Delta t}{t}\right] + S(t)\frac{\Delta t}{t}$$

Taking limits as Δt tends to zero

$$dA(t) = \frac{S(t) - A(t)}{t}dt$$

The process for $A(t)$ has a stochastic drift and no dz term. The process makes sense intuitively. Once some time has passed, the change in S in the next small portion of time has only a second order effect on the average. If S equals A the average has no drift; if $S > A$ the average is drifting up; if $S < A$ the average is drifting down.

Problem 22.11.

In an Asian option the payoff becomes more certain as time passes and the delta always approaches zero as the maturity date is approached. This makes delta hedging easy. Barrier options cause problems for delta hedgers when the asset price is close to the barrier because delta is discontinuous.

Problem 22.12.

The value of the option is given by the formula in the text

$$V_0 e^{-q_2 T} N(d_1) - U_0 e^{-q_1 T} N(d_2)$$

where

$$d_1 = \frac{\ln(V_0/U_0) + (q_1 - q_2 + \sigma^2/2)T}{\sigma\sqrt{T}}$$

$$d_2 = d_1 - \sigma\sqrt{T}$$

and

$$\sigma = \sqrt{\sigma_1^2 + \sigma_2^2 - 2\rho\sigma_1\sigma_2}$$

In this case, $V_0 = 380$, $U_0 = 400$, $q_1 = 0$, $q_2 = 0$, $T = 1$, and

$$\sigma = \sqrt{0.2^2 + 0.2^2 - 2 \times 0.7 \times 0.2 \times 0.2} = 0.1549$$

Because $d_1 = -0.2537$ and $d_2 = -0.4086$, the option price is

$$380N(-0.2537) - 400N(-0.4086) = 15.38$$

or $15.38.

Problem 22.13.

No. If the future's price is above the spot price during the life of the option, it is possible that the spot price will hit the barrier when the futures price does not.

Problem 22.14.

(a) The put–call relationship is
$$cc + K_1 e^{-rT_1} = pc + c$$

where cc is the price of the call on the call, pc is the price of the put on the call, c is the price today of the call into which the options can be exercised at time T_1, and K_1 is the exercise price for cc and pc. The proof is similar to that in Chapter 9 for the usual put–call parity relationship. Both sides of the equation represent the values of portfolios that will be worth $\max(c, K_1)$ at time T_1. Because

$$M(a,b;\rho) = N(a) - M(a,-b;-\rho) = N(b) - M(-a,b,;-\rho)$$

and

$$N(x) = 1 - N(-x)$$

we obtain

$$cc - pc = Se^{-qT_2}N(b_1) - K_2e^{-rT_2}N(b_2) - K_1e^{-rT_1}$$

Since

$$c = Se^{-qT_2}N(b_1) - K_2e^{-rT_2}N(b_2)$$

put–call parity is consistent with the formulas.

(b) The put–call relationship is

$$cp + K_1e^{-rT_1} = pp + p$$

where cp is the price of the call on the put, pp is the price of the put on the put, p is the price today of the put into which the options can be exercised at time T_1, and K_1 is the exercise price for cp and pp. The proof is similar to that in Chapter 9 for the usual put–call parity relationship. Both sides of the equation represent the values of portfolios that will be worth $\max(p, K_1)$ at time T_1. Because

$$M(a,b;\rho) = N(a) - M(a,-b;-\rho) = N(b) - M(-a,b,;-\rho)$$

and

$$N(x) = 1 - N(-x)$$

it follows that

$$cp - pp = -Se^{-qT_2}N(-b_1) + K_2e^{-rT_2}N(-b_2) - K_1e^{-rT_1}$$

Because

$$p = -Se^{-qT_2}N(-b_1) + K_2e^{-rT_2}N(-b_2)$$

put–call parity is consistent with the formulas.

Problem 22.15.

As we increase the frequency we observe a more extreme minimum which increases the value of a lookback call.

Problem 22.16.

As we increase the frequency with which the asset price is observed, the asset price becomes more likely to hit the barrier and the value of a down-and-out call goes down. For a similar reason the value of a down-and-in call goes up. The adjustment mentioned in the text, suggested by Broadie, Glasserman, and Kou, moves the barrier further out as the asset price is observed less frequently. This increases the price of a down-and-out option and reduces the price of a down-and-in option.

Problem 22.17.

If the barrier is reached the down-and-out option is worth nothing while the down-and-in option has the same value as a regular option. If the barrier is not reached the down-and-in option is worth nothing while the down-and-out option has the same value as a regular option. This is why a down-and-out call option plus a down-and-in call option is worth the same as a regular option. A similar argument cannot be used for American options.

Problem 22.18.

This is a cash-or-nothing call. The value is $100N(d_2)e^{-0.08 \times 0.5}$ where

$$d_2 = \frac{\ln(960/1000) + (0.08 - 0.03 - 0.2^2/2) \times 0.5}{0.2 \times \sqrt{0.5}} = -0.1826$$

Since $N(d_2) = 0.4276$ the value of the derivative is $41.08.

Problem 22.19.

This is a regular call with a strike price of $20 that ceases to exist if the futures price hits $18. With the notation in the text $H = 18$, $K = 20$, $S = 19$, $r = 0.05$, $\sigma = 0.4$, $q = 0.05$, $T = 0.25$. From this $\lambda = 0.5$ and

$$y = \frac{\ln[18^2/(19 \times 20)]}{0.4\sqrt{0.25}} + 0.5 \times 0.4\sqrt{0.25} = -0.69714$$

The value of a down-and-out call plus a down-and-in call equals the value of a regular call. Substituting into the formula given when $H < K$ we get $c_{di} = 0.4638$. The regular Black–Scholes formula gives $c = 1.0902$. Hence $c_{do} = 0.6264$. (These answers can be checked with DerivaGem.)

Problem 22.20.

DerivaGem shows that the value is 53.38. Note that the Minimum to date and Maximum to date should be set equal to the current value of the index for a new deal. (See material on DerivaGem at the end of the book.)

Problem 22.21.

We can use the analytic approximation given in the text.

$$M_1 = \frac{(e^{0.05 \times 0.5} - 1) \times 30}{0.05 \times 0.5} = 30.378$$

Also $M_2 = 936.9$ so that $\sigma = 17.41\%$. The option can be valued as a futures option with $F_0 = 30.378$, $K = 30$, $r = 5\%$, $\sigma = 17.41\%$, and $t = 0.5$. The price is 1.637.

Problem 22.22.

   (a) The price of a regular European call option is 7.116.

   (b) The price of the down-and-out call option is 4.696.

   (c) The price of the down-and-in call option is 2.419.

The price of a regular European call is the sum of the prices of down-and-out and down-and-in options.

Problem 22.23.

When $r = q$ in the expression for a lookback call in Section 22.8 $a_1 = a_3$ and $Y_1 = \ln(S_0/S_{\min})$ so that the expression for a lookback call becomes

$$S_0 e^{-qT} N(a_1) - S_{\min} e^{-rT} N(a_2)$$

As q approaches r in Section 22.10 we get

$$M_1 = S_0$$

$$M_2 = \frac{2e^{\sigma^2 T} S_0^2}{\sigma^4 T^2} - \frac{2S_0^2}{T^2} \frac{1 + \sigma^2 T}{\sigma^4}$$

Chapter 23

Weather, Energy, and Insurance Derivatives

SOLUTIONS TO QUESTIONS AND PROBLEMS

Problem 23.1.

A day's HDD is $\max(0, 65 - A)$ and a day's CDD is $\max(0, A - 65)$ where A is the average of the highest and lowest temperature during the day at a specified weather station, measured in degrees Fahrenheit.

Problem 23.2.

It is an agreement by one side to delivery a specified amount of gas at a roughly uniform rate during a month to a particular hub for a specified price.

Problem 23.3.

The historical data approach to valuing an option involves calculating the expected payoff using historical data and discounting the payoff at the risk-free rate. The risk-neutral approach involves calculating the expected payoff in a risk-neutral world and discounting at the risk-free rate. The two approaches give the same answer when percentage changes in the underlying market variables have zero correlation with stock market returns. (In these circumstances all risks can be diversified away.)

Problem 23.4.

The average temperature each day is $75°$. The CDD each day is therefore 10 and the cumulative CDD for the month is $10 \times 31 = 310$. The payoff from the call option is therefore $(310 - 250) \times 5,000 = \$300,000$.

Problem 23.5.

Unlike most commodities electricity cannot be stored easily. If the demand for electricity exceeds the supply, as it sometimes does during the air conditioning season, the price of electricity in a deregulated environment will skyrocket. When supply and demand become matched again the price will return to former levels.

Problem 23.6.

There is no systematic risk (i.e., risk that is priced by the market) in weather derivatives and CAT bonds.

Problem 23.7.

HDD is $\max(65 - A, 0)$ where A is the average of the maximum and minimum temperature during the day. This is the payoff from a put option on A with a strike price of 65. CDD is $\max(A - 65, 0)$. This is the payoff from call option on A with a strike price of 65.

Problem 23.8.

It would be useful to calculate the cumulative CDD for July of each year of the last 50 years. A linear regression relationship

$$\text{CDD} = a + bt + e$$

could then be estimated where a and b are constants, t is the time in years measured from the start of the 50 years, and e is the error. This relationship allows for linear trends in temperature through time. The expected CDD for next year (year 51) is then $a + 51b$. This could be used as an estimate of the forward CDD.

Problem 23.9.

The volatility of the three-month forward price will be less than the volatility of the spot price. This is because, when the spot price changes by a certain amount, mean reversion will cause the forward price will change by a lesser amount.

Problem 23.10.

The price of the energy source will show big changes, but will be pulled back to its long-run average level fast. Electricity is an example of an energy source with these characteristics.

Problem 23.11.

The energy producer faces quantity risks and price risks. It can use weather derivatives to hedge the quantity risks and energy derivatives to hedge against the price risks.

Problem 23.12.

A 5×8 contract for May, 2005 is a contract to provide electricity for five days per week during the off-peak period (11PM to 7AM). When daily exercise is specified, the holder of the option is able to choose each weekday whether he or she will buy electricity at the strike price at the agreed rate. When there is monthly exercise, he or she chooses once at the beginning of the month whether electricity is to be bought at the strike price at the agreed rate for the whole month. The option with daily exercise is worth more.

Problem 23.13.

CAT bonds (catastrophe bonds) are an alternative to reinsurance for an insurance company that has taken on a certain catastrophic risk (e.g., the risk of a hurricane or an earthquake) and wants to get rid of it. CAT bonds are issued by the insurance company. They provide a higher rate of interest than government bonds. However, the bondholders agree to forego interest, and possibly principal, to meet any claims against the insurance company that are within a prespecified range.

Problem 23.14.

The CAT bond has very little systematic risk. Whether a particular type of catastrophe occurs is independent of the return on the market. The risks in the CAT bond are likely to be largely "diversified away" by the other investments in the portfolio. A B-rated bond does have systematic risk that cannot be diversified away. It is likely therefore that the CAT bond is a better addition to the portfolio.

Chapter 24

More on Models and Numerical Procedures

SOLUTIONS TO QUESTIONS AND PROBLEMS

Problem 24.1.

It follows immediately from the equations in Section 24.1 that

$$p - c = Ke^{-rT} - S_0 e^{-qT}$$

in all cases.

Problem 24.2.

The probability of N jumps in time Δt is

$$\frac{e^{-\lambda \Delta t}(\lambda \Delta t)^N}{N!}$$

When Δt is small we can ignore terms of order $(\Delta t)^2$ and higher so that the probability of no jumps is $1 - \lambda \Delta t$ and the probability of one jump is $\lambda \Delta t$. During each time step of length Δt we first sample a random number between 0 and 1 to determine whether a jump takes place. Suppose for example that $\lambda = 0.8$ and $\Delta t = 0.1$ so that the probability of no jumps is 0.92 and the probability of one jump is 0.08. If the random number is between 0 and 0.92 there is no jump; if it is between 0.92 and 1, there is one jump. If there is a jump we sample from the appropriate distribution to determine the size of the jump. The change in the asset price in time Δt is then given by

$$\frac{\Delta S}{S} = (\mu - \lambda k)\Delta t + \sigma \varepsilon \sqrt{\Delta t} + Q$$

where $Q = 0$ if there is no jump and Q is the size of the jump if a jump takes place. We can adjust this procedure to sample $\ln S$ rather than S and to allow for more than one jump in time Δt.

Problem 24.3.

With the notation in the text the value of a call option, c is

$$\sum_{n=0}^{\infty} \frac{e^{-\lambda' T}(\lambda' T)^n}{n!} c_n$$

where c_n is the Black–Scholes price of a call option where the variance rate is

$$\sigma^2 + \frac{ns^2}{T}$$

and the risk-free rate is

$$r - \lambda k + \frac{n\gamma}{T}$$

where $\gamma = \ln(1+k)$. Similarly the value of a put option p is

$$\sum_{n=0}^{\infty} \frac{e^{-\lambda'T}(\lambda'T)^n}{n!} p_n$$

where p_n is the Black–Scholes price of a put option with this variance rate and risk-free rate. It follows that

$$p - c = \sum_{n=0}^{\infty} \frac{e^{-\lambda'T}(\lambda'T)^n}{n!}(p_n - c_n)$$

From put–call parity

$$p_n - c_n = Ke^{(-r+\lambda k)T} e^{-n\gamma} - S_0 e^{-qT}$$

Because

$$e^{-n\gamma} = (1+k)^{-n}$$

it follows that

$$p - c = \sum_{n=0}^{\infty} \frac{e^{-\lambda'T+\lambda kT}(\lambda'T/(1+k))^n}{n!}Ke^{-rT} - \sum_{n=0}^{\infty} \frac{e^{-\lambda'T}(\lambda'T)^n}{n!}S_0 e^{-qT}$$

Using $\lambda' = \lambda(1+k)$ this becomes

$$\frac{1}{e^{\lambda T}} \sum_{n=0}^{\infty} \frac{(\lambda T)^n}{n!}Ke^{-rT} - \frac{1}{e^{\lambda'T}} \sum_{n=0}^{\infty} \frac{(\lambda'T)^n}{n!}S_0 e^{-qT}$$

From the expansion of the exponential function we get

$$e^{\lambda T} = \sum_{n=0}^{\infty} \frac{(\lambda T)^n}{n!}$$

$$e^{\lambda'T} = \sum_{n=0}^{\infty} \frac{(\lambda'T)^n}{n!}$$

Hence

$$p - c = Ke^{-rT} - S_0 e^{-qT}$$

showing that put–call parity holds.

Problem 24.4.

The average variance rate is

$$\frac{6 \times 0.2^2 + 6 \times 0.22^2 + 12 \times 0.24^2}{24} = 0.0509$$

The volatility used should be $\sqrt{0.0509} = 0.2256$ or 22.56%.

Problem 24.5.

In a risk-neutral world the process for the asset price exclusive of jumps is

$$\frac{dS}{S} = (r - q - \lambda k)\, dt + \sigma\, dz$$

In this case $k = -1$ so that the process is

$$\frac{dS}{S} = (r - q + \lambda)\, dt + \sigma\, dz$$

The asset behaves like a stock paying a dividend yield of $q - \lambda$. This shows that, conditional on no jumps, call price

$$S_0 e^{-(q-\lambda)T} N(d_1) - K e^{-rT}$$

where

$$d_1 = \frac{\ln(S_0/K) + (r - q + \lambda + \sigma^2/2)T}{\sigma\sqrt{T}}$$

$$d_2 = d_1 - \sigma\sqrt{T}$$

There is a probability of $e^{-\lambda T}$ that there will be no jumps and a probability of $1 - e^{-\lambda T}$ that there will be one or more jumps so that the final asset price is zero. It follows that there is a probability of $e^{-\lambda T}$ that the value of the call is given by the above equation and $1 - e^{-\lambda T}$ that it will be zero. Because jumps have no systematic risk it follows that the value of the call option is

$$e^{-\lambda T}[S_0 e^{-(q-\lambda)T} N(d_1) - K e^{-rT}]$$

or

$$S_0 e^{-qT} N(d_1) - K e^{-(r+\lambda)T}$$

This is the required result. The value of a call option is an increasing function of the risk-free interest rate (see Chapter 9). It follows that the possibility of jumps increases the value of the call option in this case.

Problem 24.6.

(a) Suppose that S_1 is the stock price at time t_1 and S_T is the stock price at time T. From equation (13.3), it follows that in a risk-neutral world:

$$\ln S_1 - \ln S_0 \sim \phi \left[\left(r_1 - \frac{\sigma_1^2}{2} \right) t_1, \, \sigma_1 \sqrt{t_1} \right]$$

$$\ln S_T - \ln S_1 \sim \phi \left[\left(r_2 - \frac{\sigma_2^2}{2} \right) t_2, \, \sigma_2 \sqrt{t_2} \right]$$

Since the sum of two independent normal distributions is normal with mean equal to the sum of the means and variance equal to the sum of the variances

$$\ln S_T - \ln S_0 = (\ln S_T - \ln S_1) + (\ln S_1 - \ln S_0)$$

$$\sim \phi \left(r_1 t_1 + r_2 t_2 - \frac{\sigma_1^2 t_1}{2} - \frac{\sigma_2^2 t_2}{2}, \, \sqrt{\sigma_1^2 t_1 + \sigma_2^2 t_2} \right)$$

(b) Because

$$r_1 t_1 + r_2 t_2 = \bar{r} T$$

and

$$\sigma_1^2 t_1 + \sigma_2^2 t_2 - \bar{V} T$$

it follows that:

$$\ln S_T - \ln S_0 \sim \phi \left[\left(\bar{r} - \frac{\bar{V}}{2} \right) T, \, \sqrt{\bar{V} T} \right]$$

(c) If σ_i and r_i are the volatility and risk-free interest rate during the ith subinterval ($i = 1, 2, 3$), an argument similar to that in (a) shows that:

$$\ln S_T - \ln S_0 \sim \phi \left(r_1 t_1 + r_2 t_2 + r_3 t_3 - \frac{\sigma_1^2 t_1}{2} - \frac{\sigma_2^2 t_2}{2} - \frac{\sigma_3^2 t_3}{2}, \, \sqrt{\sigma_1^2 t_1 + \sigma_2^2 t_2 + \sigma_3^2 t_3} \right)$$

where t_1, t_2 and t_3 are the lengths of the three subintervals. It follows that the result in (b) is still true.

(d) The result in (b) remains true as the time between time zero and time T is divided into more subintervals, each having its own risk-free interest rate and volatility. In the limit, it follows that, if r and σ are known functions of time, the stock price distribution at time T is the same as that for a stock with a constant interest rate and variance rate with the constant interest rate equal to the average interest rate and the constant variance rate equal to the average variance rate.

Problem 24.7.

The equations are:

$$S(t+\Delta t) = S(t)\exp[(r-q-V(t)/2)\Delta t + \varepsilon_1 \sqrt{V(t)\Delta t}]$$
$$V(t+\Delta t) - V(t) = a[V_L - V(t)]\Delta t + \xi\varepsilon_2 V(t)^\alpha \sqrt{\Delta t}$$

Problem 24.8.

The IVF model is designed to match the volatility surface today. There is no guarantee that the volatility surface given by the model at future times will be the same as today—or that it will be even reasonable.

Problem 24.9.

The IVF model ensures that the risk-neutral probability distribution of the asset price at any future time conditional on its value today is correct (or at least consistent with the market prices of options). When a derivative's payoff depends on the value of the asset at only one time the IVF model therefore calculates the expected payoff from the asset correctly. The value of the derivative is the present value of the expected payoff. When interest rates are constant the IVF model calculates this present value correctly.

Problem 24.10.

In this case $S_0 = 1.6$, $r = 0.05$, $r_f = 0.08$, $\sigma = 0.15$, $T = 1.5$, $\Delta t = 0.5$. This means that.

$$u = e^{0.15\sqrt{0.5}} = 1.1119$$

$$d = \frac{1}{u} = 0.8994$$

$$a = e^{(0.05-0.08)\times 0.5} = 0.9851$$

$$p = \frac{a-d}{u-d} = 0.4033$$

$$1 - p = 0.5967$$

The option pays off

$$S_T - S_{\min}$$

The tree is shown in Figure S24.1. At each node, the upper number is the exchange rate, the middle number(s) are the minimum exchange rate(s) so far, and the lower number(s) are the value(s) of the option. The tree shows that the value of the option today is 0.131.

Problem 24.11.

As v tends to zero the value of g becomes T with certainty. This can be demonstrated using the GAMMADIST function in Excel. By using a series expansion for the ln function we see that

Figure S24.1: Binomial tree for Problem 24.10.

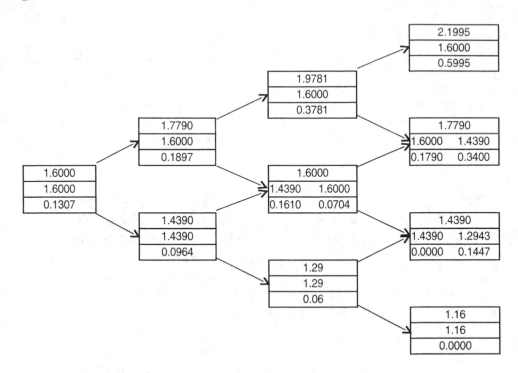

ω becomes $-\theta T$. In the limit the distribution of $\ln S_T$ therefore has a mean of $\ln S_0 + (r - q)T$ and a standard deviation of $\sigma \sqrt{T}$ so that the model becomes geometric Brownian motion.

Problem 24.12.

In this case $S_0 = 40$, $K = 40$, $r = 0.1$, $\sigma = 0.35$, $T = 0.25$, $\Delta t = 0.08333$. This means that

$$u = e^{0.35\sqrt{0.08333}} = 1.1063$$

$$d = \frac{1}{u} = 0.9039$$

$$a = e^{0.1 \times 0.08333} = 1.008368$$

$$p = \frac{a - d}{u - d} = 0.5161$$

$$1 - p = 0.4839$$

The option pays off

$$40 - \overline{S}$$

Figure S24.2: Binomial tree for Problem 24.12.

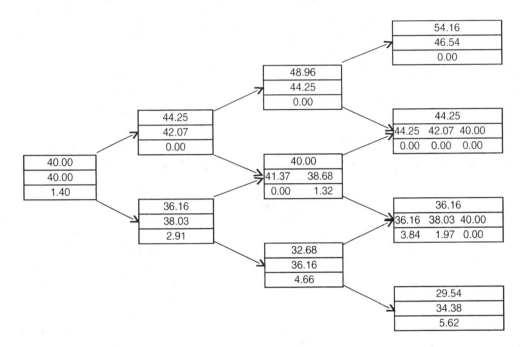

where $\overline{S}$ denotes the geometric average. The tree is shown in Figure S24.2. At each node, the upper number is the stock price, the middle number(s) are the geometric average(s), and the lower number(s) are the value(s) of the option. The geometric averages are calculated using the first, the last and all intermediate stock prices on the path. The tree shows that the value of the option today is $1.40.

Problem 24.13.

As mentioned in Section 24.4, for the procedure to work it must be possible to calculate the value of the path function at time $\tau + \Delta t$ from the value of the path function at time τ and the value of the underlying asset at time $\tau + \Delta t$. When S_{ave} is calculated from time zero until the end of the life of the option (as in the example considered in Section 24.4) this condition is satisfied. When it is calculated over the last three months it is not satisfied. This is because, in order to update the average with a new observation on S, it is necessary to know the observation on S from three months ago that is now no longer part of the average calculation.

Problem 24.14.

We consider the situation where the average at node X is 53.83. If there is an up movement to node Y the new average becomes:

$$\frac{53.83 \times 5 + 54.68}{6} = 53.97$$

Interpolating, the value of the option at node Y when the average is 53.97 is

$$\frac{(53.97 - 51.12) \times 8.635 + (54.26 - 53.97) \times 8.101}{54.26 - 51.12} = 8.586$$

Similarly if there is a down movement the new average will be

$$\frac{53.83 \times 5 + 45.72}{6} = 52.48$$

In this case the option price is 4.416. The option price at node X when the average is 53.83 is therefore:

$$8.586 \times 0.5056 + 4.416 \times 0.4944)e^{-0.1 \times 0.05} = 6.492$$

Problem 24.15.

Under the least squares approach we exercise at time $t = 1$ in paths 4, 6, 7, and 8. We exercise at time $t = 2$ for none of the paths. We exercise at time $t = 3$ for path 3. Under the exercise boundary parameterization approach we exercise at time $t = 1$ for paths 6 and 8. We exercise at time $t = 2$ for path 7. We exercise at time $t = 3$ for paths 3 and 4. For the paths sampled the exercise boundary parameterization approach gives a higher value for the option. However, it may be biased upward. As mentioned in the text, once the early exercise boundary has been determined in the exercise boundary parameterization approach a new Monte Carlo simulation should be carried out.

Problem 24.16.

If the average variance rate is 0.06, the value of the option is given by Black-Scholes with a volatility of $\sqrt{0.06} = 24.495\%$; it is 12.460. If the average variance rate is 0.09, the value of the option is given by Black-Scholes with a volatility of $\sqrt{0.09} = 30.000\%$; it is 14.655. If the average variance rate is 0.12, the value of the option is given by Black-Scholes with a volatility of $\sqrt{0.12} = 34.641\%$; it is 16.506. The value of the option is the Black-Scholes price integrated over the probability distribution of the average variance rate. It is

$$0.2 \times 12.460 + 0.5 \times 14.655 + 0.3 \times 16.506 = 14.77$$

Problem 24.17.

Suppose that there are two horizontal barriers, H_1 and H_2, with $H_1 > H_2$ and that the underlying stock price follows geometric Brownian motion. In a trinomial tree, there are three possible movements in the asset's price at each node: up by a proportional amount u; stay the same;

Figure S24.3: Tree with nodes lying on each of two barriers

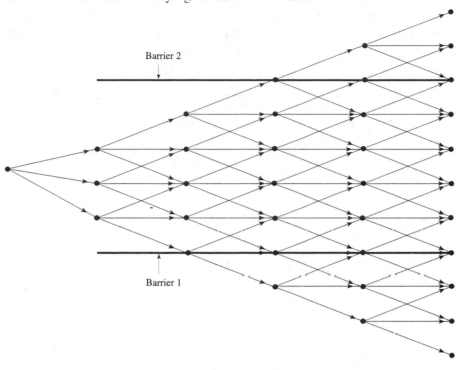

and down by a proportional amount d where $d = 1/u$. We can always choose u so that nodes lie on both barriers. The condition that must be satisfied by u is

$$H_2 = H_1 u^N$$

or

$$\ln H_2 = \ln H_1 + N \ln u$$

for some integer N.

When discussing trinomial trees in Section 17.4, the value suggested for u was $e^{\sigma\sqrt{3\Delta t}}$ so that $\ln u = \sigma\sqrt{3\Delta t}$. In the situation considered here, a good rule is to choose $\ln u$ as close as possible to this value, consistent with the condition given above. This means that we set

$$\ln u = \frac{\ln H_2 - \ln H_1}{N}$$

where

$$N = \text{int}\left[\frac{\ln H_2 - \ln H_1}{\sigma\sqrt{3\Delta t}} + 0.5\right]$$

and $\text{int}(x)$ is the integral part of x.

Normally, the trinomial stock price tree is constructed so that the central node is the initial stock price. In this case, there is likely to be no node corresponding to the stock price and the tree will have the form shown in Figure S24.3. The probabilities on all branches of the tree are chosen, as usual, to match the first two moments of the stochastic process followed by the asset price. The approach works well except when the initial asset price is close to a barrier.

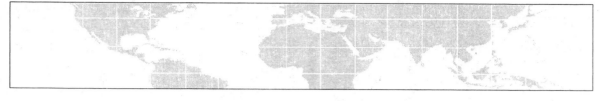

Chapter 25

Martingales and Measures

SOLUTIONS TO QUESTIONS AND PROBLEMS

Problem 25.1.

The market price of risk for a variable that is not the price of a traded security is the market price of risk of a traded security whose price is instantaneously perfectly positively correlated with the variable.

Problem 25.2.

If its market price of risk is zero, gold must, after storage costs have been paid, provide an expected return equal to the risk-free rate of interest. In this case, the expected return after storage costs must be 6% per annum. It follows that the expected growth rate in the price of gold must be 7% per annum.

Problem 25.3.

The market price of risk is

$$\frac{\mu - r}{\sigma}$$

This is the same for both securities. From the first security we know it must be

$$\frac{0.08 - 0.04}{0.15} = 0.26667$$

The volatility, σ for the second security is given by

$$\frac{0.12 - 0.04}{\sigma} = 0.26667$$

The volatility is 30%.

Problem 25.4.

It can be argued that the market price of risk for the second variable is zero. This is because the risk is unsystematic, i.e., it is totally unrelated to other risks in the economy. To put this another way, there is no reason why investors should demand a higher return for bearing the risk since the risk can be totally diversified away.

Problem 25.5.

Suppose that the price, f, of the derivative depends on the prices, S_1 and S_2, of two traded securities. Suppose further that:

$$dS_1 = \mu_1 S_1 dt + \sigma_1 S_1 dz_1$$
$$dS_2 = \mu_2 S_2 dt + \sigma_2 S_2 dz_2$$

where dz_1 and dz_2 are Wiener processes with correlation ρ. From Itô's lemma [see equation (25A.3)]

$$df = \left(\mu_1 S_1 \frac{\partial f}{\partial S_1} + \mu_2 S_2 \frac{\partial f}{\partial S_2} + \frac{\partial f}{\partial t} + \frac{1}{2}\sigma_1^2 S_1^2 \frac{\partial^2 f}{\partial S_1^2} + \frac{1}{2}\sigma_2^2 S_2^2 \frac{\partial^2 f}{\partial S_2^2} \right.$$
$$\left. + \rho\sigma_1\sigma_2 S_1 S_2 \frac{\partial^2 f}{\partial S_1 \partial S_2} \right) dt + \sigma_1 S_1 \frac{\partial f}{\partial S_1} dz_1 + \sigma_2 S_2 \frac{\partial f}{\partial S_2} dz_2$$

To eliminate the dz_1 and dz_2 we choose a portfolio, Π, consisting of

$$\begin{aligned} -1 : &\quad \text{derivative} \\ +\tfrac{\partial f}{\partial S_1} : &\quad \text{first traded security} \\ +\tfrac{\partial f}{\partial S_2} : &\quad \text{second traded security} \end{aligned}$$

$$\Pi = -f + \frac{\partial f}{\partial S_1} S_1 + \frac{\partial f}{\partial S_2} S_2$$
$$d\Pi = -df + \frac{\partial f}{\partial S_1} dS_1 + \frac{\partial f}{\partial S_2} dS_2$$
$$= -\left(\frac{\partial f}{\partial t} + \frac{1}{2}\sigma_1^2 S_1^2 \frac{\partial^2 f}{\partial S_1^2} + \frac{1}{2}\sigma_2^2 S_2^2 \frac{\partial^2 f}{\partial S_2^2} + \rho\sigma_1\sigma_2 S_1 S_2 \frac{\partial^2 f}{\partial S_1 \partial S_2} \right) dt$$

Since the portfolio is instantaneously risk-free it must instantaneously earn the risk-free rate of interest. Hence

$$d\Pi = r\Pi dt$$

Combining the above equations

$$-\left[\frac{\partial f}{\partial t} + \frac{1}{2}\sigma_1^2 S_1^2 \frac{\partial^2 f}{\partial S_1^2} + \frac{1}{2}\sigma_2^2 S_2^2 \frac{\partial^2 f}{\partial S_2^2} + \rho\sigma_1\sigma_2 S_1 S_2 \frac{\partial^2 f}{\partial S_1 \partial S_2} \right] dt = r\left[-f + \frac{\partial f}{\partial S_1} S_1 + \frac{\partial f}{\partial S_2} S_2 \right] dt$$

so that:

$$\frac{\partial f}{\partial t} + rS_1 \frac{\partial f}{\partial S_1} + rS_2 \frac{\partial f}{\partial S_2} + \frac{1}{2}\sigma_1^2 S_1^2 \frac{\partial^2 f}{\partial S_1^2} + \frac{1}{2}\sigma_2^2 S_2^2 \frac{\partial^2 f}{\partial S_2^2} + \rho\sigma_1\sigma_2 S_1 S_2 \frac{\partial^2 f}{\partial S_1 \partial S_2} = rf$$

Problem 25.6.

The process for x can be written

$$\frac{dx}{x} = \frac{a(x_0 - x)}{x}dt + \frac{c}{\sqrt{x}}dz$$

Hence the expected growth rate in x is:

$$\frac{a(x_0 - x)}{x}$$

and the volatility of x is

$$\frac{c}{\sqrt{x}}$$

In a risk neutral world the expected growth rate should be changed to

$$\frac{a(x_0 - x)}{x} - \lambda\frac{c}{\sqrt{x}}$$

so that the process is

$$\frac{dx}{x} = \left[\frac{a(x_0 - x)}{x} - \lambda\frac{c}{\sqrt{x}}\right]dt + \frac{c}{\sqrt{x}}dz$$

i.e.

$$dx = \left[a(x_0 - x) - \lambda c\sqrt{x}\right]dt + c\sqrt{x}dz$$

Hence the drift rate should be reduced by $\lambda c\sqrt{x}$.

Problem 25.7.

As suggested in the hint we form a new security f^* which is the same as f except that all income produced by f is reinvested in f. Assuming we start doing this at time zero, the relationship between f and f^* is

$$f^* = fe^{qt}$$

If μ^* and σ^* are the expected return and volatility of f^*, Itô's lemma shows that

$$\mu^* = \mu + q$$

$$\sigma^* = \sigma$$

From equation (25.9)

$$\mu^* - r = \lambda\sigma^*$$

It follows that

$$\mu + q - r = \lambda\sigma$$

Problem 25.8.

As suggested in the hint, we form two new securities f^* and g^* which are the same as f and g at time zero, but are such that income from f is reinvested in f and income from g is reinvested in g. By construction f^* and g^* are non-income producing and their values at time t are related to f and g by

$$f^* = fe^{q_f t} \qquad\qquad g^* = ge^{q_g t}$$

From Itô's lemma, the securities g and g^* have the same volatility. We can apply the analysis given in Section 25.3 to f^* and g^* so that from equation (25.15)

$$f_0^* = g_0^* E_g\left(\frac{f_T^*}{g_T^*}\right)$$

or

$$f_0 = g_0 E_g\left(\frac{f_T e^{q_f T}}{g_T e^{q_g T}}\right)$$

or

$$f_0 = g_0 e^{(q_f - q_g)T} E_g\left(\frac{f_T}{g_T}\right)$$

Problem 25.9.

This statement implies that the interest rate has a negative market price of risk. Since bond prices and interest rates are negatively correlated, the statement implies that the market price of risk for a bond price is positive. The statement is reasonable. When interest rates increase, there is a tendency for the stock market to decrease. This implies that interest rates have negative systematic risk, or equivalently that bond prices have positive systematic risk.

Problem 25.10.

(a) In the traditional risk-neutral world the process followed by S is

$$dS = (r - q)S\,dt + \sigma_S S\,dz$$

where r is the instantaneous risk-free rate. The market price of dz-risk is zero.

(b) In the traditional risk-neutral world for currency B the process is

$$dS = (r - q + \rho_{QS}\sigma_S\sigma_Q)S\,dt + \sigma_S S\,dz$$

where Q is the exchange rate (units of A per unit of B), σ_Q is the volatility of Q and ρ_{QS} is the coefficient of correlation between Q and S. The market price of dz-risk is $\rho_{QS}\sigma_Q$.

(c) In a world that is forward risk neutral with respect to a zero-coupon bond in currency A maturing at time T

$$dS = (r - q + \sigma_S\sigma_P)S\,dt + \sigma_S S\,dz$$

where σ_P is the bond price volatility. The market price of dz-risk is σ_P.

(d) In a world that is forward risk neutral with respect to a zero-coupon bond in currency B maturing at time T

$$dS = (r - q + \sigma_S \sigma_P + \rho_{FS} \sigma_S \sigma_F) S \, dt + \sigma_S S \, dz$$

where F is the forward exchange rate, σ_F is the volatility of F (units of A per unit of B, and ρ_{FS} is the correlation between F and S. The market price of dz-risk is $\sigma_P + \rho_{FS} \sigma_F$.

Problem 25.11.

The forward value of a stock price, commodity price, or exchange rate is the delivery price in a forward contract that causes the value of the forward contract to be zero. A forward bond price is calculated in this way. However, a forward interest rate is the interest rate implied by the forward bond price.

Problem 25.12.

Equation (25A.4) in the appendix to Chapter 25 gives:

$$d \ln f = \left[r + \sum_{i=1}^{n} (\lambda_i \sigma_{f,i} - \sigma_{f,i}^2/2) \right] dt + \sum_{i=1}^{n} \sigma_{f,i} dz_i$$

$$d \ln g = \left[r + \sum_{i=1}^{n} (\lambda_i \sigma_{g,i} - \sigma_{g,i}^2/2) \right] dt + \sum_{i=1}^{n} \sigma_{g,i} dz_i$$

so that

$$d \ln \frac{f}{g} = d(\ln f - \ln g) = \left[\sum_{i=1}^{n} (\lambda_i \sigma_{f,i} - \lambda_i \sigma_{g,i} - \sigma_{f,i}^2/2 + \sigma_{g,i}^2/2) \right] dt + \sum_{i=1}^{n} (\sigma_{f,i} - \sigma_{g,i}) dz_i$$

Applying Itô's lemma again

$$d \frac{f}{g} = \frac{f}{g} \left[\sum_{i=1}^{n} (\lambda_i \sigma_{f,i} - \lambda_i \sigma_{g,i} - \sigma_{f,i}^2/2 + \sigma_{g,i}^2/2) + (\sigma_{f,i} - \sigma_{g,i})^2 \right] dt + \frac{f}{g} \sum_{i=1}^{n} (\sigma_{f,i} - \sigma_{g,i}) dz_i$$

When $\lambda_i = \sigma_{g,i}$ the coefficient of dt is zero and f/g is a martingale.

Problem 25.13.

Consider the case where v depends on m traded securities $f_i, f_2, \ldots, f_m$ and the ith component of the volatility of f_j is $\sigma_{i,j}$. With the notation in Section 25.7 when the numeraire changes from g to h the expected growth rate of f_j changes by

$$\sum_{i=1}^{n} (\sigma_{h,i} - \sigma_{g,i}) \sigma_{i,j}$$

Equation (25A.5) shows that the drift rate v changes by

$$\sum_{j=1}^{m} \frac{\partial v}{\partial f_j} \sum_{i=1}^{n} (\sigma_{h,i} - \sigma_{g,i}) \sigma_{i,j} f_j$$

The ith component of the volatility of v, $\sigma_{v,i}$ is from equation (25A.5) given by

$$v\sigma_{v,i} = \sum_{j=1}^{m} \frac{\partial v}{\partial f_j} \sigma_{i,j} f_j$$

so that the drift rate of v changes by

$$\sum_{i=1}^{n} (\sigma_{h,i} - \sigma_{g,i}) v\sigma_{v,i}$$

This is the same as saying that the growth rate of v changes by

$$\sum_{i=1}^{n} (\sigma_{h,i} - \sigma_{g,i}) \sigma_{v,i}$$

and proves equation (25.33).

Problem 25.14.

Equation (25A.4) in the appendix to Chapter 25 gives:

$$d \ln h = \ldots + \sum_{i=1}^{n} \sigma_{h,i} dz_i$$

$$d \ln g = \ldots + \sum_{i=1}^{n} \sigma_{g,i} dz_i$$

so that

$$d \ln \frac{h}{g} = \ldots + \sum_{i=1}^{n} (\sigma_{h,i} - \sigma_{g,i}) dz_i$$

Applying Itô's lemma again

$$d\frac{h}{g} = \ldots + \frac{h}{g} \sum_{i=1}^{n} (\sigma_{h,i} - \sigma_{g,i}) dz_i$$

This proves the result.

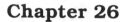

Chapter 26

Interest Rate Derivatives: The Standard Market Models

SOLUTIONS TO QUESTIONS AND PROBLEMS

Problem 26.1.

An amount
$$\$20,000,000 \times 0.02 \times 0.25 = \$100,000$$

would be paid out 3 months later.

Problem 26.2.

A swap option (or swaption) is an option to enter into an interest rate swap at a certain time in the future with a certain fixed rate being used. An interest rate swap can be regarded as the exchange of a fixed-rate bond for a floating-rate bond. A swaption is therefore the option to exchange a fixed-rate bond for a floating-rate bond. The floating-rate bond will be worth its face value at the beginning of the life of the swap. The swaption is therefore an option on a fixed-rate bond with the strike price equal to the face value of the bond.

Problem 26.3.

In this case, $F_0 = (125 - 10)e^{0.1 \times 1} = 127.09$, $K = 110$, $P(0,T) = e^{-0.1 \times 1}$, $\sigma_B = 0.08$, and $T = 1.0$.

$$d_1 = \frac{\ln(127.09/110) + (0.08^2/2)}{0.08} = 1.8456$$
$$d_2 = d_1 - 0.08 = 1.7656$$

The value of the put option is

$$110e^{-0.1 \times 1}N(-1.7656) - 115N(-1.8456) = 0.12$$

or $0.12.

Problem 26.4.

When spot volatilities are used to value a cap, a different volatility is used to value each caplet. When flat volatilities are used, the same volatility is used to value each caplet within a given cap. Spot volatilities are a function of the maturity of the caplet. Flat volatilities are a function of the maturity of the cap.

Problem 26.5.

In this case $L = 1000$, $\delta_k = 0.25$, $F_k = 0.12$, $R_K = 0.13$, $r = 0.115$, $\sigma_k = 0.12$, $t_k = 1.25$, $P(0, t_{k+1}) = 0.8416$.

$$L\delta_k = 250$$

$$d_1 = \frac{\ln(0.12/0.13) + 0.12^2 \times 1.25/2}{0.12\sqrt{1.25}} = -0.5295$$
$$d_2 = -0.5295 - 0.12\sqrt{1.25} = -0.6637$$

The value of the option is

$$250 \times 0.8416 \times [0.12N(-0.5295) - 0.13N(-0.6637)]$$

$$= 0.59$$

or $0.59.

Problem 26.6.

The implied volatility measures the standard deviation of the logarithm of the bond price at the maturity of the option divided by the square root of the time to maturity. In the case of a five year option on a ten year bond, the bond has five years left at option maturity. In the case of a nine year option on a ten year bond it has one year left. The standard deviation of a one year bond price observed in nine years can be normally be expected to be considerably less than that of a five year bond price observed in five years. (See Figure 26.1.) We would therefore expect the price to be too high.

Problem 26.7.

The present value of the principal in the four year bond is $100e^{-4\times0.1} = 67.032$. The present value of the coupons is, therefore, $102 - 67.032 = 34.968$. This means that the forward price of the five-year bond is

$$(105 - 34.968)e^{4\times0.1} = 104.475$$

The parameters in Black's model are therefore $F_0 = 104.475$, $K = 100$, $r = 0.1$, $T = 4$, and $\sigma = 0.02$.

$$d_1 = \frac{\ln 1.04475 + 0.5 \times 0.02^2 \times 4}{0.02\sqrt{4}} = 1.1144$$
$$d_2 = d_1 - 0.02\sqrt{4} = 1.0744$$

The price of the European call is

$$e^{-0.1 \times 4}[104.475 N(1.1144) - 100 N(1.0744)] = 3.19$$

or $3.19.

Problem 26.8.

The option should be valued using Black's model in equations (26.1) and (26.2) with the bond price volatility being
$$4.2 \times 0.07 \times 0.22 = 0.0647$$

or 6.47%.

Problem 26.9.

A 5-year zero-cost collar where the strike price of the cap equals the strike price of the floor is the same as an interest rate swap agreement to receive floating and pay a fixed rate equal to the strike price. The common strike price is the swap rate. Note that the swap is actually a forward swap that excludes the first exchange. (See Business Snapshot 26.1.)

Problem 26.10.

There are two way of expressing the put–call parity relationship for bond options. The first is in terms of bond prices:
$$c + I + Ke^{-RT} = p + B$$

where c is the price of a European call option, p is the price of the corresponding European put option, I is the present value of the bond coupon payments during the life of the option, K is the strike price, T is the time to maturity, B is the bond price, and R is the risk-free interest rate for a maturity equal to the life of the options. To prove this we can consider two portfolios. The first consists of a European put option plus the bond; the second consists of the European call option, and an amount of cash equal to the present value of the coupons plus the present value of the strike price. Both can be seen to be worth the same at the maturity of the options.

The second way of expressing the put–call parity relationship is

$$c + Ke^{-RT} = p + F_0 e^{-RT}$$

where F_0 is the forward bond price. This can also be proved by considering two portfolios. The first consists of a European put option plus a forward contract on the bond plus the present value of the forward price; the second consists of a European call option plus the present value of the strike price. Both can be seen to be worth the same at the maturity of the options.

Problem 26.11.

The put–call parity relationship for European swap options is

$$c + V = p$$

where c is the value of a call option to pay a fixed rate of s_K and receive floating, p is the value of a put option to receive a fixed rate of s_K and pay floating, and V is the value of the forward swap underlying the swap option where s_K is received and floating is paid. This can be proved by considering two portfolios. The first consists of the put option; the second consists of the call option and the swap. Suppose that the actual swap rate at the maturity of the options is greater than s_K. The call will be exercised and the put will not be exercised. Both portfolios are then worth zero. Suppose next that the actual swap rate at the maturity of the options is less than s_K. The put option is exercised and the call option is not exercised. Both portfolios are equivalent to a swap where s_K is received and floating is paid. In all states of the world the two portfolios are worth the same at time T. They must therefore be worth the same today. This proves the result.

Problem 26.12.

Suppose that the cap and floor have the same strike price and the same time to maturity. The following put–call parity relationship must hold:

$$\text{cap} + \text{swap} = \text{floor}$$

where the swap is an agreement to receive the cap rate and pay floating over the whole life of the cap/floor. If the implied Black volatilities for the cap equals that for the floor, the Black formulas show that this relationship holds. In other circumstances it does not hold and there is an arbitrage opportunity. The broker quotes in Table 26.1 do not present an arbitrage opportunity because the cap offer is always higher than the floor bid and the floor offer is always higher than the cap bid.

Problem 26.13.

Yes. If a zero-coupon bond price at some future time is lognormal, there is some chance that the price will be above par. This in turn implies that the yield to maturity on the bond is negative.

Problem 26.14.

In equation (26.15), $L = 10,000,000$, $s_K = 0.05$, $s_0 = 0.05$, $d_1 = 0.2\sqrt{4}/2 = 0.2$, $d_2 = -.2$, and

$$A = \frac{1}{1.05^5} + \frac{1}{1.05^6} + \frac{1}{1.05^7} = 2.2404$$

The value of the swap option (in millions of dollars) is

$$10 \times 2.2404[0.05N(0.2) - 0.05N(-0.2)] = 0.178$$

This is the same as the answer given by DerivaGem. (For the purposes of using the DerivaGem software note that the interest rate is 4.879% with continuous compounding for all maturities.)

Problem 26.15.

The price of the bond at time t is $e^{-R(T-t)}$ where T is the time when the bond matures. Using Itô's lemma the volatility of the bond price is

$$\sigma \frac{\partial}{\partial R} e^{-R(T-t)} = -\sigma(T-t)e^{-R(T-t)}$$

This tends to zero as t approaches T.

Problem 26.16.

The cash price of the bond is

$$4e^{-0.05 \times 0.50} + 4e^{-0.05 \times 1.00} + \ldots + 4e^{-0.05 \times 10} + 100e^{-0.05 \times 10} = 122.82$$

As there is no accrued interest this is also the quoted price of the bond. The interest paid during the life of the option has a present value of

$$4e^{-0.05 \times 0.5} + 4e^{-0.05 \times 1} + 4e^{-0.05 \times 1.5} + 4e^{-0.05 \times 2} = 15.04$$

The forward price of the bond is therefore

$$(122.82 - 15.04)e^{0.05 \times 2.25} = 120.61$$

The duration of the bond at option maturity is

$$\frac{0.25 \times 4e^{-0.05 \times 0.25} + \ldots + 7.75 \times 4e^{-0.05 \times 7.75} + 7.75 \times 100e^{-0.05 \times 7.75}}{4e^{-0.05 \times 0.25} + 4e^{-0.05 \times 0.75} + \ldots + 4e^{-0.05 \times 7.75} + 100e^{-0.05 \times 7.75}}$$

or 5.99. The bond price volatility is therefore $5.99 \times 0.05 \times 0.2 = 0.0599$. We can therefore value the bond option using Black's model with $F_0 = 120.61$, $P(0, 2.25) = e^{-0.05 \times 2.25} = 0.8936$, $\sigma = 5.99\%$, and $T = 2.25$. When the strike price is the cash price $K = 115$ and the value of the option is 1.78. When the strike price is the quoted price $K = 117$ and the value of the option is 2.41.

Problem 26.17.

We choose the Caps and Swap Options worksheet of DerivaGem and choose Cap/Floor as the Underlying Type. We enter the 1-, 2-, 3-, 4-, 5-year zero rates as 6%, 6.4%, 6.7%, 6.9%, and 7.0% in the Term Structure table. We enter Semiannual for the Settlement Frequency, 100 for the Principal, 0 for the Start (Years), 5 for the End (Years), 8% for the Cap/Floor Rate, and $3 for the Price. We select Black-European as the Pricing Model and choose the Cap button. We check the Imply Volatility box and Calculate. The implied volatility is 24.79%. We then uncheck Implied Volatility, select Floor, check Imply Breakeven Rate. The floor rate that is calculated is 6.71%. This is the floor rate for which the floor is worth $3. A collar when the floor rate is 6.71% and the cap rate is 8% has zero cost.

Problem 26.18.

We prove this result by considering two portfolios. The first consists of the swap option to receive s_K; the second consists of the swap option to pay s_K and the forward swap. Suppose that the actual swap rate at the maturity of the options is greater than s_K. The swap option to pay s_K will be exercised and the swap option to receive s_K will not be exercised. Both portfolios are then worth zero since the swap option to pay s_K is neutralized by the forward swap. Suppose next that the actual swap rate at the maturity of the options is less than s_K. The swap option to receive s_K is exercised and the swap option to pay s_K is not exercised. Both portfolios are then equivalent to a swap where s_K is received and floating is paid. In all states of the world the two portfolios are worth the same at time T_1. They must therefore be worth the same today. This proves the result. When s_K equals the current forward swap rate $f = 0$ and $V_1 = V_2$. A swap option to pay fixed is therefore worth the same as a similar swap option to receive fixed when the fixed rate in the swap option is the forward swap rate.

Problem 26.19.

We choose the Caps and Swap Options worksheet of DerivaGem and choose Swap Option as the Underlying Type. We enter 100 as the Principal, 1 as the Start (Years), 6 as the End (Years), 6% as the Swap Rate, and Semiannual as the Settlement Frequency. We choose Black-European as the pricing model, enter 21% as the Volatility and check the Pay Fixed button. We do not check the Imply Breakeven Rate and Imply Volatility boxes. The value of the swap option is 5.63.

Problem 26.20.

(a) To calculate flat volatilities from spot volatilities we choose a strike rate and use the spot volatilities to calculate caplet prices. We then sum the caplet prices to obtain cap prices and imply flat volatilities from Black's model. The answer is slightly dependent on the strike price chosen. This procedure ignores any volatility smile in cap pricing.

(b) To calculate spot volatilities from flat volatilities the first step is usually to interpolate between the flat volatilities so that we have a flat volatility for each caplet payment date. We choose a strike price and use the flat volatilities to calculate cap prices. By subtracting successive cap prices we obtain caplet prices from which we can imply spot volatilities. The answer is slightly dependent on the strike price chosen. This procedure also ignores any volatility smile in caplet pricing.

Chapter 27

Convexity, Timing, and Quanto Adjustments

SOLUTIONS TO QUESTIONS AND PROBLEMS

Problem 27.1.

The value of the derivative is $100R_{4.5}P(0,5)$ where $P(0,t)$ is the value of a t-year zero-coupon bond today and R_{t_1,t_2} is the forward rate for the period between t_1 and t_2, expressed with annual compounding. If the payoff is made in four years the value is $100(R_{4.5} + c)P(0,4)$ where c is the convexity adjustment given by equation (27.2). the formula for the convexity adjustment is:

$$c = \frac{4R_{4.5}^2 \sigma_{4.5}^2}{(1 + R_{4.5})}$$

where σ_{t_1,t_2} is the volatility of the forward rate between times t_1 and t_2.

The expression $100(R_{4.5} + c)$ is the expected payoff in a world that is forward risk neutral with respect to a zero-coupon bond maturing at time four years. If the payoff is made in six years, the value is from equation (27.4) given by

$$100(R_{4.5} + c)P(0,6)\exp\left[-\frac{4\rho\,\sigma_{4.5}\sigma_{4.6}R_{4.6} \times 2}{1 + R_{4.6}}\right]$$

where ρ is the correlation between the (4,5) and (4,6) forward rates. As an approximation we can assume that $\rho = 1$, $\sigma_{4.5} = \sigma_{4.6}$, and $R_{4.5} = R_{4.6}$. Approximating the exponential function we then get the value of the derivative as $100(R_{4.5} - c)P(0,6)$.

Problem 27.2.

(a) A convexity adjustment is necessary for the swap rate

(b) No convexity or timing adjustments are necessary.

Problem 27.3.

There are two differences. The discounting is done over a 1.0-year period instead of over a 1.25-year period. Also a convexity adjustment to the forward rate is necessary. From equation (27.2) the convexity adjustment is:

$$\frac{0.07^2 \times 0.2^2 \times 0.25 \times 1}{1 + 0.25 \times 0.07} = 0.00005$$

or about half a basis point.

In the formula for the caplet we set $F_k = 0.07005$ instead of 0.07. This means that $d_1 = -0.5642$ and $d_2 = -0.7642$. With continuous compounding the 15-month rate is 6.5% and the forward rate between 12 and 15 months is 6.94%. The 12 month rate is therefore 6.39%. The caplet price becomes

$$0.25 \times 10,000 e^{-0.069394 \times 1.0} [0.07005 N(-0.5642) - 0.08 N(-0.7642)] = 5.29$$

or $5.29.

Problem 27.4.

The convexity adjustment discussed in Section 27.1 leads to the instrument being worth an amount slightly different from zero. Define $G(y)$ as the value as seen in five years of a two-year bond with a coupon of 10% as a function of its yield.

$$G(y) = \frac{0.1}{1+y} + \frac{1.1}{(1+y)^2}$$

$$G'(y) = -\frac{0.1}{(1+y)^2} - \frac{2.2}{(1+y)^3}$$

$$G''(y) = \frac{0.2}{(1+y)^3} + \frac{6.6}{(1+y)^4}$$

It follows that $G'(0.1) = -1.7355$ and $G''(0.1) = 4.6582$ and the convexity adjustment that must be made for the two-year swap- rate is

$$0.5 \times 0.1^2 \times 0.2^2 \times 5 \times \frac{4.6582}{1.7355} = 0.00268$$

We can therefore value the instrument on the assumption that the swap rate will be 10.268% in five years. The value of the instrument is

$$\frac{0.268}{1.1^5} = 0.167$$

or $0.167.

Problem 27.5.

In this case we have to make a timing adjustment as well as a convexity adjustment to the forward swap rate. For **(a)**, equation (27.4) shows that the timing adjustment involves multiplying the swap rate by

$$\exp\left[-\frac{0.8 \times 0.20 \times 0.20 \times 0.1 \times 5}{1 + 0.1}\right] = 0.9856$$

so that it becomes $10.268 \times 0.9856 = 10.120$. The value of the instrument is

$$\frac{0.120}{1.1^5} = 0.075$$

or \$0.075.

For **(b)**, equation (27.4) shows that the timing adjustment involves multiplying the swap rate by

$$\exp\left[-\frac{0.95 \times 0.2 \times 0.2 \times 0.1 \times 2 \times 5}{1+0.1}\right] = 0.9660$$

so that it becomes $10.268 \times 0.966 = 9.919$. The value of the instrument is now

$$-\frac{0.081}{1.1^5} = 0.050$$

or $-\$0.050$.

Problem 27.6.

(a) The process for y is

$$dy = \alpha y\, dt + \sigma_y y\, dz$$

The forward bond price is $G(y)$. From Itô's lemma, its process is

$$d[G(y)] = [G'(y)\alpha y + \frac{1}{2}G''(y)\sigma_y^2 y^2]\, dt + G'(y)\sigma_y y\, dz$$

(b) Since the expected growth rate of $G(y)$ is zero

$$G'(y)\alpha y + \frac{1}{2}G''(y)\sigma_y^2 y^2 = 0$$

or

$$\alpha = -\frac{1}{2}\frac{G''(y)}{G'(y)}\sigma_y^2 y$$

(c) Assuming as an approximation that y always equals its initial value of y_0, this shows that the growth rate of y is

$$-\frac{1}{2}\frac{G''(y_0)}{G'(y_0)}\sigma_y^2 y_0$$

The variable y starts at y_0 and ends as y_T. The convexity adjustment to y_0 when we are calculating the expected value of y_T in a world that is forward risk neutral with respect to a zero-coupon bond maturing at time T is approximately $y_0 T$ times this or

$$-\frac{1}{2}\frac{G''(y_0)}{G'(y_0)}\sigma_y^2 y_0^2 T$$

This is consistent with equation (27.1).

Problem 27.7.

(a) In the traditional risk-neutral world the process followed by S is

$$dS = (r-q)S\,dt + \sigma_S S\,dz$$

where r is the instantaneous risk-free rate. The market price of dz-risk is zero.

(b) In the traditional risk-neutral world for currency B the process is

$$dS = (r-q+\rho_{QS}\sigma_S\sigma_Q)S\,dt + \sigma_S S\,dz$$

where Q is the exchange rate (units of A per unit of B), σ_Q is the volatility of Q and ρ_{QS} is the coefficient of correlation between Q and S. The market price of dz-risk is $\rho_{QS}\sigma_Q$.

(c) In a world that is forward risk neutral with respect to a zero-coupon bond in currency A maturing at time T

$$dS = (r-q+\sigma_S\sigma_P)S\,dt + \sigma_S S\,dz$$

where σ_P is the bond price volatility. The market price of dz-risk is σ_P.

(d) In a world that is forward risk neutral with respect to a zero-coupon bond in currency B maturing at time T

$$dS = (r-q+\sigma_S\sigma_P+\rho_{FS}\sigma_S\sigma_F)S\,dt + \sigma_S S\,dz$$

where F is the forward exchange rate, σ_F is the volatility of F (units of A per unit of B, and ρ_{FS} is the correlation between F and S. The market price of dz-risk is $\sigma_P + \rho_{FS}\sigma_F$.

Problem 27.8.

Define

$P(t,T):$ Price in yen at time t of a bond paying 1 yen at time T

$E_T(\cdot):$ Expectation in world that is forward risk neutral with respect to $P(t,T)$

$F:$ Dollar forward price of gold for a contract maturing at time T

$F_0:$ Value of F at time zero

$\sigma_F:$ Volatility of F

$G:$ Forward exchange rate (dollars per yen)

$\sigma_G:$ Volatility of G

We assume that S_T is lognormal. We can work in a world that is forward risk neutral with respect to $P(t,T)$ to get the value of the call as

$$P(0,T)[E_T(S_T)N(d_1) - N(d_2)]$$

where

$$d_1 = \frac{\ln[E_T(S_T)/K] + \sigma_F^2 T/2}{\sigma_F\sqrt{T}}$$

$$d_2 = \frac{\ln[E_T(S_T)/K] - \sigma_F^2 T/2}{\sigma_F\sqrt{T}}$$

The expected gold price in a world that is forward risk-neutral with respect to a zero-coupon dollar bond maturing at time T is F_0. It follows from equation (27.6) that

$$E_T(S_T) = F_0(1 + \rho\sigma_F\sigma_G T)$$

Hence the option price, measured in yen, is

$$P(0,T)[F_0(1 + \rho\sigma_F\sigma_G T)N(d_1) - KN(d_2)]$$

where

$$d_1 = \frac{\ln[F_0(1 + \rho\sigma_F\sigma_G T)/K] + \sigma_F^2 T/2}{\sigma_F\sqrt{T}}$$

$$d_2 = \frac{\ln[F_0(1 + \rho\sigma_F\sigma_G T)/K] - \sigma_F^2 T/2}{\sigma_F\sqrt{T}}$$

Problem 27.9.

(a) The value of the option can be calculated by setting $S_0 = 400$, $K = 400$, $r = 0.06$; $q = 0.03$, $\sigma = 0.2$, and $T = 2$. With 100 time steps the value (in Canadian dollars) is 52.92.

(b) The growth rate of the index using the CDN numeraire is $0.06 - 0.03$ or 3%. When we switch to the USD numeraire we increase the growth rate of the index by $0.4 \times 0.2 \times 0.06$ or 0.48% per year to 3.48%. The option can therefore be calculated using DerivaGem with $S_0 = 400$, $K = 400$, $r = 0.04$, $q = 0.04 - 0.0348 = 0.0052$, $\sigma = 0.2$, and $T = 2$. With 100 time steps DerivaGem gives the value as 57.51.

Chapter 28

Interest Rate Derivatives: Models of the Short Rate

SOLUTIONS TO QUESTIONS AND PROBLEMS

Problem 28.1.

Equilibrium models usually start with assumptions about economic variables and derive the behavior of interest rates. The initial term structure is an output from the model. In a no-arbitrage model the initial term structure is an input. The behavior of interest rates in a no-arbitrage model is designed to be consistent with the initial term structure.

Problem 28.2.

In Vasicek's model the standard deviation stays at 1%. In the Rendleman and Bartter model the standard deviation is proportional to the level of the short rate. When the short rate increases from 4% to 8% the standard deviation increases from 1% to 2%. In the Cox, Ingersoll, and Ross model the standard deviation of the short rate is proportional to the square root of the short rate. When the short rate increases from 4% to 8% the standard deviation of the short rate increases from 1% to 1.414%.

Problem 28.3.

If the price of a traded security followed a mean-reverting or path-dependent process there would be a market inefficiency. The short-term interest rate is not the price of a traded security. In other words we cannot trade something whose price is always the short-term interest rate. There is therefore no market inefficiency when the short-term interest rate follows a mean-reverting or path-dependent process. We can trade bonds and other instruments whose prices do depend on the short rate. The prices of these instruments do not follow mean-reverting or path-dependent processes.

Problem 28.4.

In a one-factor model there is one source of uncertainty driving all rates. This usually means that in any short period of time all rates move in the same direction (but not necessarily by the same amount). In a two-factor model, there are two sources of uncertainty driving all rates. The first source of uncertainty usually gives rise to a roughly parallel shift in rates. The second gives rise to a twist where long and short rates moves in opposite directions.

Problem 28.5.

No. The approach in Section 28.4 relies on the argument that, at any given time, all bond prices are moving in the same direction. This is not true when there is more than one factor.

Problem 28.6.

In Vasicek's model, $a = 0.1$, $b = 0.1$, and $\sigma = 0.02$ so that

$$B(t, t+10) = \frac{1}{0.1}(1 - e^{-0.1 \times 10}) = 6.32121$$

$$A(t, t+10) = \exp\left[\frac{(6.32121 - 10)(0.1^2 \times 0.1 - 0.0002)}{0.01} - \frac{0.0004 \times 6.32121^2}{0.4}\right]$$

$$= 0.71587$$

The bond price is therefore $0.71587e^{-6.32121 \times 0.1} = 0.38046$.

In the Cox, Ingersoll, and Ross model, $a = 0.1$, $b = 0.1$ and $\sigma = 0.02/\sqrt{0.1} = 0.0632$. Also

$$\gamma = \sqrt{a^2 + 2\sigma^2} = 0.13416$$

Define

$$\beta = (\gamma + a)(e^{10\gamma} - 1) + 2\gamma = 0.92992$$

$$B(t, t+10) = \frac{2(e^{10\gamma} - 1)}{\beta} = 6.07650$$

$$A(t, t+10) = \left(\frac{2\gamma e^{5(a+\gamma)}}{\beta}\right)^{2ab/\sigma^2} = 0.69746$$

The bond price is therefore $0.69746e^{-6.07650 \times 0.1} = 0.37986$.

Problem 28.7.

Using the notation in the text, $s = 3$, $T = 1$, $L = 100$, $K = 87$, and

$$\sigma_P = \frac{0.015}{0.1}(1 - e^{-2 \times 0.1})\sqrt{\frac{1 - e^{-2 \times 0.1 \times 1}}{2 \times 0.1}} = 0.025886$$

From equation (28.6) $P(0, 1) = 0.94988$, $P(0, 3) = 0.85092$, and $h = 1.14277$ so that equation (28.20) gives the call price as call price is

$$100 \times 0.85092 \times N(1.14277) - 87 \times 0.94988 \times N(1.11688) = 2.59$$

or \$2.59.

Problem 28.8.

As mentioned in the text, equation (28.20) for a call option is essentially the same as Black's model.[2] By analogy with Black's formulas corresponding expression for a put option is

$$KP(0,T)N(-h+\sigma_P)-LP(0,s)N(-h)$$

In this case the put price is

$$87 \times 0.94988 \times N(-1.11688) - 100 \times 0.85092 \times N(-1.14277) = 0.14$$

Since the underlying bond pays no coupon, put–call parity states that the put price plus the bond price should equal the call price plus the present value of the strike price. The bond price is 85.09 and the present value of the strike price is $87 \times 0.94988 = 82.64$. Put–call parity is therefore satisfied:

$$82.64 + 2.59 = 85.09 + 0.14$$

Problem 28.9.

As explained in Section 28.4, the first stage is to calculate the value of r at time 2.1 years which is such that the value of the bond at that time is 99. Denoting this value of r by r^*, we must solve

$$2.5A(2.1,2.5)e^{-B(2.1,2.5)r^*} + 102.5A(2.1,3.0)e^{-B(2.1,3.0)r^*} = 99$$

where the A and B functions are given by equations (28.7) and (28.8). The solution to this is $r^* = 0.066$. Since

$$2.5A(2.1,2.5)e^{-B(2.1,2.5)\times 0.066} = 2.43473$$

and

$$102.5A(2.1,3.0)e^{-B(2.1,3.0)\times 0.063} = 96.56438$$

the call option on the coupon-bearing bond can be decomposed into a call option with a strike price of 2.43473 on a bond that pays off 2.5 at time 2.5 years and a call option with a strike price of 96.56438 on a bond that pays off 102.5 at time 3.0 years. Equation (28.20) shows that the value of the first option is 0.009085 and the value of the second option is 0.806143. The total value of the option is therefore 0.815238.

Problem 28.10.

Put-call parity shows that:[3]

$$c + I + PV(K) = p + B_0$$

or

$$p = c + PV(K) - (B_0 - I)$$

[2]Problem 28.8 should refer to Problem 28.7 (not 23.7). There is a typo in the first printing of the book.
[3]Problem 28.10 should refer to Problem 28.9 (not 23.9). There is a typo in the first printing of the book.

where c is the call price, K is the strike price, I is the present value of the coupons, and B_0 is the bond price. In this case $c = 0.8152$, $PV(K) = 99 \times P(0, 2.1) = 87.1222$, $B_0 - I = 2.5 \times P(0, 2.5) + 102.5 \times P(0, 3) = 87.4730$ so that the put price is

$$0.8152 + 87.1222 - 87.4730 = 0.4644$$

Problem 28.11.

Using the notation in the text $P(0, T) = e^{-0.1 \times 1} = 0.9048$ and $P(0, s) = e^{-0.1 \times 5} = 0.6065$. Also

$$\sigma_P = \frac{0.01}{0.08}(1 - e^{-4 \times 0.08})\sqrt{\frac{1 - e^{-2 \times 0.08 \times 1}}{2 \times 0.08}} = 0.0329$$

and $h = -0.4192$ so that the call price is

$$100 \times 0.6065 N(h) - 68 \times 0.9048 N(h - \sigma_P) = 0.439$$

Problem 28.12.

The relevant parameters for the Hull–White model are $a = 0.05$ and $\sigma = 0.015$. Setting $\Delta t = 0.4$

$$\hat{B}(2.1, 3) = \frac{B(2.1, 3)}{B(2.1, 2.5)} \times 0.4 = 0.88888$$

Also from equation (28.26), $\hat{A}(2.1, 3) = 0.99925$ The first stage is to calculate the value of R at time 2.1 years which is such that the value of the bond at that time is 99. Denoting this value of R by R^*, we must solve

$$2.5 e^{-R^* \times 0.4} + 102.5 \hat{A}(2.1, 3) e^{-\hat{B}(2.1, 3) R^*} = 99$$

The solution to this for R^* turns out to be 6.626%. The option on the coupon bond is decomposed into an option with a strike price of 96.565 on a zero-coupon bond with a principal of 102.5 and an option with a strike price of 2.435 on a zero-coupon bond with a principal of 2.5. The first option is worth 0.0105 and the second option is worth 0.9341. The total value of the option is therefore 0.9446.

Problem 28.13.

We will consider instantaneous forward and futures rates. (A more general result involving the forward and futures rate applying to a period of time between T_1 and T_2 is proved in Technical Note 1 on the author's site.)

Because $P(t, T) = A(t, T)e^{-r(T-t)}$ the process for $P(t, T)$ is from Itô's lemma

$$dP(t, T) = \ldots - \sigma(T - t)P(t, T)dz$$

Define $F(t, T)$ as the instantaneous forward rate for maturity T. The process for $F(0, T)$ is from Itô's lemma

$$dF(0, T) = \ldots + \sigma\, dz$$

The instantaneous forward rate with maturity T has a drift of zero in a world that is forward risk neutral with respect to $P(t,T)$. This is a world where the market price of risk is $-\sigma(T-t)$. When we move to a world where the market price of risk is zero the drift of the forward rate increases to $\sigma^2(T-t)$. Integrating this between $t=0$ and $t=T$ wee see that the forward rate grows by a total of $\sigma^2 T^2/2$ between time 0 and time T in a world where the market price of risk is zero. The futures price has zero growth rate in this world. At time T the forward price equals the futures price. It follows that the futures price must exceed the forward price by $\sigma^2 T^2/2$ at time zero. This is consistent with the formula in Section 6.4.

Define $F(0,t)$ and $G(0,t)$ as the instantaneous forward and futures rate for maturity t so that

$$G(0,t) - F(0,t) = \sigma^2 t^2/2$$

and

$$G_t(0,t) - F_t(0,t) = \sigma^2 t$$

In the traditional risk-neutral world the expected value of r at time t is the futures rate, $G(0,t)$. This means that the expected growth in r at time t must be $G_t(0,t)$ so that $\theta(t) = G_t(0,t)$. It follows that

$$\theta(t) = F_t(0,t) + \sigma^2 t$$

This is equation (28.11).

Problem 28.14.

In this case we have $P(t,T) = A(t,T)e^{-B(t,T)r}$ so that from Itô's lemma

$$dP(t,T) = \ldots - \sigma B(t,T)P(t,T)dz$$

Define $F(t,T)$ as the instantaneous forward rate for maturity T. The process for $F(0,T)$ is from Itô's lemma

$$dF(0,T) = \ldots + \sigma e^{-a(T-t)}dz$$

This has drift of zero in a world that is forward risk neutral with respect to $P(t,T)$. This is a world where the market price of risk is $-\sigma B(t,T)$. When we move to a world where the market price of risk is zero the drift of $F(0,T)$ increases to $\sigma^2 e^{-a(T-t)}B(t,T)$. Integrating this between $t=0$ and $t=T$ wee see that the forward rate grows by a total of

$$\frac{\sigma^2}{2a^2}(1-e^{-aT})^2$$

between time 0 and time T in a world where the market price of risk is zero. The futures price has zero growth rate in this world. At time T the forward price equals the futures price. It follows that the futures price must exceed the forward price by

$$\frac{\sigma^2}{2a^2}(1-e^{-aT})^2$$

at time zero.[4]

Define $F(0,t)$ and $G(0,t)$ as the instantaneous forward and futures rate for maturity t so that

$$G(0,t) - F(0,t) = \frac{\dot\sigma^2}{2a^2}(1 - e^{-at})^2$$

and

$$G_t(0,t) - F_t(0,t) = \frac{\sigma^2}{a}(1 - e^{-at})e^{-at}$$

In the traditional risk-neutral world the expected value of r at time t is the futures rate, $G(0,t)$. This means that the expected growth in r at time t must be $G_t(0,t) - a[r - G(0,t)]$ so that $\theta(t) - ar = G_t(0,t) - a[r - G(0,t)]$. It follows that

$$\theta(t) = G_t(0,t) + aG(0,t)]$$

$$= F_t(0,t) + aF(0,t) + \frac{\sigma^2}{a}(1 - e^{-at})e^{-at} + \frac{\sigma^2}{2a}(1 - e^{-at})^2$$

$$= F_t(0,t) + aF(0,t) + \frac{\sigma^2}{2a}(1 - e^{-2at})$$

This proves equation (28.14).

Problem 28.15.

The time step, Δt, is 1 so that $\Delta r = 0.015\sqrt{3} = 0.02598$. Also $j_{max} = 4$ showing that the branching method should change four steps from the center of the tree. With only three steps we never reach the point where the branching changes. The tree is shown in Figure S28.1.

---

[4]To produce a result relating the futures rate for the period between times T_1 and T_2 to the forward rate between this period we can proceed as in Technical Note 1 on the author's web site. The drift of the forward rate is

$$\frac{\sigma^2 B(t,T_2)^2 - \sigma^2 B(t,T_1)^2}{2(T_2 - T_1)}$$

$$= \frac{\sigma^2}{2a^2(T_2 - T_1)}[e^{at}(-2e^{-aT_2} + 2e^{-aT_1}) + e^{2at}[e^{-2aT_2} - e^{-2aT_1}]$$

Integrating between time 0 and time T_1 we get

$$\frac{\sigma^2}{2a^2(T_2 - T_1)}[(e^{aT_1} - 1)(-2e^{-aT_2} + 2e^{-aT_1})/a + (e^{2aT_1} - 1)(e^{-2aT_2} - e^{-2aT_1})/(2a)]$$

$$= \frac{\sigma^2 B(T_1,T_2)}{4a^2(T_2 - T_1)}[4(1 - e^{-aT_1}) - (1 - e^{-2aT_1})(1 + e^{a(T_2-T_1)})]$$

$$= \frac{B(T_1,T_2)}{T_2 - T_1}[B(T_1,T_2)(1 - e^{-2aT_1}) + 2aB(0,T_1)^2]\frac{\sigma^2}{4a}$$

This is the amount by which the futures price exceeds the forward price at time zero.

Figure S28.1: Tree for Problem 28.15.

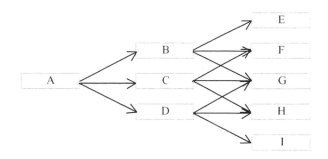

Node	A	B	C	D	E	F	G	H	I
r	10.00%	12.61%	10.01%	7.41%	15.24%	12.64%	10.04%	7.44%	4.84%
p_u	0.1667	0.1429	0.1667	0.1929	0.1217	0.1429	0.1667	0.1929	0.2217
p_m	0.6666	0.6642	0.6666	0.6642	0.6567	0.6642	0.6666	0.6642	0.6567
p_d	0.1667	0.1929	0.1667	0.1429	0.2217	0.1929	0.1667	0.1429	0.1217

Problem 28.16.

A two-year zero-coupon bond pays off $100 at the ends of the final branches. At node B it is worth $100e^{-0.12\times1} = 88.69$. At node C it is worth $100e^{-0.10\times1} = 90.48$. At node D it is worth $100e^{-0.08\times1} = 92.31$. It follows that at node A the bond is worth

$$(88.69 \times 0.25 + 90.48 \times 0.5 + 92.31 \times 0.25)e^{-0.1\times1} = 81.88$$

or $81.88.

Problem 28.17.

A two-year zero-coupon bond pays off $100 at time two years. At node B it is worth $100e^{-0.0693\times1} = 93.30$. At node C it is worth $100e^{-0.0520\times1} = 94.93$. At node D it is worth $100e^{-0.0347\times1} = 96.59$. It follows that at node A the bond is worth

$$(93.30 \times 0.167 + 94.93 \times 0.666 + 96.59 \times 0.167)e^{-0.0382\times1} = 91.37$$

or $91.37. Because $91.37 = 100e^{-0.04512\times2}$, the price of the two-year bond agrees with the initial term structure.

Problem 28.18.

An 18-month zero-coupon bond pays off $100 at the final nodes of the tree. At node E it is worth $100e^{-0.088\times0.5} = 95.70$. At node F it is worth $100e^{-0.0648\times0.5} = 96.81$. At node G it is

Chapter 29

Interest Rate Derivatives: HJM and LMM

SOLUTIONS TO QUESTIONS AND PROBLEMS

Problem 29.1.

In a Markov model the expected change and volatility of the short rate at time t depend only on the value of the short rate at time t. In a non-Markov model they depend on the history of the short rate prior to time t.

Problem 29.2.

Equation (29.1) becomes

$$dP(t,T) = r(t)P(t,T)\,dt + \sum_k v_k(t,T,\Omega_t)P(t,T)\,dz_k(t)$$

so that

$$d\ln[P(t,T_1)] = \left[r(t) - \sum_k \frac{v_k(t,T_1,\Omega_t)^2}{2}\right]dt + \sum_k v_k(t,T_1,\Omega_t)\,dz_k(t)$$

and

$$d\ln[P(t,T_2)] = \left[r(t) - \sum_k \frac{v_k(t,T_2,\Omega_t)^2}{2}\right]dt + v_k(t,T_2,\Omega_t)\,dz_k(t)$$

From equation (29.2)

$$df(t,T_1,T_2) = \frac{\sum_k[v_k(t,T_2,\Omega_t)^2 - v_k(t,T_1,\Omega_t)^2]}{2(T_2 - T_1)}\,dt + \sum_k \frac{v_k(t,T_1,\Omega_t) - v_k(t,T_2,\Omega_t)}{T_2 - T_1}\,dz_k(t)$$

Putting $T_1 = T$ and $T_2 = T + \Delta t$ and taking limits as Δt tends to zero this becomes

$$dF(t,T) = \sum_k \left[v_k(t,T,\Omega_t)\frac{\partial v_k(t,T,\Omega_t)}{\partial T}\right]dt - \sum_k \left[\frac{\partial v_k(t,T,\Omega_t)}{\partial T}\right]dz_k(t)$$

Using $v_k(t,t,\Omega_t) = 0$

$$v_k(t,T,\Omega_t) = \int_t^T \frac{\partial v_k(t,\tau,\Omega_t)}{\partial \tau}\,d\tau$$

worth $100e^{-0.0477 \times 0.5} = 97.64$. At node H it is worth $100e^{-0.0351 \times 0.5} = 98.26$. At node I it is worth $100e^{0.0259 \times 0.5} = 98.71$. At node B it is worth

$$(0.118 \times 95.70 + 0.654 \times 96.81 + 0.228 \times 97.64)e^{-0.0564 \times 0.5} = 94.17$$

Similarly at nodes C and D it is worth 95.60 and 96.68. The value at node A is therefore

$$(0.167 \times 94.17 + 0.666 \times 95.60 + 0.167 \times 96.68)e^{-0.0343 \times 0.5} = 93.92$$

The 18-month zero rate is $0.08 - 0.05e^{-0.18 \times 1.5} = 0.0418$. This gives the price of the 18-month zero-coupon bond as $100e^{-0.0418 \times 1.5} = 93.92$ showing that the tree agrees with the initial term structure.

Problem 28.19.

The calibration of a one-factor interest rate model involves determining its volatility parameters so that it matches the market prices of actively traded interest rate options as closely as possible.

Problem 28.20.

The option prices are 0.1302, 0.0814, 0.0580, and 0.0274. The implied Black volatilities are 14.28%, 13.64%, 13.24%, and 12.81%.

Problem 28.21.

From equation (28.15)

$$P(t, t + \Delta t) = A(t, t + \Delta t)e^{-r(t)B(t, t + \Delta t)}$$

Also

$$P(t, t + \Delta t) = e^{-R(t)\Delta t}$$

so that

$$e^{-R(t)\Delta t} = A(t, t + \Delta t)e^{-r(t)B(t, t + \Delta t)}$$

or

$$e^{-r(t)B(t,T)} = \frac{e^{-R(t)B(t,T)\Delta t / B(t, t + \Delta t)}}{A(t, t + \Delta t)^{B(t,T)/B(t, t + \Delta t)}}$$

Hence equation (28.25) is true with

$$\hat{B}(t, T) = \frac{B(t, T)\Delta t}{B(t, t + \Delta t)}$$

and

$$\hat{A}(t, T) = \frac{A(t, T)}{A(t, t + \Delta t)^{B(t,T)/B(t, t + \Delta t)}}$$

or

$$\ln \hat{A}(t, T) = \ln A(t, T) - \frac{B(t, T)}{B(t, t + \Delta t)} \ln A(t, t + \Delta t)$$

Substituting for $\ln A(t, T)$ and $\ln A(t, t + \Delta t)$ we obtain equation (28.26).

The result in equation (29.6) follows by substituting

$$s_k(t,T,\Omega_t) = \frac{\partial v_k(t,T,\Omega_t)}{\partial T}$$

Problem 29.3.

Using the notation in Section 29.1, when s is constant,[5]

$$v_T(t,T) = s \qquad v_{TT}(t,T) = 0$$

Integrating $v_T(t,T)$

$$v(t,T) = sT + \alpha(t)$$

for some function α. Using the fact that $v(T,T) = 0$, we must have

$$v(t,T) = s(T-t)$$

Using the notation from Chapter 28, in Ho–Lee $P(t,T) = A(t,T)e^{-r(T-t)}$. The standard deviation of the short rate is constant. It follows from Itô's lemma that the standard deviation of the bond price is a constant times the bond price times $T-t$. The volatility of the bond price is therefore a constant times $T-t$. This shows that Ho–Lee is consistent with a constant s.

Problem 29.4.

Using the notation in Section 29.1, when $v_T(t,T) = s(t,T) = \sigma e^{-a(T-t)}$ [4]

$$v_{TT}(t,T) = -a\sigma e^{-a(T-t)}$$

Integrating $v_T(t,T)$

$$v(t,T) = -\frac{1}{a}\sigma e^{-a(T-t)} + \alpha(t)$$

for some function α. Using the fact that $v(T,T) = 0$, we must have

$$v(t,T) = \frac{\sigma}{a}[1 - e^{-a(T-t)}] = \sigma B(t,T)$$

Using the notation from Chapter 28, in Hull–White $P(t,T) = A(t,T)e^{-rB(t,T)}$. The standard deviation of the short rate is constant, σ. It follows from Itô's lemma that the standard deviation of the bond price is $\sigma P(t,T)B(t,T)$. The volatility of the bond price is therefore $\sigma B(t,T)$. This shows that Hull-White is consistent with $s(t,T) = \sigma e^{-a(T-t)}$.

Problem 29.5.

LMM is a similar model to HJM.[6] It has the advantage over HJM that it involves forward rates that are readily observable. HJM involves instantaneous forward rates.

[5]In the first printing of this book the references to LMM should be to HJM.
[6]In the first printing of this book the references to BGM should be to HJM.

Problem 29.6.

A ratchet cap tends to provide relatively low payoffs if a high (low) interest rate at one reset date is followed by a high (low) interest rate at the next reset date. High payoffs occur when a low interest rate is followed by a high interest rate. As the number of factors increase, the correlation between successive forward rates declines and there is a greater chance that a low interest rate will be followed by a high interest rate.

Problem 29.7.

Equation (29.10) can be written

$$dF_k(t) = \zeta_k(t)F_k(t) \sum_{i=m(t)}^{k} \frac{\delta_i F_i(t)\zeta_i(t)}{1+\delta_i F_i(t)} dt + \zeta_k(t)F_k(t) dz$$

As δ_i tends to zero, $\zeta_i(t)F_i(t)$ becomes the standard deviation of the instantaneous t_i-maturity forward rate at time t. Using the notation of Section 29.1 this is $s(t,t_i,\Omega_t)$. As δ_i tends to zero

$$\sum_{i=m(t)}^{k} \frac{\delta_i F_i(t)\zeta_i(t)}{1+\delta_i F_i(t)}$$

tends to

$$\int_{\tau=t}^{t_k} s(t,\tau,\Omega_t)\, d\tau$$

Equation (29.10) therefore becomes

$$dF_k(t) = \left[s(t,t_k,\Omega_t) \int_{\tau=t}^{t_k} s(t,\tau,\Omega_t)\, d\tau \right] dt + s(t,t_k,\Omega_t)\, dz$$

This is the HJM result.

Problem 29.8.

In a ratchet cap, the cap rate equals the previous reset rate, R, plus a spread. In the notation of the text it is $R_j + s$. In a sticky cap the cap rate equal the previous capped rate plus a spread. In the notation of the text it is $\min(R_j, K_j) + s$. The cap rate in a ratchet cap is always at least a great as that in a sticky cap. Since the value of a cap is a decreasing function of the cap rate, it follows that a sticky cap is more expensive.

Problem 29.9.

When prepayments increase, the principal is received sooner. This increases the value of a PO. When prepayments increase, less interest is received. This decreases the value of an IO.

Problem 29.10.

A bond yield is the discount rate that causes the bond's price to equal the market price. The same discount rate is used for all maturities. An OAS is the parallel shift to the Treasury zero curve that causes the price of an instrument such as a mortgage-backed security to equal its market price.

Problem 29.11.

When there are p factors equation (29.7) becomes

$$dF_k(t) = \sum_{q=1}^{p} \zeta_{k,q}(t)F_k(t)dz_q$$

Equation (29.8) becomes

$$dF_k(t) = \sum_{q=1}^{p} \zeta_{k,q}(t)[v_{m(t),q} - v_{k+1,q}]F_k(t)dt + \sum_{q=1}^{p} \zeta_{k,q}(t)(F_k(t)dz_q$$

Equation coefficients of dz_q in

$$\ln P(t,t_i) - \ln P(t,t_{i+1}) = \ln[1 + \delta_i F_i(t)]$$

Equation (29.9) therefore becomes

$$v_{i,q}(t) - v_{i+1,q}(t) = \frac{\delta_i F_i(t)\zeta_{i,q}}{1 + \delta_i F_i(t)}$$

Equation (29.15) follows.

Problem 29.12.

From the equations on page 688

$$s(t) = \frac{P(t,T_0) - P(t,T_N)}{\sum_{i=0}^{N-1} \tau_i P(t,T_{i+1})}$$

and

$$\frac{P(t,T_i)}{P(t,T_0)} = \prod_{j=0}^{i-1} \frac{1}{1 + \tau_j G_j(t)}$$

so that

$$s(t) = \frac{1 - \prod_{j=0}^{N-1} \frac{1}{1+\tau_j G_j(t)}}{\sum_{i=0}^{N-1} \tau_i \prod_{j=0}^{i} \frac{1}{1+\tau_j G_j(t)}}$$

(We employ the convention that empty sums equal zero and empty products equal one.) Equivalently,

$$s(t) = \frac{\prod_{j=0}^{N-1}[1 + \tau_j G_j(t)] - 1}{\sum_{i=0}^{N-1} \tau_i \prod_{j=i+1}^{N-1}[1 + \tau_j G_j(t)]}$$

or

$$\ln s(t) = \ln \left\{ \prod_{j=0}^{N-1} [1 + \tau_j G_j(t)] - 1 \right\} - \ln \left\{ \sum_{i=0}^{N-1} \tau_i \prod_{j=i+1}^{N-1} [1 + \tau_j G_j(t)] \right\}$$

so that

$$\frac{1}{s(t)} \frac{\partial s(t)}{\partial G_k(t)} = \frac{\tau_k \gamma_k(t)}{1 + \tau_k G_k(t)}$$

where

$$\gamma_k(t) = \frac{\prod_{j=0}^{N-1} [1 + \tau_j G_j(t)]}{\prod_{j=0}^{N-1} [1 + \tau_j G_j(t)] - 1} - \frac{\sum_{i=0}^{k-1} \tau_i \prod_{j=i+1}^{N-1} [1 + \tau_j G_j(t)]}{\sum_{i=0}^{N-1} \tau_i \prod_{j=i+1}^{N-1} [1 + \tau_j G_j(t)]}$$

From Itô's lemma the qth component of the volatility of $s(t)$ is

$$\sum_{k=0}^{N-1} \frac{1}{s(t)} \frac{\partial s(t)}{\partial G_k(t)} \beta_{k,q}(t) G_k(t)$$

or

$$\sum_{k=0}^{N-1} \frac{\tau_k \beta_{k,q}(t) G_k(t) \gamma_k(t)}{1 + \tau_k G_k(t)}$$

The variance rate of $s(t)$ is therefore

$$V(t) = \sum_{q=1}^{p} \left[\sum_{k=0}^{N-1} \frac{\tau_k \beta_{k,q}(t) G_k(t) \gamma_k(t)}{1 + \tau_k G_k(t)} \right]^2$$

Problem 29.13.

$$1 + \tau_j G_j(t) = \prod_{m=1}^{M} [1 + \tau_{j,m} G_{j,m}(t)]$$

so that

$$\ln[1 + \tau_j G_j(t)] = \sum_{m=1}^{M} \ln[1 + \tau_{j,m} G_{j,m}(t)]$$

Equating coefficients of dz_q

$$\frac{\tau_j \beta_{j,q}(t) G_j(t)}{1 + \tau_j G_j(t)} = \sum_{m=1}^{M} \frac{\tau_{j,m} \beta_{j,m,q}(t) G_{j,m}(t)}{1 + \tau_{j,m} G_{j,m}(t)}$$

If we assume that $G_{j,m}(t) = G_{j,m}(0)$ for the purposes of calculating the swap volatility we see from equation (29.17) that the volatility becomes

$$\sqrt{\frac{1}{T_0} \int_{t=0}^{T_0} \sum_{q=1}^{p} \left[\sum_{k=n}^{N-1} \sum_{m=1}^{M} \frac{\tau_{k,m} \beta_{k,m,q}(t) G_{k,m}(0) \gamma_k(0)}{1 + \tau_{k,m} G_{k,m}(0)} \right]^2 dt}$$

This is equation (29.19).

Chapter 30
Swaps Revisited

SOLUTIONS TO QUESTIONS AND PROBLEMS

Problem 30.1.

The target payment dates are July 11, 2004; January 11, 2005; July 11, 2005; January 11, 2006; July 11, 2006; January 11, 2007; July 11, 2007; January 11, 2008; July 11, 2008; January 11, 2009. These occur on Sunday, Tuesday, Monday, Wednesday, Tuesday, Thursday, Wednesday, Friday, Friday, and Sunday respectively with no holidays. The actual payment dates are therefore July 12, 2004; January 11, 2005; July 11, 2005; January 11, 2006; July 11, 2006; January 11, 2007; July 11, 2007; January 11, 2008; July 11, 2008; January 12, 2009. The fixed rate day count convention is Actual/365. There are 182 days between January 11, 2004 and July 11, 2004. This means that the fixed payments on July 11, 2004 is

$$\frac{182}{365} \times 0.06 \times 100,000,000 = \$2,991,781$$

Similarly subsequent fixed cash flows are: \$3,024,658, \$2,975,342, \$3,024,658, \$2,975,342, \$3,024,658, \$2,975,342 \$3,024,658, \$2,991,781 \$3,024,658.

Problem 30.2.

Yes. The swap is the same as one on twice the principal where half the fixed rate is exchanged for the LIBOR rate.

Problem 30.3.

The final fixed payment is in millions of dollars:

$$[(4 \times 1.0415 + 4) \times 1.0415 + 4] \times 1.0415 + 4 = 17.0238$$

The final floating payment assuming forward rates are realized is

$$[(4.05 \times 1.041 + 4.05) \times 1.041 + 4.05] \times 1.041 + 4.05 = 17.2238$$

The value of the swap is therefore $-0.2000/(1.04^4) = -0.1710$ or $-\$171,000$.

Problem 30.4.

The value is zero. The receive side is the same as the pay side with the cash flows compounded forward at LIBOR. Compounding cash flows forward at LIBOR does not change their value.

Problem 30.5.

In theory, a new floating-for-floating swap should involve exchanging LIBOR in one currency for LIBOR in another currency (with no spreads added). In practice, macroeconomic effects give rise to spreads. Financial institutions often adjust the discount rates they use to allow for this. Suppose that USD LIBOR is always exchanged Swiss franc LIBOR plus 15 basis points. Financial institutions would discount USD cash flows at USD LIBOR and Swiss franc cash flows at LIBOR plus 15 basis points. This would ensure that the floating-for-floating swap is valued consistently with the market.

Problem 30.6.

In this case $y_i = 0.05$, $\sigma_{y,i} = 0.13$, $\tau_i = 0.5$, $F_i = 0.05$, $\sigma_{F,i} = 0.18$, and $\rho_i = 0.7$ for all i. It is still true that $G_i'(y_i) = -437.603$ and $G_i''(y_i) = 2261.23$. Equation (30.2) gives the total convexity/timing adjustment as $0.0000892t_i$ or 0.892 basis points per year until the swap rate is observed. The swap rate in three years should be assumed to be 5.0268%. The value of the swap is \$119,069.

Problem 30.7.

In a plain vanilla swap we can enter into a series of FRAs to exchange the floating cash flows for their values if the "assume forward rates are realized rule" is used. In the case of a compounding swap Section 30.2 shows that we are able to enter into a series of FRAs that exchange the final floating rate cash flow for its value when the "assume forward rates are realized rule" is used. There is no way of entering into FRAs so that the floating-rate cash flows in a LIBOR-in-arrears swap are exchanged for their values when the "assume forward rates are realized rule" is used.

Problem 30.8.

Suppose that the fixed rate accrues only when the floating reference rate is below R_X and above R_Y where $R_Y < R_X$. In this case the swap is a regular swap plus two series of binary options, one for each day of the life of the swap. Using the notation in the text, the risk-neutral probability that LIBOR will be above R_X on day i is $N(d_2)$ where

$$d_2 = \frac{\ln(F_i/R_X) - \sigma_i^2 t_i^2/2}{\sigma_i \sqrt{t_i}}$$

The probability that it will be below R_Y where $R_Y < R_X$ is $N(-d_2')$ where

$$d_2' = \frac{\ln(F_i/R_Y) - \sigma_i^2 t_i^2/2}{\sigma_i \sqrt{t_i}}$$

From the viewpoint of the party paying fixed, the swap is a regular swap plus binary options. The binary options corresponding to day i have a total value of

$$\frac{QL}{n_2} P(0, s_i)[N(d_2) + N(-d_2')]$$

(This ignores the small timing adjustment mentioned in Section 30.6.)

Chapter 31

Real Options

SOLUTIONS TO QUESTIONS AND PROBLEMS

Problem 31.1.

In the net present value approach, cash flows are estimated in the real world and discounted at a risk-adjusted discount rate. In the risk-neutral valuation approach, cash flows are estimated in the risk-neutral world and discounted at the risk-free interest rate. The risk-neutral valuation approach is arguably more appropriate for valuing real options because it is very difficult to determine the appropriate risk-adjusted discount rate when options are valued.

Problem 31.2.

In a risk-neutral world the expected price of copper in six months is 75 cents. This corresponds to an expected growth rate of $2\ln(75/80) = -12.9\%$ per annum. The decrease in the growth rate when we move from the real world to the risk-neutral world is the volatility of copper times its market price of risk. This is $0.2 \times 0.5 = 0.1$ or 10% per annum. It follows that the expected growth rate of the price of copper in the real world is -2.9%.

Problem 31.3.

In this case

$$\frac{dS}{S} = \mu(t)\,dt + \sigma\,dz$$

or

$$d\ln S = [\mu(t) - \sigma^2/2]\,dt + \sigma\,dz$$

so that $\ln S_T$ is normal with mean

$$\ln S_0 + \int_{t=0}^{T} \mu(t)dt - \sigma^2 T/2$$

and standard deviation $\sigma\sqrt{T}$. Section 28.5 shows that

$$\mu(t) = \frac{\partial}{\partial t}[\ln F(t)]$$

so that

$$\int_{t=0}^{T} \mu(t)dt = \ln F(T) - \ln F(0)$$

Since $F(0) = S_0$ the result follows.

Problem 31.4.

We explained the concept of a convenience yield for a commodity in Chapter 3. It is a measure of the benefits realized from ownership of the physical commodity that are not realized by the holders of a futures contract. If y is the convenience yield and u is the storage cost, equation (5.17) shows that the commodity behaves like an investment asset that provides a return equal to $y - u$. In a risk-neutral world its growth is, therefore,

$$r - (y - u) = r - y + u$$

The convenience yield of a commodity can be related to its market price of risk. From Section 28.2, the expected growth of the commodity price in a risk-neutral world is $m - \lambda s$, where m is its expected growth in the real world, s its volatility, and λ is its market price of risk. It follows that

$$m - \lambda s = r - y + u$$

or

$$y = r + u - m + \lambda s$$

Problem 31.6.

In equation (31.2) $\rho = 0.2$, $\mu_m - r = 0.06$, and $\sigma_m = 0.18$. It follows that the market price of risk lambda is

$$\frac{0.2 \times 0.06}{0.18} = 0.067$$

Problem 31.6.

The option can be valued using Black's model. In this case $F_0 = 24$, $K = 25$, $r = 0.05$, $\sigma = 0.2$, and $T = 3$. The value of a option to purchase one barrel of oil at $25 is

$$e^{-rT}[F_0 N(d_1) - KN(d_2)]$$

where

$$d_1 = \frac{\ln(F_0/K) + \sigma^2 T/2}{\sigma\sqrt{T}}$$

$$d_2 = \frac{\ln(F_0/K) - \sigma^2 T/2}{\sigma\sqrt{T}}$$

This is 2.489. The value of the option to purchase one million barrels is therefore $2,489,000.

Problem 31.7.

The expected growth rate of the car price in a risk-neutral world is $-0.25 - (-0.1 \times 0.15) = -0.235$ The expected value of the car in a risk-neutral world in four years, $\hat{E}(S_T)$, is therefore $30,000e^{-0.235 \times 4} = \$11,719$. Using the result in the appendix to Chapter 13 the value of the option is

$$e^{-rT}[\hat{E}(S_T)N(d_1) - KN(d_2)]$$

where

$$d_1 = \frac{\ln(\hat{E}(S_T)/K) + \sigma^2 T/2}{\sigma\sqrt{T}}$$

$$d_2 = \frac{\ln(\hat{E}(S_T)/K) - \sigma^2 T/2}{\sigma\sqrt{T}}$$

$r = 0.06$, $\sigma = 0.15$, $T = 4$, and $K = 10,000$. It is \$1,832.